The Road to Total War

Frederick M. Sallagar

RAND CORPORATION

The Road to Total War was originally published by Van Nostrand Reinhold Company in 1969. This RAND edition reflects the original layout.

Library of Congress Cataloging-in-Publication Data

978-0-8330-4228-6

Cover Design by Peter Soriano

Published 2007 by the RAND Corporation
1776 Main Street, P.O. Box 2138, Santa Monica, CA 90407-2138
1200 South Hayes Street, Arlington, VA 22202-5050
4570 Fifth Avenue, Suite 600, Pittsburgh, PA 15213-2665
RAND URL: http://www.rand.org/
To order RAND documents or to obtain additional information, contact
Distribution Services: Telephone: (310) 451-7002;
Fax: (310) 451-6915; Email: order@rand.org

to the memory
of
E.F.S.

Preface

We like to think that total war can never happen again. The carnage and devastation of World War II, and the lasting damage it did to the fabric of Western society are grim enough warning against a repetition. And if such havoc could be wrought with the relatively puny weapons of that time, what would be the consequences of total war in the nuclear age? This unimaginable prospect alone is counted upon to restrain future belligerents.

The fact that both nuclear giants now have the means to make the prospect come true appears to support the current American belief that in the unlikely event of a nuclear war, both sides will find it in their own self-interest to fight it in a carefully controlled and restrained fashion. But this could turn out to be a false hope, unless leaders are more willing to learn from the past than they have given evidence so far. The mere wish to avoid a total war, even if shared by the belligerents, is not enough to prevent it from happening.

In the beginning of World War II, both sides wished to limit the conflict, for different reasons. Yet both acted, or reacted, in ways that eventually caused it to become total. The Nazis, as one would expect, were mainly responsible. Their instinct for extreme violence and Hitler's unbridled ambitions inevitably won out over more practical considerations. As the self-styled prophet of total war, he was not deterred by its horrors so long as he could hope to confine them to the other side.

But the British also contributed to the escalation. That their humanitarian scruples were overridden by the passions of war is less remarkable than that, unlike the Germans, they expected their own country to be devastated in a total war. Their image of what would happen, though it turned out to be grossly exaggerated, came as close to our current image of a nuclear holocaust as the imagination could conceive prior to Hiroshima. It is a chilling portent of the future that they nevertheless played a part in allowing the war to escalate.

Was it therefore inevitable that World War II became total? In one sense it was, given the circumstances and personalities involved. For the leaders on both sides became prisoners of events that tempted them to respond to immediate problems with actions whose consequences were often neither planned nor foreseen. Total war was not willed so much as it was allowed to happen.

This book attempts to show how and why it happened. It may thus throw light on the larger question to which I have not addressed myself directly although it is the reason why this inquiry into the past was undertaken: would escalation be equally uncontrollable in a future nuclear war? The Soviets, for reasons of their own, maintain that it would. American leaders believe, or hope, that it would not. The facts set down here may help the reader to form his own judgment.

The past does not enable us to predict the future, but it can teach us to shape it to the extent that fallible human beings can be masters of their own fate. Future leaders may be unable, or unwilling, to control the events that caused their predecessors in World War II to come as close to destroying Western civilization as the weapons of that time would permit. But they might benefit from knowing about them.

This book was originally written as a Rand Corporation report for the United States Air Force. My purpose was not to unearth new historical facts but to interpret those we already have. I am indebted to my friends at Rand who assisted me in various ways, and especially to Dr. Alfred Goldberg and Dr. Hans Speier who shared their knowledge and insight so generously with me. Their valuable contributions are gratefully acknowledged.

FMS

Contents

The Road to Total War

1

Introduction: The Problem

THE JOINT CHIEFS OF STAFF define "general war" as "Armed conflict between the major powers of the communist and free worlds in which the total resources of the belligerents are employed, and the national survival of a major belligerent is in jeopardy."* Considering the means of destruction now available to the major powers, the prospect of a war in which they actually would use their "total resources" staggers the imagination. For some years, therefore, the defense community has been exploring alternatives to an all-out war between the Soviet Union and the United States; there has been a search for a form of war in which both sides would limit the level of violence so as to avoid the mutual annihilation implied in the JCS definition of general war.

So far, the search has yielded no agreement on what such a war -- often referred to as a "controlled general war"** -- would be like, beyond the fact that it would be fought with restraint. There is no consensus on what the permissible level of violence would be, what forms the restraints would take, or how they

*The Joint Chiefs of Staff, *Dictionary of U.S. Military Terms for Joint Usage,* JCS Publication No. 1, Washington, D.C., 1966.

**Among other names suggested by different authors are: "limited strategic war," "tactical nuclear war," "controlled counterforce war," "controlled" or "flexible response," and combinations of these and similar words. See Klaus Knorr and Thornton Read, *Limited Strategic War,* Frederick A. Praeger, Inc., New York, 1962, Chap. 1, esp. pp. 4-10. The term "controlled general war," though not approved by the JCS for official use, seems preferable to me because it is less restrictive than the other names. It conveys the only two characteristics on which there is general agreement: (1) that the war would be a major armed conflict between the great powers, as connoted by the words "general war," and (2) that it would be less than an all-out war, since military force would be used in a "controlled" or restrained fashion.

would be enforced. Nor have we resolved the far more basic issue whether the concept of such a war itself is viable.

Although no definite resolution may be possible short of the actual test, it is essential that we explore the viability of the concept as best we can before embracing a strategy that may turn out to be self-deluding. Proponents of the concept usually defend it by stressing the imperative need for restraint in a world of thermonuclear weapons. But the necessity for restraint need not be argued; it argues for itself. The crucial question is whether restraint is feasible in a major war. Would the belligerents adhere to self-imposed limitations if it meant keeping the level of violence below what, in the heat of battle, might seem appropriate or advantageous to them? And, if both sides were in favor of such limitations, could not circumstances or the pressure of events cause them to act against their own better judgment?

Such intractable questions cannot be answered through logical analysis alone. But history may come to our aid, for the problem of trying to exercise restraint in a major war is not without precedent. World War II started out with some of the same features we now associate with a "controlled general war." In the beginning, both sides observed limitations on the level of violence, and it was only gradually that the conflict turned into an all-out war of the kind envisaged in the JCS definition of general war. It may be that the attempts to exercise restraint were half-hearted or misdirected. But then again, they could have been frustrated by something that is inherent in the nature of modern population wars.

By examining the reasons for the failure of these attempts in World War II, the reasons why the war became total, we may be able to gain insight into the kind of problems that belligerents are likely to face in trying to exercise restraint in a future war. This would not answer the basic question whether such restraint will prove feasible in the future. But it would give us a better basis for judging the likelihood of success or failure than if we had to rely on mere speculation. It was with this thought in mind that this inquiry into the escalation of World War II was undertaken.

Although World War II corresponds to the popular image of total war, purists may object that it was not really total. While it did reach the highest level of violence then known to man, the escalation did not go as far as it might have gone. The belligerents, with the possible exception of Britain, did not mobilize their "total resources" for the war effort. They did not even use all the weapons at their command, for they abstained from chemical or biological warfare. The fact that poison gas was not used is sometimes cited as proof that restraint is indeed feasible, and that a major war need not become total any more than World War II was a total war in the strict sense of the term.

This argument, however, is based on a wrong premise. It would be meaningless to define total war as one in which the belligerents employ, literally, their "total resources." Mobilization can never be total because of deficiencies in knowledge, skill, and managerial talent, because there is rarely enough time for full conversion, and because, even in an authoritarian country, institutional and social constraints prevent it. It is equally unreasonable to hinge the definition on the use of every weapon available to the belligerents, since there are usually some weapons that turn out to be inappropriate or disadvantageous to the user, no matter what the scale of the war.

What characterizes an all-out, or total, war is that it is fought for such high stakes that the belligerents are willing, or compelled, to employ, not *all* weapons they possess, but *any* weapons they consider appropriate and advantageous to them. It is a war in which no holds are barred, although, for one reason or another, not all holds may be used. This is what is commonly understood by total war, and this is the sense in which the term is used here.

That both sides refrained from using poison gas in World War II is therefore not inconsistent with its designation as a total war. The Allies were morally and legally inhibited from initiating chemical or biological warfare; it would not have been appropriate for them to resort to such weapons except in retaliation. It would not have been to their advantage either, since they were ill equipped for gas warfare. The Nazis might have had no scruples about using poison gas, but in the early part of the war they, too, were inadequately prepared, and the use of gas would have conflicted with their Blitzkrieg tactics. Later in the war, when they were better prepared, and when chemical weapons might have been tactically useful to them in defending static positions, they no longer had air superiority and feared retaliation against their cities. "At no time during World War II, in the opinion of the German military leaders, was the situation favorable for the initiation of gas warfare."* It is also said that Hitler had a personal antipathy to the use of poison gas, probably stemming from his own World War I injuries.

Since both sides considered chemical warfare disadvantageous and did not wish to resort to it, we cannot regard its not being used in World War II as an example of restraint; one is restrained only from something that one wishes to do. Another error would be to conclude from this case that belligerents in future wars will be equally circumspect in ruling out forms of warfare that would be disadvantageous to them, such as the all-out use of thermonuclear weapons.

The story of escalation in World War II shows several instances in which one side or the other allowed escalation to happen, or actively contributed to it, when it was not to its advantage to do so. Sometimes this was done for an immediate military benefit, real or imagined, that was out of proportion to the price that had to be paid for it later. There were also occasions when emotional and other pressures drove the belligerents to take actions that were even against their most immediate interest, because the leaders either did not foresee the consequences of their decisions or

*Brooks E. Kleber and Dale Birdsell, *The Chemical Warfare Services: Chemical in Combat,* in the series "United States Army in World War II," published by the Office of the Chief of Military History, U.S. Army, Washington, D.C., 1966, p. 655. The rest of my paragraph on this subject is based on the same source, specifically the section entitled "Why Gas Was Not Used," pp. 652-657.

deliberately ignored them. That chemical warfare proved the exception in being recognized as disadvantageous may have been partly due, as already suggested, to a combination of inadequate capabilities and the fact that even Hitler abhorred its use.

The concept of a "controlled general war" rests on the basic assumption that unwanted escalation can be avoided if both sides recognize that it is in their mutual interest to avoid it, and act accordingly. But it is one thing for the leaders to recognize this before the war has actually occurred, and another for them to act on such a recognition under the pressure of wartime events. This is why the instances in World War II when escalation occurred against the best interests of the side that instigated it will be given special emphasis in this inquiry.

The escalation of World War II was a cumulative process, as is likely to be the case in future wars as well. Some steps in this process were relatively harmless in themselves, in that they did not exceed the bounds tacitly accepted by both sides as permissible in war. They enlarged the scale of the conflict, geographically or otherwise, but did not change its character; they did not cross a "firebreak," to use the current phrase. The battle for air superiority over Britain, for instance, was an important geographical expansion of the war but was accepted by the British as a legitimate military operation of the kind they themselves might have undertaken if they had had the capability. It was an escalation in degree but not in kind. Yet it started a chain of circumstances that contributed to a much more fateful step of escalation: the deliberate bombing of cities by both sides. This was a change in the character of the conflict and completed its transition to a total war in which no holds were barred.

In studying the examples of World War II, we therefore must be concerned with the entire process of escalation, and not only with those steps that directly resulted in changing the level of violence through the adoption of forms of warfare that the belligerents had theretofore avoided. We are concerned with it, however, primarily as it bears on the air war, which is the main focus of this inquiry. It was the adoption of indiscriminate air warfare which signaled the transition to total war, and was the nearest equivalent, in World War II, to the kind of escalation that the proponents of "controlled general war" hope to prevent in a future conflict. This is why the story of the air war occupies a dominant place in the historical analysis presented in Part One of this study; other forms of escalation have been included only to indicate the military and political pressures that influenced the decisions pertaining to air warfare.

While there will be many parallels between World War II and a possible war between the nuclear powers, there will also be important differences. Even where force was used without restraint in World War II, it was kept within bounds by the relatively puny weapons available at the time. The next major war would be the first in the history of modern warfare in which the belligerents would have at their disposal means of destruction likely to exceed even the most ambitious military requirements. Moderation thus will no longer be imposed by a shortage of means but will require a deliberate policy decision.

It is possible that the new element introduced by the advent of nuclear weapons will prove to have changed the nature of warfare in such a way as to invalidate the lessons sought in this inquiry into the past. Whether the forces that made for escalation in World War II are or are not likely to prevail in a future war is of course a matter of judgment. But first we must know what these forces were. We may find that some of them are so deeply rooted in human conduct that they could be operative even in the face of threatened extinction. If they were, it would not be the first time that nations had been tempted into a course of action that predictably led to their downfall; it happened when Japan decided to attack Pearl Harbor.

Part One

THE EVIDENCE

We all were sea-swallow'd, though some cast again,
And by that destiny to perform an act
Whereof what's past is prologue, what to come
In yours and my discharge.

Shakespeare, *The Tempest*

2

Prewar Developments – Britain

THE ACTIONS of both sides in World War II were taken in response to the political and military pressures that the conflict had generated or had made more acute. But the nature of the response was also influenced by the national characteristics of the belligerents and by basic attitudes toward warfare whose roots went back into the past. One of the important questions, therefore, to be asked about the escalation of World War II is to what extent it was preordained or brought about by the events of the conflict itself.

Chapters 2 and 3 of this book, dealing with the prewar thinking of the two sides, are intended to help us answer this question. They are the necessary background for our understanding of the influence that such thinking exercised on the events that will be described in the remaining chapters.

On the British side, it is not difficult to find out what the military and civilian leaders, or the general public, thought about the coming war. Here the main problem is to isolate among the diverse and conflicting views those dominant trends that were later reflected in Britain's wartime actions. We face quite a different task when we deal with the German side, a closed society headed by a despotic leader and protected by a curtain of secrecy and deception.

A Peacetime Debate Over Strategic Air Warfare

In the brief interval of peace during the 1920s, the victors of World War I were more concerned with disarmament than with planning for a possible future war. In such an atmosphere, the thinking even of military professionals becomes unrealistic and their debates over strategy take on an academic flavor. This was true of one of the important prewar debates in Britain, in May 1928, when the British service chiefs exchanged a series of memoranda on the subject of strategic air warfare.*

The debate was launched with a memorandum from the Chief of the Air Staff, Marshal of the Royal Air Force Sir Hugh (later Lord) Trenchard, the famous and controversial British prophet of strategic air power.** He propounded the now familiar but then still unorthodox doctrine that air power should be used for direct attack on the enemy's *sources* of power, instead of being frittered away in an effort to defeat the hostile armies and navies, which are only the *manifestations* of his power.

> It is not, however, necessary for an air force, in order to defeat the enemy nation, to defeat its armed forces first. Air power can dispense with that intermediate step, can pass over the enemy navies and armies, and penetrate the air defences and attack direct the centres of production, transportation and communication from which the enemy war effort is maintained.***

The lengthy memorandum went on to disclaim the notion that "the Air by itself can finish the war." However, it would be one of the principal means for putting pressure on the enemy. It would do so in two ways: By attacking the enemy's means for waging war, air power would contribute substantially toward destruction of his *ability* to resist. At the same time, these attacks would weaken the enemy's *will* to resist through what Trenchard called the "moral effects" of strategic bombardment.**** Industrial targets are usually located in populated areas, where frequent heavy air attacks would produce panic among the civilian workers and thus interfere with war production. This feeling of panic was likely to spread to other elements of the population and might eventually force the government to call a halt.

We know that Lord Trenchard considered the "moral" effects of strategic bombing more important than the physical effects and sometimes put the ratio as high as 20:1.***** He did not say so in his memorandum, however, but contented himself with invoking Marshal Foch's authority by quoting him on this point:

*Sir Charles Webster and Noble Frankland, *The Strategic Air Offensive against Germany, 1939-1945* (hereafter cited as *Air Offensive),* in *History of the Second World War,* United Kingdom Military Series, Her Majesty's Stationery Office, London, 1961, Vol. 4, App. 2.

**For a biography of this remarkable man, whom Britain honored with burial in Westminster Abbey, see Andrew Boyle, *Trenchard,* W. W. Norton & Co. Inc., New York, 1962.

****Air Offensive,* Vol. 4, App. 2, p. 72.

****He used the term "moral" as the equivalent of "morale." In this context it has no ethical connotation.

*****Noble Frankland, *The Bombing Offensive against Germany: Outlines and Perspectives,* Faber and Faber, London, 1965, p. 40.

> The potentialities of aircraft attacks on a large scale are almost incalculable, but it is clear that such attack, owing to its crushing moral effect on a Nation, may impress the public opinion to a point of disarming the Government and thus becoming decisive.*

The views expressed in Lord Trenchard's memorandum were not new. They had begun to evolve in World War I and were shared by such advocates of strategic air power as Field Marshal Smuts and Winston Churchill in England, Giulio Douhet in Italy, and Billy Mitchell in the United States. But the doctrine was still opposed on many grounds, not least because the older services saw it as relegating them to a subsidiary role. The most frequent and most violent criticism, however, was that strategic bombing represented an inhumane and illegal method of warfare. The Trenchard memorandum took note of this charge and rejected it with the argument that workers who provide the sinews of war were a legitimate military objective.

> What is illegitimate, as being contrary to the dictates of humanity, is the indiscriminate bombing of a city for the sole purpose of terrorising the civilian population. It is an entirely different matter to terrorise munition workers (men and women) into absenting themselves from work or stevedores into abandoning the loading of a ship with munitions through fear of air attack upon the factory or dock concerned. Moral effect is created by the bombing in such circumstances but it is the inevitable result of a lawful operation of war -- the bombing of a military objective.**

This fine distinction between munition workers and the civilians who feed, clothe, and house them, or who sustain the war effort in other ways, may seem far-fetched and disingenuous to us. But it must be remembered that this was written in 1928, when the difference between a combat area and a rear area, between open and defended towns, had not yet lost its meaning.

In their official replies, the Army and Navy chiefs flatly rejected the Trenchard thesis of strategic air warfare on the grounds of both expediency and humanity. Their objections were well-reasoned and expressed in temperate language. If these men were influenced by parochial service loyalties, this would only be natural.

Their most telling argument, persuasively put forward by CIGS,*** was that Britain would be clearly at a disadvantage in a war in which both sides resorted to unrestricted air warfare. Geography was against her. Unlike the major cities of France and Germany, which were located deep inland, Britain's coastal cities would get practically no warning of an enemy air attack. London, the financial and distribution center of the country, could be reached by short-range aircraft based in the Low Countries or in France, whereas British bombers would need to be of much longer range to attack enemy capitals on the Continent. Moreover, unrestricted air

Air Offensive, Vol. 4, App. 2, p. 75.

***Ibid.*, p. 73.

***Chief of the Imperial General Staff (Army).

warfare was likely to lead to unrestricted warfare at sea as well. This would put Britain at an even greater disadvantage relative to a potential enemy, since she was uniquely dependent on keeping the sea lanes open. For these and other reasons, both service chiefs argued that Britain should never be the one to initiate unrestricted air warfare, should do all she could to oppose it, and should resort to it only if the enemy started it.

As for Trenchard's defense of strategic bombing against the charge that it was an illegal and inhumane method of warfare, CIGS commented as follows:

> As regards the ethical aspects of his [Trenchard's] proposals, it is for His Majesty's Government to accept or to refuse a doctrine which, put into plain English, amounts to one which advocates unrestricted warfare against the civil population of one's enemy.*

Since expediency argued against a method of warfare in which Britain would be at a disadvantage, one is tempted to question the sincerity of the moral objections that were raised against it. But it would be a mistake to underrate the strong feelings of military professionals against making war on civilians. It is of course impossible to separate expediency and humanity when both argue for the same course. In World War II, their respective influence was to become clearer after hostilities had started, when the two were sometimes at variance. Until we reach this point in our narrative, it would be well to withhold judgment.

Though the Army and Navy chiefs took up the points in Trenchard's memorandum one by one, they did not address themselves to the most important issue he had raised when he asserted that unrestricted air warfare *would* be employed by both sides, regardless of what opinions one might have as to its desirability, legality, or moral acceptability. The views he had expressed on this point are exceedingly germane to this study:

> There may be many who, realising that this new warfare will extend to the whole community the horrors and suffering hitherto confined to the battlefield would urge that the Air offensive should be restricted to the zone of the opposing armed forces. If this restriction were feasible, I should be the last to quarrel with it; but it is not feasible. In a vital struggle all available weapons always have been used and always will be used. All sides made a beginning in the last war, and what has been done will be done.
>
> . . . . .
>
> Whatever we may wish or hope, or whatever course of action we may decide, whatever be the views held as to the legality, or the humanity, or the military wisdom and expediency of such operations, there is not the slightest doubt that in the next war both sides will send their aircraft out without scruple to bomb those objectives which they consider the most suitable.

**Air Offensive,* Vol. 4, App. 2, p. 81.

> I would, therefore, urge most strongly that we accept this fact and face it; that we do not bury our heads in the sand like ostriches; but that we train our officers and men, and organise our Services, so that they may be prepared to meet and to counter these inevitable air attacks.*

When this was written, in 1928, there was no enemy threatening Britain. Communist Russia, though hostile, was in no position militarily to fight a modern power. Germany had not yet emerged as a potential enemy. Disarmament and pacificism were the order of the day. Military planning in Britain -- what there was of it -- was shackled by the "Ten-Year Rule,"** and, in the absence of a specific enemy, it naturally lacked focus and realism.

In this atmosphere, the debate over strategic air warfare, important as it was, had almost no effect on practical decisions, at least not at the time. No attempt was made by the Government to deal with the basic issue Lord Trenchard had raised: his prediction that strategic air warfare *would* be employed in the next war no matter what one might think about it. Even after the advent of Hitler had brought the prospect of war much closer, the Government still made no effort to determine what British bombing policy in the event of war should be. Yet there could be little doubt in Britain what German policy on aerial warfare would be. It would be ruthless and unrestrained by humanitarian considerations of any kind. Hitler's actions as soon as he came to power had made this clear for all who wished to see.

The British Image of a Future War

As the war clouds began to gather over Europe in the thirties, the British public shared with its leaders the belief that a future war would be short and ferocious. It would begin with a slaughter of innocent civilians through aerial bombardment of cities on a vast scale. London which, in Mr. Churchill's words, was like "a tremendous fat cow, a valuable fat cow tied up to attract the beasts of prey,"*** would be the first target. The results of an attack on such a vulnerable, densely populated city would be catastrophic. Casualties in the hundreds of thousands would be inflicted in a few days, and millions of Londoners would be driven out into the open countryside to escape the bombardment.

**Ibid.*, pp. 75-76.

**After the close of World War I the British Government directed that all military planning be done on the assumption that there would be no major war for ten years. The "Ten-Year Rule" was applied on a rolling basis, always extending ten years from the respective planning date. The Rule had a paralyzing and cumulatively worsening effect on military plans and preparations. It was maintained until 1932, but its consequences were felt for a decade longer. The memoirs of British military leaders who were planners in the prewar days are replete with references to the effects of the Ten-Year Rule. See Norman Gibbs, "British Strategic Doctrine 1918-1939," in Michael Howard (ed.), *The Theory and Practice of War: Essays Presented to Captain B. H. Liddell Hart on His Seventieth Birthday*, Frederick A. Praeger, Inc., New York, 1966.

***J. M. Spaight, *Air Power and War Rights*, 3d ed., Longmans, Green and Co., London, 1947, p. 31.

These were not the lurid imaginings of excitable journalists but the expectations held by sober and responsible statesmen. In 1933 Lord Cecil said in a House of Lords debate:

> The amount of destruction that can be wrought by a concentrated attack by a considerable Air Force is so great that it may well be that one or two such attacks will decide the whole ultimate course of the war. . . .There is no doubt that a strong attack made on this city and on the other great centres of our life might absolutely cripple us in, I might say, forty-eight hours.*

In 1934 Mr. Churchill estimated that "under the pressure of continuous air attack upon London, at least 3,000,000 or 4,000,000 people would be driven out into the open country around the metropolis."**

The prevailing estimate of the German threat was shared by the government agencies concerned with air raid precautions and civil defense. But it would have been clearly impossible to evacuate 3 or 4 million people from London alone in a short period and with little or no warning. When more concrete and more realistic plans were made after the Munich crisis in 1938, the figures were scaled down considerably. The new plans provided for the evacuation of approximately 4 million people throughout the United Kingdom, of whom 1.4 million were to be from London alone.

The civil defense planners relied on the British Air Staff for estimates of the expected weight of German attacks and of the damage they were likely to inflict. In 1934 the Air Staff had calculated that by 1942 the Germans would be able to drop a maximum of 150 tons of bombs per 24 hours over a sustained period of several weeks. As the strength of the German Air Force continued to increase during the thirties at a much faster rate than foreseen, the estimates had to be revised upwards. In 1939 the Air Staff expected the Germans to be able to deliver 700 tons daily on a sustained basis. More ominous was the prediction that an aerial assault might be initiated with an attempted "knockout blow" in which as much as 3500 tons could be delivered in the first 24 hours.

For a number of years, the Air Staff had estimated casualties at the rate of 50 per ton of bomb delivered -- a figure of questionable validity which was based on the German bombing of London in World War I. After the bombing of Barcelona and Guernica during the Spanish Civil War, the multiplier was increased from 50 to 72 casualties per ton of bomb, with one-third dead, one-third seriously injured, and one-third slightly injured. Combining this rate with the expected weight of enemy attack, the Air Staff estimated that civilian casualties (mortalities and seriously injured) could be as high as 165,000 in the first 24 hours, and on the order of 35,000 daily for several weeks thereafter. To these figures, which were based on

Ibid., p. 30.

**Richard M. Titmuss, *Problems of Social Policy*, in *History of the Second World War*, United Kingdom Civil Series, His Majesty's Stationery Office, London, 1950, p. 9.

the effects of H.E. (high explosive) bombs alone, would have to be added casualties from incendiaries and gas, both of which the British also expected the Germans to use.*

These being official estimates used by British planners, it is not surprising that popular writers of the period painted an even more lurid picture of the coming war -- one not very different from the present generation's vision of a future nuclear war. In the thirties, the image held by the British public was that the war would start with a German knockout blow from the air that would turn London and other British cities into rubble, kill or maim uncounted numbers of civilians, and send millions more wandering homeless through a devastated countryside, vainly searching for food, shelter, and medical care. A contemporary writer described the results of an attack against London with H.E. bombs, incendiaries, and gas: "London, with its environs and suburbs, had become a place of ruin and sepulture so vast that in comparison Sodom and Gomorrah, Herculaneum and Pompeii, were but ant-heaps scattered by the feet of children."**

That these images, public and official alike, were based on a gross exaggeration of what air power could do *at the time* is beside the point. They were what people expected to happen. They undoubtedly contributed to Chamberlain's appeasement policy. They were also responsible for the panicky behavior of the British public during the Munich crisis -- so different from its behavior later on, in the face of the real thing -- when the roads out of London were jammed with automobiles and 150,000 people fled to Wales in an unauthorized evacuation.

The panic flight from London during the Munich crisis confirmed the Government's worst fears about the effects of strategic bombing on civilian morale. These fears dated back to World War I, when the feeble German Zeppelin raids on London created a panic that was out of all proportion to the small damage inflicted. Ever since, British leaders had been obsessed with the notion that civilian morale was potentially fragile and would break under air attack. As we have seen, the notion was shared by Lord Trenchard in his emphasis on the "moral effects" of strategic bombing.

The erroneous belief that civilian morale was the most vulnerable target for strategic bombing dominated British government policy both before World War II and during it. The belief was not abandoned even after the British people had proved that their morale would stand up under continuous air attack. It was merely transferred to the German people, whose morale was not expected to stand up as the British had done because the Germans were fighting in an ignoble cause and were widely believed to be ruled by a government not of their own choice.

*For the casualty estimates used by British planning agencies and their derivation, my main source was Titmuss, Chaps. 1 and 2. For the expectations of the British public regarding a future war, see also Spaight, Chap. 2, and *Air Offensive,* Vol. 1, Chap. 2.

**Spaight, p. 31.

British Plans Under the Shadow of War

Starting in 1934, the possibility of war with Germany could no longer be ignored by the British planners. Many people in Britain -- and elsewhere in the West -- still dismissed Hitler as a temporary aberration from which the German people would recover sooner or later. But German rearmament could not be so easily dismissed. When formation of the German Luftwaffe under Göring was officially announced, in 1935, the general speculation in Britain was that Hitler intended to use his new weapon for a knockout blow against British cities.

The time for academic debates on strategy was over. Increasingly, as the thirties wore on, the question for the military planners -- if not for their civilian superiors -- was not whether there would be war but when. There was no longer any doubt who the enemy would be. The relative merits of different strategies now had to be assessed in terms of a realistic appraisal of what Britain could do with the weapons it had and those it could procure in whatever time would be available for undoing the damage caused by years of neglect. The outlook was not encouraging.

Since Germany was expected to begin a future war with an aerial attack on British cities, one strategy would have been for Britain to concentrate on building up a powerful bomber force of her own, so as to deter Germany from carrying out such an attack or be able to retaliate against it if the deterrence should fail. This is what Lord Trenchard had urged in the twenties and what his disciples continued to urge in the thirties. (Trenchard had been replaced as Chief of the Air Staff in December 1929.) But long-range strategic bombers are expensive and take years to develop and build. Fighters could be built more cheaply and more quickly. Should Britain, therefore, concentrate on a defensive strategy in the air and give highest priority to building up her fighter defenses against the expected German aerial attack?

Some planners disagreed with the basic estimate that the war would begin with attack on Britain. They thought that the Germans were more likely to launch a ground assault against the Low Countries and France. If this were the case, British forces would be involved in a long ground war on the Continent of Europe. Britain therefore would need to give a high priority to rebuilding her Army, which had been sadly neglected during the lean years, and to strengthening the Navy, which would have to guard Britain's lifelines to the outside world. The role of the Air Force in such a war would be primarily that of supporting the ground battle.

The choice among these different claimants would have been difficult to make even if unlimited funds and unlimited time had been available. But time was short -- though no one knew exactly how short -- and funds were still being doled out sparingly by a government that was far less convinced of the imminence of war -- at least prior to Munich -- than were the military professionals.

Although piecemeal decisions to deal with the worst shortages were made all along, it was not until 1937 that the planners succeeded in coming up with a general war plan that was acceptable to all concerned, including the Chiefs of Staff, the

Committee of Imperial Defence, and the Cabinet.* In the circumstances, it is not surprising that the Plan was a compromise among all the divergent viewpoints on how a future war should be fought. That it lacked realism and was based on wishful thinking more than a sound appreciation of what was actually feasible is not surprising either. Democracies don't normally face up to hard facts until a crisis forces them to. In 1937 the crisis had not yet happened.

So far as over-all strategy was concerned, the Plan envisaged an initial phase during which Britain would be on the defensive. The main burden of defending the island against German aerial attacks would have to be borne by the fighter defenses, which would need to be given the highest priority. Bombers would be required to assist in the defense by operating in a counterair role against the airfields and maintenance organization of the Luftwaffe in order to reduce the weight of the German attack. If the Germans began the war not with a knockout blow against Britain but with a ground invasion of the Low Countries and France, the British bombers would be used primarily to assist the Allied ground forces in repelling the attack.

In the initial phase, therefore, the bomber force would not be playing the offensive role Lord Trenchard had advocated, but would be used defensively. However, the Trenchard doctrine was not repudiated entirely. In the second phase of the war, "after Germany's initial offensive is held," British bombers would attack strategic targets in Germany so as to soften up the enemy for his eventual defeat by the Allied ground forces. Unrealistic as the Plan was in the light of Britain's military capabilities at the time, it turned out to be a surprisingly good blueprint of the basic strategy the Allies eventually used for the defeat of Germany.

Just how unrealistic the Plan was was brought home to the Air Staff and to Bomber Command as they approached the difficult task of trying to prepare concrete operational plans for implementing the general strategy laid down in the Plan. Now they had to consider the numbers of aircraft that would be available and their ranges and payloads; operational crew requirements and training needs; target characteristics and bombing accuracy; navigation problems and expected enemy defenses. Wherever they looked, there were glaring deficiencies which only money and time could correct. Even the reduced role that the Plan assigned to strategic bombers was far beyond the resources that could be made available in the foreseeable future. The most ardent advocates of the Trenchard doctrine of air warfare themselves were now forced -- many for the first time -- to consider strategy not in terms of what was theoretically desirable but what was practically feasible. It was a painful but salutary process, which brought them down to earth and often revolutionized their thinking.

There was no doubt that the British bomber force was, and would remain for some time to come, woefully inadequate to carrying out the counterair and interdiction missions assigned to it in the Plan, let alone deep inland penetrations against

**Air Offensive*, Vol. 1, pp. 89*ff.* For the Joint Planners Appreciation from which the Plan was derived, see *ibid.*, Vol. 4, App. 4, pp. 88-95.

heavily defended targets in Germany. The Air Staff estimated that by 1939 only 17 of the 33 operational squadrons scheduled for Bomber Command would be equipped with aircraft even remotely suited for attacks against the Continent from British bases (Whitleys, Hampdens, and Wellingtons).* Heavier and longer-range aircraft (Stirlings, Halifaxes, and Lancasters) were on order but were not expected to come into the inventory until 1943.**

The stark implications of these facts were driven home during the Munich crisis, in the autumn of 1938, when the prospect arose that the Plan might have to be put into execution immediately. Bomber Command was well aware that its inadequate force could contribute little toward reducing the weight of a German aerial attack on British cities. The burden of defense would have to be borne by fighters. The Air Staff admitted as much when it agreed, at least for the time being, to the higher priority that the Cabinet had assigned to Fighter Command.***

Not only was the role assigned to Bomber Command beyond its capabilities, but in attempting it the bombers were likely to suffer losses out of all proportion to the possible gains. This realization dealt a blow to another cherished aspect of the Trenchard doctrine, the assumption that "the bomber will always get through." Certainly the dictum did not apply to the kinds of bombers then available to Britain. The situation was epitomized when Sir Edgar Ludlow-Hewitt, who then headed Bomber Command, made the courageous but heretical suggestion that long-range fighters be developed to escort the bombers.****

Since it was apparent to the enemy that the bombers available to Britain during the thirties would not be capable of an effective air offensive against Germany, there was nothing to deter Hitler from destroying British cities if he wished to do so. The only hope was that he might be reluctant to initiate such attacks out of concern for world opinion. Slim as this hope was, it meant that Britain would have to confine her own air operations to "strictly military" objectives so as not to free Hitler from any self-imposed constraints he might be willing to observe.

> In view of the British air inferiority it is not surprising to find that the possibility of restricting bombing to purely military objectives now [at the time of Munich] received fresh and sympathetic consideration. . . .Both the Air Officer Commanding-in-Chief, Bomber Command and the Air Ministry were of opinion that restrictions on bombing would be an advantage and official orders were sent to the former to confine his attacks to the W.A. [Western Air] 1 and W.A. 4 plans which were obviously aimed at military objectives.

*This turned out to be an overly optimistic estimate. When war broke out in September 1939, only a total of 140 aircraft of these three types were in serviceable condition and manned by operational crews. *Air Offensive,* Vol. 4, App. 38 and 39, pp. 400-428.

**This estimate proved pessimistic. The first of these aircraft actually entered the inventory in 1941.

****Air Offensive,* Vol. 1, pp. 92 and 102.

*****Ibid.*, p. 96.

> Even then he was to do nothing that might be construed as an attack on civilians and so give the enemy an excuse to do likewise.*

Thus, on the grounds of expediency alone, a strategic bombing campaign against Germany of the kind advocated by Lord Trenchard was out of the question during the early part of a future war. Even if it had not been ruled out by Britain herself, it would have been ruled out by her French ally. The French General Staff was bitterly opposed to any action that might lead to the unrestricted bombing of targets in France. The French Air Force was in much worse shape than the British and was intended for strictly tactical use in support of the ground forces. The French General Staff could conceive of no other use for air power and wanted all available British aircraft, bombers as well as fighters, to be employed in the same way. Since British bombers would have to operate from French bases for any but the most shallow penetrations of the Continent, French objections could have effectively vetoed strategic bombing of Germany.**

Thus there were strong reasons why Britain should not plan to rely on strategic air warfare in a future war but should instead channel her scarce resources into strengthening her defenses and building up the Army and Navy. Yet the plans for the strategic bombing of Germany were kept alive in spite of the dim prospects of carrying them out, and the gradual buildup of Bomber Command continued, though at a slow pace, even when it competed for resources with more urgent needs. What accounts for this apparent paradox?

One possible explanation may be that British leaders had vivid memories of the horrible trench warfare of World War I and were trying to find a better alternative. The senseless slaughter on the Western front had cut deeply into a whole generation of British manhood and was not to be allowed to happen again. Some thought that the only alternative was to abolish war altogether through disarmament and dedication to pacifism. But those who were more realistic and understood that war was coming were searching for a strategy that could terminate such a war quickly and without the appalling losses suffered in 1914-1918.

The Trenchard doctrine of strategic air warfare against the enemy's ability and will to resist seemed to provide such an alternative. As it had never been tried before, it was hard to dispute the claims made by its advocates. Also, it had a good

*_Ibid._, p. 99. The W.A. [Western Air] Plans were a series of target directives. W.A. 1 dealt with attacks on German Air Force targets; W.A. 4 dealt with interdiction attacks on German troop concentrations and LOCs [Line of Communications] during a ground campaign in the Low Countries and France.

**On June 11, 1940, while France was still nominally fighting as Britain's ally, at the very moment that Winston Churchill was in France to confer with Premier Reynaud and General deGaulle, the French were piling up physical obstacles on the runways of the airfields used by the British Air Forces in France to prevent them from taking off on bombing missions which might bring retaliation against French towns. This little-known incident is reported by Sir Edward Spears, *Assignment to Catastrophe,* Vol. 2, *The Fall of France,* The Windmill Press, Kingswood, Surrey, England, 1954, pp. 162*ff;* also Winston S. Churchill, *The Second World War,* Vol. 2, *Their Finest Hour,* Houghton Mifflin Company, Boston, Mass., 1949, p. 156.

deal of similarity with the principle of naval blockade -- as Noble Frankland put it, strategic warfare was "in essence, naval blockade writ new" -- and appealed on the same ground. But the naval blockade of World War I, though ultimately effective, had been too slow, so that in the meantime the armed forces of the belligerents had fought each other to exhaustion. Strategic bombing seemed to offer a better, faster-acting attrition strategy.

British leaders regarded Germany as particularly vulnerable to such a strategy. Hitler had succeeded only too well in hammering home his point that the "Versailles *Diktat,*" by truncating Germany, had made her into a "have-not" nation. Spurious as this argument was, it played on the guilt feelings of the victor nations and convinced them that Germany lacked some of the essential resources needed to fight a protracted war. Her hoarded stocks would be quickly depleted and would be difficult to replenish if she were subjected to a combination of strategic bombing, naval blockade, and economic warfare in its new and more sophisticated forms.

No one could foretell how effective strategic air warfare would be. Most of its advocates overrated its effectiveness. They believed that strategic bombing could bring Germany to her knees by depriving her war machine of oil and other critical resources, while at the same time inflicting such hardships on the civilian population as to cause it to revolt against the "unpopular" Hitler government. Even those who thought that the war would be fought along more traditional lines, with armies and navies bearing the brunt of the battle, were inclined to believe that strategic bombing would affect the fighting capability of the opposing forces and so prevent a repetition of the mass slaughter of World War I.

When Britain entered the war, in September 1939, she lacked the means to conduct an effective bombing offensive and the plans made for it were hopelessly unrealistic. But the ground had been prepared, and during the period that Britain stood alone, strategic bombing was to become the principal, indeed almost the sole, means by which she was able to maintain her war effort against the German homeland.

3

Prewar Developments – Germany

IN NAZI GERMANY, an intramural debate such as the British controversy over strategic air warfare would have been unthinkable. The Führer had his own ideas on strategy and came to rely less and less on the advice of his military professionals. In the early years, his top generals sometimes succeeded in challenging his plans, but, after he had won his showdown with the Reichswehr in 1938, even senior commanders rarely dared to express any disagreement with him. There certainly were no dissenters among the toadies with whom he surrounded himself in his personal headquarters, the OKW *(Oberkommando der Wehrmacht)*. In the Byzantine atmosphere of what Trevor-Roper called Hitler's "groveling court," the function of men like Keitel and Jodl was not to debate strategy with the Führer but to provide an admiring audience for his monologues.

So far as the operative German views on the nature of the coming war were concerned, we are therefore dealing mainly with the thoughts and plans of a single man. When he chose to communicate them, he usually did so in harangues to his senior military commanders or in informal remarks to his courtiers. The members of this privileged audience were in the habit of making extensive notes right after the event and checking them with each other for accuracy.*

Some of these diaries have come to light since the war. Unfortunately, the insight they provide into Hitler's thinking on strategic matters is not as good as one would wish. Even where his words are reproduced almost verbatim, it is often difficult to

*The methods used to record the Führer's thoughts are described by the official OKW diarist, a professional historian who managed to maintain a reasonably objective approach. Helmuth Greiner, *Die Oberste Wehrmachtführung, 1939-1943* (The Supreme Command of the Wehrmacht), Limes Verlag, Wiesbaden, Germany, 1951.

disentangle his thoughts from the vague or purposely deceptive statements in which he chose to express them. As we know, Hitler lied to his closest subordinates, and probably to himself as well. His uncouth and sloppy use of the German language adds to the difficulty.

Hitler's Plans for a Limited War

Since democracies tend to overrate the efficiency of their authoritarian opponents, the British assumed that Germany had entered the war with a set of complete and detailed plans for its conduct. But this was true only so far as the campaign against Poland was concerned. Hitler had made no concrete plans or preparations for a major war with the Western Allies. He realized that such a war might be "forced upon him," as he put it, but his preference was for a local war with Poland.

In common with other aggressors, Hitler favored what are now called "salami-tactics." He wanted to reach his objectives piecemeal, through a succession of quick local wars in which he could defeat his opponents one by one. He hoped to avoid having to fight the combined power of his enemies simultaneously in a long-drawn-out conflict, for which Germany lacked the staying power.*

The Führer's one-slice-at-a-time method already had yielded him the Rhineland, Austria, and Czechoslovakia, without his having to fight for them. The next slice was to be Poland, and for that slice Hitler *wanted* to fight. He admitted this in a long secret address to his top generals at the Berghof on August 22, 1939, when he said that he considered it "of the greatest importance to test the instrument of the new German Wehrmacht in a limited conflict, prior to a final reckoning with the victors of World War I."** He was so determined to have his little war that he was "only afraid that some *Schweinehund* will make a proposal for mediation."***

Mediation was one way through which Hitler's plans for a limited war could be upset.**** The other was that the war might not remain limited, a contingency he wanted to avoid at all cost. His plans for the invasion of Poland were based on the proviso that "there must be no simultaneous conflict with the Western powers."

That Hitler wished to limit the conflict to Poland, and that he wanted to avoid a world war *at that time,* was of course no tribute to his sense of moderation.

*A thoroughly documented account of Hitler's views on this subject is given in Andreas Hillgruber, *Hitlers Strategie: Politik und Kriegführung 1940-1941* (Hitler's Strategy: Politics and the Conduct of the War, 1940-1941), Bernard & Graefe Verlag für Wehrwesen, Frankfurt, Germany, 1965, pp. 27-45.

**Greiner, p. 40.

***This phrase is not included in Greiner's paraphrase of the speech. It can be found in the longer version used at the Nuremberg Trials. See Doc. No. 798, *The Trial of Major War Criminals before the International Military Tribunal,* cited in F. H. Hinsley, *Hitler's Strategy,* Cambridge University Press, Cambridge, England, 1951, p. 25.

****A dissenting view is expressed by A. J. P. Taylor, who suggests that Hitler might have been satisfied with a peaceful settlement of the Danzig problem on his own terms. A. J. P. Taylor, *The Origins of the Second World War,* Atheneum, New York, 1962, Chap. 11.

He simply wanted to limit his risk. To blood the as yet untested German Wehrmacht in a short, easy war with Poland was one thing; to plunge it into a two-front war involving the Western powers -- a war for which Germany was as yet ill-prepared -- was quite another matter.

Hitler had always intended to attack the West eventually, but in his own good time. In one of his early discourses on the subject, in 1937,* he speculated that 1943-1945 might be the right time, and probably the latest possible date, for a "final reckoning" with the West. Germany would then be at peak strength, with her reserves fully built up and equipped, while British and French rearmament would not yet have reached the point where it might threaten German superiority.

In 1937 Hitler had a right to think that he could pick his own time for the showdown with the West. But two years later, when it came to be Poland's turn after the rape of Austria and Czechoslovakia, he could no longer be sure. Britain and France had given Poland a solemn promise of support in case of an armed attack against her independence. Hitler professed not to believe that the "decadent democracies" would honor their promise. But as the date set for the attack on Poland approached, his dismissal of Western intervention sounded more and more hollow. The popular mood in Britain had begun to change shortly after Munich, and had hardened further during 1939, when Hitler's behavior seemed almost calculated to dispel any notion that one could do business with him.** Nevertheless, Hitler still made no concrete plans for a war that might involve Britain and France. If he was no longer entirely confident that the Allies would refuse to fight, he may have relied on an intuitive feeling that, if worst came to worst, the West would give him time to make his plans.

He had considered two possible courses of action.*** One was to attack the West first, and leave Poland until later. If he did that, he ran the risk that, while he was engaged in the West, Poland might "stab him in the back" as he put it. The alternative was to go ahead with the invasion of Poland, to which he had become emotionally committed, and to rely on his intuition that Britain and France would again sit by and do nothing. This also was a risk, but one he seemed willing to accept.

Hitler believed -- and was confirmed in this belief by the tendentious reports he was getting from his experts, including Foreign Minister von Ribbentrop -- that the Western powers were not ready for war and would not risk a world war over an issue like Poland. *"Pourquoi mourir pour Danzig?"* was the question being asked in

*Reported in the "Hossbach Minutes." (Colonel Hossbach was Hitler's aide-de-camp.) The Minutes are extensively quoted in Peter de Mendelssohn, *Design for Aggression,* Harper & Brothers, New York, 1946, p. 19.

**Examples of Hitler's recent conduct were his press campaign against England, brutality against the Czechs, and renewed Jewish pogroms in Germany.

***This is a composite of Hitler's thoughts as he expressed them at different times while his plans for the Polish campaign were maturing, primarily in the already-cited speech of August 1939 and in an earlier speech to a similar audience on May 3, 1939. Based on Mendelssohn, Hinsley, and Greiner.

France. And if it should turn out that he had miscalculated and the Western powers did intervene, there was not much they could do to hurt Germany militarily, at least not in the short run. The speedy conquest of Poland, and the pact Hitler was planning to conclude with the Soviet Union, would vitiate the effects of any naval blockade England might try to impose. An invasion of German territory from France was dismissed by him as hardly credible for "psychological reasons" and because it could not succeed unless the Allies violated Belgian and Dutch neutrality, a possibility which he ruled out as inconceivable.

In his all-day harangue of August 22, 1939, Hitler assured his senior commanders that British threats of intervention on the side of Poland were nothing but bluff. (It was always Britain that loomed in Hitler's thoughts, not France, which he despised.) He explained that the Chamberlain Government had been severely criticized in Britain for having capitulated prematurely during the Munich crisis. This time, therefore, it would keep up its bluff until the last moment, in the hope of frightening off Germany. But in the end, when confronted with Hitler's iron determination, Chamberlain would again give in and do nothing but talk. Whether Hitler actually believed this or was merely trying to reassure his commanders who were worried at the prospect of a two-front war, will never be known.

As it turned out, Hitler miscalculated in one respect -- in his belief that Britain and France would not go to war over Poland -- but he was right in discounting the risk that they would intervene militarily while German forces were engaged in the Polish campaign. To reduce the risk even further, he had instructed his military commanders that, in the unlikely event of a declaration of war by the Western powers, the weak German forces in the West were not to open hostilities. They were to be scrupulous in respecting the neutrality of the Low Countries, and leave it to the other side to initiate military action. If attacked, they were to respond only with defensive measures.

His having gambled on the democracies' making no military move, even if they did declare war, can be explained only by Hitler's utter contempt for their political and military leaders and for their woeful state of unpreparedness. How certain he was that his gamble would pay off is demonstrated by the fact that he had not planned against the possibility that France and Britain might force him to fight them in earnest.*

What thinking he had done about a war with the West, and he had done a good deal, was about the kind of war he would fight when he could choose his time for the "final reckoning."** It would be a war to the finish. He would "smash" decadent France. He would "force Britain to her knees" by strangling her seaborne supply routes, mining her harbors, and cutting her off from the Continent, where

*Hillgruber, p. 45.

**His thoughts were expressed in secret briefings and informal remarks throughout the latter part of the thirties. They are paraphrased here from quotations in Mendelssohn, Hinsley, and Greiner.

Germany would then reign supreme. So far as we know, he did not at that time consider the possibility that Britain might have to be invaded.

Strategic bombing played a negligible role in Hitler's thoughts about a future war. In common with most of his military associates, he was oriented toward a ground strategy and did not understand either sea power or air power. The latter he regarded primarily as an adjunct of the army. Certainly, humanitarian considerations were not the reason that strategic air warfare figured so little in his planning; that he would not hesitate to bomb cities was demonstrated when the German Condor Legion bombed Guernica during the Spanish Civil War.

There were some references to strategic bombing in the war plans made by the German Army General Staff before Hitler himself monopolized the strategic planning function. A 1937 plan prepared under the direction of Field Marshal von Blomberg, who was then Minister of War, contains this phrase: "[Air] attacks on targets of mainly political importance, such as Paris, need my [Blomberg's] special consent in every case."*

A later plan (CASE GREEN) for the contemplated invasion of Czechoslovakia, prepared in 1938 under Hitler's own direction, warned commanders that "Retaliatory [air] attacks against the population will be carried out only with my [Hitler's] permission." Another version of the same plan (EXTENDED CASE GREEN) dealt with a war against the Western powers that might be set off by the invasion of Czechoslovakia. This plan directed the Luftwaffe to prepare implementing plans and target folders for the bombing of London, Hull, and other industrial targets.**

One of the few hints that Hitler was at least aware of the threat value of strategic bombing was given shortly before the outbreak of war, in August 1939, when he conferred with the Italian Foreign Minister, Count Ciano. On this occasion, the Führer pointed out the vulnerability of British cities to aerial bombing and the lack of adequate antiaircraft defenses in Britain.

The references to strategic bombing in routine contingency plans are significant but do not add up to anything like the British image of a Germany busily engaged in plans and preparations for an aerial knockout blow against Britain. The British had made the mistake, common before the war, of overrating German efficiency. Hitler was too busy with his piecemeal conquests in the East to spare much thought for a possible war in the West which he did not think was imminent. Like other one-man managements, his could only handle one crisis at a time. But even if he had actively planned for a war with the West, strategic bombing probably would not have had much of a part in it, any more than it did when the actual plan for

*This particular plan (CASE RED, for a two-front war) was one of a series of routine war plans for different contingencies, such as are prepared by all major powers. It did not mean that Germany at that time actually intended to attack the West.

**The references to German war plans are taken from Mendelssohn, especially pp. 8, 46, 182, and 96.

the war with the West (CASE YELLOW) was prepared after the conclusion of the Polish campaign.*

Since the Nazis were not likely to be restrained by moral scruples, there had to be other reasons why the plans for CASE RED and CASE GREEN prohibited the bombing of civilians without express permission. The mention of Paris in the Blomberg directive was probably intended as a generic reference to open cities of such importance that attacks on them might have undesirable repercussions for Germany. It is also possible that Hitler had special plans for Paris in his dream of a postwar Europe. The prohibition against population attacks in Czechoslovakia without his express permission may have been because Hitler wished to spare Czech industry and its skilled workers for use in his own armament effort.

If Hitler had any compunction about killing civilians, we know that it did not extend to the Poles. These "subhumans," as he used to call them, were to be got out of the way so as to provide new *Lebensraum* for the racially superior Germans. The thoughts he expressed on the conduct of the Polish campaign in his address of August 22, 1939, as paraphrased by Greiner, speak for themselves:

> . . .He [Hitler] would find some propaganda device to provide an excuse for starting the war. Never mind if it was credible or not; legality was unimportant, only victory mattered. *Therefore there must be no mercy, no humanitarian qualms.* He had a duty to the German people who could no longer exist in their limited space. . . . Military operations were to be conducted with the single aim of producing a quick decision. . .new Polish units were to be smashed as soon as they were formed, and *the enemy was to be softened up through the ruthless employment of the Luftwaffe. . . .***

*See below, pp. 33*ff.*

**Greiner, p. 43. Italics mine.

4

Blitzkrieg and Sitzkrieg

The Polish Campaign

THE GERMAN invasion of Poland began at dawn on September 1, 1939. In the course of the day, reports began to reach Western capitals that the Germans were bombing Warsaw and other Polish cities. After these reports had been confirmed by Ambassador Biddle in Warsaw and Ambassador Bullitt in Paris, President Roosevelt decided that same day to issue an appeal to all belligerents to refrain from "bombardment from the air of civilian populations or unfortified cities." The President's appeal was promptly welcomed in an Anglo-French Declaration which stated that the two governments had given "explicit instructions to the commanders of their armed forces prohibiting the bombardment, whether from the air or the sea, or by artillery on land, of any except strictly military objectives in the narrowest sense of the word."* Hitler replied in a similar vein, expressing his "unqualified agreement," since he had always advocated "in all circumstances to avoid bombing non-military objectives during military operations."** Each side made the promise contingent upon its observance by the other side. The big question left open was, of course, how to define a "military objective."

The Polish campaign was over in three weeks. This first demonstration of German Blitzkrieg tactics awed Western observers and confirmed their worst fears of Nazi military might and ruthlessness. The Polish forces had indeed been "softened up through the ruthless employment of the Luftwaffe."

*Spaight, p. 259.

***Ibid.*, p. 260.

Reports continued to pour in that fleeing civilians had been machine-gunned from the air to spread panic and that open cities had been bombed. They came from official Polish sources and from neutral observers stationed in Poland. Ambassador Biddle cabled on September 14:

> In view of what the members of my staff and my family and I have experienced and witnessed I find it difficult in many cases to ascribe the wanton barbaric aerial bombardment by German planes to anything short of deliberate intention to terrorize the civilian population and to reduce the number of child-producing Poles irrespective of category.*

President Moscicki of Poland reported to President Roosevelt by cable the "deliberate and methodical bombing of Polish open towns by German aircraft." Roosevelt replied that he was "deeply shocked" by these reports and made public his exchange of telegrams with the Polish President. By then, however, the Polish tragedy was nearly over.

On September 17, Russian divisions invaded Poland from the East. The next day, the Polish government fled to Rumania. Organized resistance had practically ended, except for a few pockets in the southeastern portion of the country, including the city of Warsaw. Though further resistance was futile, the city held out for a few more days in spite of German artillery bombardment. In order to force a quick decision, the Germans supplemented their artillery fire with heavy air attacks, which destroyed a substantial portion of the city and forced it to surrender on September 27.

The impression that Hitler's Luftwaffe had engaged in deliberate atrocities during the Polish campaign was confirmed by the manner in which the Nazis exploited their victory. Their propaganda film "Baptism of Fire," assembled from newsreel pictures of the campaign, was widely shown to audiences of horrified neutrals to impress them with the efficiency and ruthlessness of German arms. It succeeded beyond expectations. It made a mockery of German attempts to defend the air attacks on Warsaw as the legitimate use of "vertical artillery" against a "defended fortress."

The irony is that there may have been some truth in these claims. Asher Lee, a wartime British intelligence officer, believes that the Germans did not deliberately attack nonmilitary objectives during the Polish campaign, and that they did not machine-gun fleeing civilians in Poland as they later did in the Low Countries and France. He feels that in Poland, at least, the German Air Force conducted a "model campaign" in the use of tactical air power, and that the civilian casualties inflicted were an inevitable by-product of attacks on military objectives.**

The world reaction to the Polish campaign was, of course, based on the facts as they were believed to be at the time. It is not surprising that the stories of inhumane

*Cordell Hull, *The Memoirs of Cordell Hull,* The Macmillan Company, New York, 1948, Vol. 1, p. 678.

**Asher Lee, *The German Air Force,* Harper & Brothers, New York, 1946, p. 51.

warfare against Polish noncombatants were so readily accepted, for there had been enough evidence of Nazi brutality in the years since Hitler came to power to make these stories credible. Moreover, there had been Hitler's own broadcasts prior to the war when he raved against the Poles in unbridled language.

What Hitler said in his inner circle was much worse and shocked even the Nazi officers to whom he delivered his tirades. In one of his paroxysms of rage he boasted that "our strength is in our ruthlessness and our brutality." He spoke of killing "without mercy all men, women and children of Polish race and language" and expressed admiration for Genghis Khan, who had exterminated whole populations and "had millions of women and children killed by his own will and with a gay heart."*

Though outbursts like these were reserved for his intimates, Hitler made no secret of his hatred of the Poles, and the West had ample evidence of how he customarily dealt with the objects of his rage. And those Westerners who were still unwilling to believe the worst only had to look at the picture the Nazis themselves provided in their film "Baptism of Fire" to be convinced that the Polish campaign had been waged as a deliberate war of extermination.

Regardless of what really happened, the alleged brutality of the German armed forces during the Polish campaign was believed at the time and had a lasting effect on Britain's conduct of the war. Senior British officers felt that the actions of the Luftwaffe against Polish civilians had freed Britain from the obligations she had assumed with the Anglo-French Declaration in response to the Roosevelt appeal.**

Whether or not the Wehrmacht itself had been guilty of uncivilized conduct during the military phase of the Polish campaign soon became an academic question, as reports began arriving of the unspeakable atrocities the Nazi authorities committed after their occupation of the hapless country. And later on, during the campaign against Scandinavia and in the assault on the Western front, the German armed forces themselves became guilty of the outrages of which they had perhaps been wrongly accused during the Polish campaign.

If the Luftwaffe did not deliberately use terror as a weapon in Poland, it may have been because the potentialities of this weapon had not been fully appreciated before the campaign. Asher Lee reports that a General Quade of the German Air Force gave a series of lectures to Luftwaffe officers on the lessons of the Polish war, in which he pointed out "that the terror effect of bombing on civilian morale was a military factor in air warfare."***

Although Asher Lee absolves the Luftwaffe of blame for the bombing of Warsaw, one is left to wonder if this act had really been prompted by military necessity, as the Germans claimed. As late as three years after the event, in

*John W. Wheeler-Bennett, *The Nemesis of Power: The German Army in Politics 1918-1945*, Macmillan & Co. Ltd., London, 1953, p. 461.

***Air Offensive*, Vol. 1, p. 135.

***Asher Lee, p. 51.

November 1942, when indiscriminate city bombing by both sides had become a common occurrence, Hitler still felt constrained to defend the bombing of Warsaw in one of his speeches. His argument was:

> Before I attacked Warsaw I five times asked them to capitulate, and only then did I do what is allowed by the rules of war.*

What Hitler failed to mention was that, when Warsaw was bombed, the war was already over in all but name. The Polish government had fled the country a week earlier. The bedraggled defenders of Warsaw were running out of supplies, were cut off from the rest of the country, and had no hope of reinforcements. It was only a question of time -- and a very short time, at that -- before they would have had to surrender. But Hitler was in a hurry. He wanted to be able to announce the formal conclusion of the war and redeploy his forces to the West so as to forestall a possible Anglo-French offensive. He ordered his commanders to take Warsaw by September 30, a few days from the time the air bombardment began.

Regardless of whether there was military justification for the bombing of Warsaw, it undoubtedly provided Hitler with an outlet for his rage against the Poles. According to Field Marshal von Manstein, the Führer had wanted to bomb Warsaw earlier in the war.** At that time, his field commanders had succeeded in arguing him out of it on the ground that it would not benefit their military operations and thus would be a wasteful use of the Luftwaffe. Presumably, they withdrew their objections later, when the stubborn defense of Warsaw had turned the city into a "military objective" that had to be taken by force.

The Luftwaffe actions in Poland may well have been wrongly interpreted by the Allies at the time. As we shall see, there were other occasions during the war when both sides made far-reaching decisions on the basis of their erroneous interpretation of what had happened, or why.

Prelude to the "Final Reckoning"

The end of the Polish campaign left Hitler free to turn against the West. The implications should have been obvious, but Allied leaders were still reluctant to face up to the unpleasant prospect before them.

The victory over Poland had another, less obvious consequence, which may have had an even greater bearing on the future course of the war -- the effect of that victory on Hitler himself and on his position in Germany. The brilliantly successful Polish campaign was a personal triumph for the Führer in every way. He had undertaken the venture against the advice of his military professionals, and had been vindicated by its spectacular success. He had been right in predicting that the new Wehrmacht, which he regarded as his own creation,

*Spaight, p. 265.

**Generalfeldmarschall Erich von Manstein, *Verlorene Siege* (Lost Victories), Athenäum-Verlag, Bonn, 1955, p. 51.

would pass its first test with flying colors.* And he had relied on his intuition against the judgment of those of his advisers who did not believe that the Allies would sit idly by while the German forces were engaged in the East.

Hitler's elation at his victory, and at having triumphed over his own experts, gave a boost to his already colossal ego and strengthened his belief in his infallibility. The effects were noticeable in a different attitude toward his generals. Always suspicious of the old-line professionals among them, he became markedly more assertive in dealing with them, and made little effort to hide his contempt for their conservatism or his low regard for their professional advice. The generals, in turn, were changing in their attitude toward Hitler, either because their former self-assurance had been shaken or because they were cowed by the man who was beginning to assume the role of Supreme Commander in fact as well as in name. They found themselves less and less able, and also much less willing, to argue him out of plans that they feared would bring disaster upon Germany.

The Polish victory marked an important stage in Hitler's gradual assumption of absolute control over military as well as political matters. Field Marshal von Manstein states that it was after this victory, and during the subsequent planning for the invasion of the West, that the Army High Command (OKH)** abdicated its responsibilities for the conduct of land warfare and allowed Hitler to usurp the role of *Feldherr:* "Hitler had assumed functions which, according to Schlieffen, could barely be exercised in our age by a triumvirate of king-statesman-*Feldherr.*"*** Others believe that this stage was not reached until the even more spectacular victory in France, which put Hitler at the pinnacle of his power.**** But even after the Polish campaign, the transformation was sufficiently marked to be noted by Greiner and other observers.

The change in Hitler's position meant that whatever moderating influence his military advisers might have had before the Polish campaign would now be lost. Henceforth, the broad strategy of the war and even minor details of its tactical conduct would be determined increasingly by a single man -- a man who acknowledged no moral constraints and would use any means that could serve his purpose. It was therefore a foregone conclusion that the war would reach any level of violence that Hitler considered useful in achieving his growing ambitions. But the test was not to come for another year.

Meanwhile, the Führer lost no time in demonstrating his newfound self-assurance to his inner circle. On September 27, the day Warsaw capitulated, he called a few

*Hitler flew into a rage when Field Marshal von Brauchitsch cautiously hinted that the conduct and discipline of the German troops in the Polish campaign had not been all that could be desired. See Greiner, p. 67.

**Oberkommando des Heeres.

***Von Manstein, p. 90.

****Hans-Adolf Jacobsen, *Fall Gelb: Der Kampf um den deutschen Operationsplan zur Westoffensive 1940* (CASE YELLOW: The Conflict Over the German Operations Plan for the Western Offensive, 1940), Wiesbaden, 1957, p. 153.

of his top commanders to the Chancellery and informed them that he had decided to launch an offensive in the West that autumn. It was to begin as soon as the necessary preparations were completed, unless he could come to an understanding with Britain beforehand. He had reached the decision independently, without consulting his military leaders, because he suspected, correctly, that they would try to argue him out of it.* They were stunned at this announcement, for the German troop dispositions in the West were based on a defensive strategy, and there was not enough time to complete the preparations for an offensive. But Hitler had called them in not to ask their opinion but to give them their orders. If the former corporal had in the past felt somewhat ill at ease in the presence of his top generals, there was no trace of this attitude left now.

He showed his disregard for the sensibilities of the German officer corps on other occasions, as when he ordered the Army to carry out his "solution" of the Polish problem. This was to consist, among other measures, of mass executions of the Polish intelligentsia, the nobility, and the clergy. In addition, they were to create an incident that could serve as an excuse for a wholesale massacre of the Jews. Though the liquidation of Polish undesirables was only another in the long list of crimes the Nazis had already committed in Germany, Austria, and Czechoslovakia, the Army had not thus far taken part in these atrocities. Admiral Canaris, the head of the German *Abwehr* (Counterintelligence), protested to Keitel that, if German military honor were sullied with such crimes, "The day will come when the world will hold the *Wehrmacht,* under whose eyes these events occurred, responsible for such measures."** In the event, German officers found that they could keep their honor unsullied by not carrying out the executions themselves and leaving them to the SS and the SIPO.*** The "Polish solution" bode ill for those who still had any illusions about the manner in which the war would thenceforth be conducted.

But first the world was treated by Hitler to a short-lived peace campaign. On September 19, when the Polish war had clearly been won, though the campaign was not yet over, Hitler extended the olive branch in a speech he made in Danzig. He assured Britain and France that he wanted nothing of them, that he wished to live in peace with the rest of the world, and that, if the Allies insisted on continuing the war, the responsibility for the suffering would be theirs and not his. He returned to this theme in a formal Reichstag speech on October 6. It was again a relatively conciliatory speech, though he did demand the return of the German colonies.****

Hitler's motives behind the peace campaign remain unclear. Perhaps he really expected the Allies to write off Poland and make their peace with him, though it is doubtful that he would have granted them acceptable terms. He may have hoped

*Greiner, pp. 56-57.

**Wheeler-Bennett, pp. 461-462.

****Sicherheits-Polizei* (Security Police).

****J. R. M. Butler, *Grand Strategy,* Vol. 2, *September 1939 - June 1941* (hereafter cited as *Grand Strategy),* in *History of the Second World War,* United Kingdom Military Series, Her Majesty's Stationery Office, London, 1957, p. 61.

that his professions of peace would appeal to the neutrals and influence public opinion in Britain and France, where people had become impatient with what came to be called the "twilight war," and that this might force their governments to give in or at least would undermine the already feeble war spirit in the West. Hitler also presumably was trying to show the German people that he had tried his best to make peace and that the Allies were responsible if the war continued.

It may have been coincidental that Hitler chose this particular time to step up his naval warfare against Allied merchant shipping, but he may have thought that this would make his enemies more eager to come to the conference table. On September 23, a few days after the Danzig peace speech, Hitler authorized Admiral Raeder to lift some of the restrictions on naval warfare dictated by the Hague Convention, which he had observed for fear of provoking Allied intervention while the Polish campaign was in progress. The most important was the prohibition against sinking enemy merchant vessels without warning. The decision to lift this restriction was interpreted by at least one historian as an indication that the Führer had begun to doubt that the Allies would accept his peace offers.*

Regardless of what Hitler may have expected from his peace offensive, he did not allow it to delay his planning for the continuation of the war. As we have seen, he first told his intimates of his plans for the invasion of the Low Countries and France on September 27, though he had decided on it at least tentatively two weeks earlier.** During the following weeks he called in his top leaders for a number of briefing sessions at which he elaborated on these plans and on his general scheme for the future conduct of the war. One of the most important of these meetings was held on October 10, two days before the formal Allied rejection of his peace offer was received. On this occasion Hitler read a memorandum he himself had composed for the personal use of his senior commanders, which was to serve as background for his official "Directive No. 6 for the Conduct of the War."***

Hitler's plans, as he unfolded them in the October 10 meeting and on subsequent occasions, were quite simple when stripped of the endless repetition, self-justification and geopolitical nonsense in which he embedded them. In essence, they were to defeat the Anglo-French armies in the West and to bring pressure on Britain through war at sea and in the air. Hitler's main concern was to draw the Allied armies into a full-scale ground battle *(offene Feldschlacht)*, because this was the kind of engagement in which he felt that the German superiority in the equipment, training, and

*Hinsley, pp. 31-34.

**According to authoritative OKW sources, he had mentioned his intentions in confidence to his aide-de-camp, Lieutenant Colonel Schmundt, as early as September 12. See Jacobsen, p. 7.

***A paraphrase of Hitler's memorandum and the verbatim text of Directive No. 6 are given by Greiner, pp. 61-63. My main sources for the planning sessions that Hitler held during October and November were Hinsley, pp. 38-41; Mendelssohn, pp. 113-122; Jacobsen, Chaps. 1-3; von Manstein, Chap. 4; Greiner, Chap. 2; and Hillgruber, *passim.* The greatly condensed account given here is intended to convey the general tenor of Hitler's thinking during this period.

leadership of ground forces could best be exploited. In his opinion, a decisive victory in a ground battle could bring a quick end to the war. Germany had to avoid a long war of attrition in which she would be at a disadvantage.

The German offensive in the West would begin with the invasion of Belgium, Holland, and Luxemburg. This was an essential feature of Hitler's plan and was mentioned by him in his first meeting with his commanders, on September 27. The Low Countries were needed for tactical reasons in mounting the initial German thrust, as a bastion for protection of the vital Ruhr area, and to provide bases for extended naval and air warfare against Britain.

Only a month earlier, the German government had sent a formal notification to Belgium, Luxemburg, the Netherlands, and Switzerland that their neutrality would be "unconditionally guaranteed." Hitler may have thought that his military leaders might feel somewhat squeamish about breaking yet another solumn undertaking. The justification he gave them for an invasion was that the Low Countries were "insincere" in their professions of neutrality. The proof was that Belgian fortifications were all on the Eastern boarder with Germany, while the Western border had been left open!*

Hitler was determined to have the offensive start as soon as possible, before the onset of winter. Time was of the essence. A quick victory would help to bring the reluctant Italian partner into the war. The Russians were still neutral, and it was to their interest to remain so, but they could change their minds if Germany got bogged down in a long-drawn-out war. To delay the invasion of the Low Countries would be risky, because Britain and France might move in first -- a possibility Hitler had dismissed when he was selling his military leaders on the Polish campaign. Hitler was not worried about France, but Britain was arming frantically and was getting stronger every day. The time to move was now.

The Führer was aware that the stakes were enormous. He was sure that the Allies' objective was nothing less than the "dissolution or destruction of the German Reich." His own objectives were equally unlimited. The time for salami tactics was over; he must aim for the total defeat of the enemy.

For the present, Hitler's thoughts were centered on the ground offensive: the occupation of the Low Countries and destruction of the Anglo-French armies. He seems to have done no concrete planning beyond this point. He did mention the advantages the possession of Holland and Belgium would give him for the defense of the Ruhr and as a base for U-boat operations as well as for air attacks against the industrial heart of Britain and her ports in the south and southwest. Though he spoke of dealing Britain "a mortal blow" from the air, his references to military operations other than those connected with the initial ground offensive were casual, and one gets the impression that he had not given them any real thought.

There was, however, an ominous phrase in the memorandum he had written for his top military leaders. After mentioning the importance of the Low Countries

*Greiner, p. 56.

as bases for air operations against Britain, he said: "The ruthless employment of the Luftwaffe against the heart of the British will-to-resist can and will follow at the given moment."* This phrase may be significant not so much as a plan of action but as an indication of Hitler's readiness to employ any means available. At the time he had made the statement he was probably confident that a victorious ground offensive would end Allied resistance.

Detailed plans and preparations for the offensive in the West -- which was given the code name CASE YELLOW -- were put under way, and the tentative D-day was set for November 12. That date was clearly unrealistic; it had been dictated by Hitler's impatience and did not allow enough time for adequate planning, let alone to make up the severe shortages in ammunition, heavy equipment, and training. It was therefore changed in what turned out to be the first of twenty-nine postponements. The weather was partly responsible, but another factor was the opposition of the Army leaders, who were dragging their feet as long as they could in the hope that a peaceful solution of the conflict would make the offensive unnecessary. One of the many postponements occurred in January 1940, when two German officer couriers carrying top secret invasion plans fell into Belgian hands in an aircraft accident. The offensive had to be rescheduled for March 1940, by which time other developments forced further postponements.

During the winter and early spring, Allied attention was centered on the North, first on the Russo-Finnish war and then on the problem of cutting off the German ore traffic with Sweden and Norway. On the Western front, the Germans were completing the preparations for the great offensive but were careful not to engage in any except defensive military actions. They explained the buildup of their forces as precautionary, designed to protect against an Anglo-French attack through the Low Countries. This was the period of the "phoney war," or "Sitzkrieg," which baffled people in the West and encouraged the wishful thinking of their leaders. In April 1940, only a month before the storm broke, Mr. Chamberlain declared that "Hitler has missed the bus."

The Phoney War

The Allies, for reasons of their own, had no intention of turning the twilight war into a real war. Except for their abortive venture in Norway and a proposed expedition to assist Finland, they left the initiative to Germany and waited for the next blow to fall.

While the German forces were occupied with the Polish campaign in the East, the French could have used their vastly larger armies for offensive action against the small German token force in the West. But the French Chief of Staff, General Gamelin, did not wish to provoke a German reaction until he had completed the leisurely concentration of his forces. After that was done, he would be willing, not

**Air Offensive*, Vol. 1, p. 136, fn. 2.

to attack the Siegfried Line, but to "lean against it" in order to test its strength.* By the time he was ready, the Polish campaign was in its closing days and the Germans were redeploying their first-line forces to the West. Needing no further excuse, Gamelin pulled his troops back toward their Maginot Line positions and held them inactive until the Germans were ready to move against them.

The Chamberlain Government in Britain was not eager to take the offensive either, and, besides, it lacked the means to do so. On the ground, the small British Expeditionary Force in France was, of course, unable to act without the French. Apart from small-scale naval actions and economic warfare, the only way Britain could strike at Germany was through air attack. It was questionable how effective such attacks would be, since Bomber Command was quantitatively and qualitatively inadequate to the task. Nevertheless, the Director of Plans of the Air Staff, Air Commodore Slessor, pointed out on September 7, 1939, that it might be desirable to strike at Germany while she was engaged in the East:

> Although our numerical inferiority in the air is a most important factor, it should not be allowed to obscure other potent considerations. We are now at war with a nation which possesses an imposing facade of armed might, but which, behind that facade, is politically rotten, weak in financial and economic resources, and already heavily engaged on another front. The lessons of history prove that victory does not always go to the big battalions. . . .**

Air Commodore Slessor thought that "indiscriminate attack on civilian populations as such will never form part of our policy," but he regarded attacks on power stations in the Ruhr and on oil as legitimate. His suggestion was not taken up by the Government, partly for reasons with which he and his colleagues fully agreed.

The Air Staff was well aware that it would be taking a great risk to expose the small striking force that Bomber Command could muster at the time to losses from which it might never recover. The aircraft, and especially the trained crews, were the seed corn which had to be preserved if Bomber Command was ever to grow into the kind of force the planners envisaged. At this stage of its growth, heavy losses could cripple the entire establishment. Royal Air Force leaders were also concerned that strategic bombing with ineffective results might discredit what was still a novel method of warfare.

The Government had additional reasons for ruling out air attacks on Germany for the time being. Even carefully executed precision attacks on targets in the Ruhr would inevitably inflict civilian casualties and kill women and children. British leaders were reluctant to accept the onus for having started this kind of warfare and did not want to invite retaliation in kind. Within the RAF it was felt that the Germans themselves had started it by carrying out indiscriminate air attacks in Poland and that therefore Britain was freed from the obligations she had assumed

**Grand Strategy,* Vol. 2, p. 60.

***Air Offensive,* Vol. 1, p. 135.

under the Anglo-French Declaration.* But the Government preferred to wait until the Germans engaged in strategic bombing against Britain or France, or until they violated the neutrality of the Low Countries. The decision may have been prompted by considerations of expediency or of humanity, but most likely by a combination of the two.** Whatever the reason, it is clear that the Chamberlain Government was not inclined toward offensive action in any form, much less a form of warfare so out of keeping with the British mood during the twilight war.

What may have clinched the case was again the attitude of the French, who were opposed to all strategic bombing. In October 1939 the British Chiefs of Staff had prepared a paper on future bombing policy, which was approved by the Cabinet and submitted to Generals Gamelin and Vuillemin (French Air Force) for concurrence. The paper reflected the compromise to which Britain had been driven by necessity. It proposed taking no offensive action in the air so long as the twilight war continued, and using the respite to build up the strength of Bomber Command. Only if the enemy took offensive action in the West that "looked like being decisive" would Bomber Command launch a full-scale daylight assault on the Ruhr, "without frittering away the striking force on unprofitable objectives."***

The French generals did not like anything about the British plan. Under no circumstances would they approve any British action that could invite German retaliation against French cities. Moreover, the "unprofitable objectives" on which the British did not wish to fritter away their precious heavy bombers were precisely the targets the French generals wanted to hit first in case of a German offensive. In their view, all bombers, heavy as well as medium, should be used against troop columns, LOCs, and other tactical targets of concern to a ground commander. They disagreed with the British view that, unless the bombers were used to maximum effect -- that is, for purposes other than those for which artillery was available -- the Germans would be able to occupy the Low Countries and acquire bases for the knockout blow against Britain.

As these disagreements could not be resolved by the military negotiators, they were brought up again at two meetings of the Supreme War Council, in November 1939 and in April 1940. By the time of the second meeting, the positions of the two countries had come closer together, partly because Bomber Command had lost its enthusiasm for a daylight assault on the Ruhr, and partly because the French had somewhat broadened their ideas of what constituted desirable objectives for a bombing attack. But the agreement was only on the surface; the two countries never saw eye to eye on the proper use of strategic bombers.

Another factor that may have contributed to the decision to withhold air attacks on Germany until faced with a desperate situation was the hope of British leaders that the German people would come to their senses and overthrow their bloodthirsty

*See above, p. 29.

***Air Offensive*, Vol. 1, p. 135.

****Ibid.*, pp. 136-137.

rulers. This hope was nourished through the contacts of Foreign Office emissaries with various self-appointed peacemakers in Germany who, understandably, played up the opposition to the Führer within their country. The opposition did exist, but it was not nearly as widespread or as active as it was made out to be. The conspiracies and plots against Hitler's life hatched by certain high-ranking Wehrmacht officers and old-line civilians were amateurish and often halfhearted. Yet the exaggerated reports of these conspiracies -- some planted by German counterespionage agents -- and of the extent of disaffection behind them were all too readily believed by the Chamberlain Government.* They lent support to the assumption, which stubbornly persisted throughout the war, that German morale was vulnerable and that the people were only waiting for an opportunity to turn against their leader.

It was on the basis of this assumption that the British Cabinet had authorized a leaflet campaign aimed at German morale. All during the Polish campaign and during the phoney war, British bombers flew night missions over Germany to drop leaflets. The dual purpose was to incite the German people to revolt and at the same time to show them that their homeland was open to attack from the air. Neutral observers continued to point out that the campaign was having the opposite effect from that intended; to the German people it demonstrated British impotence rather than British strength, and thus relieved their minds of any fear they might have had of the enemy. But the leaflet raids served at least one purpose: "Their chief value was probably the practice they gave to Bomber Command in navigating over Germany at night."**

The British Air Staff as well as Bomber Command were aware that the bomber crews needed all the practice they could get in night flying. The doctrine of daylight precision bombing had begun to look less and less attractive when it was examined from an operational and practical viewpoint. The slow British bombers would be easy prey for German fighters, especially when trying to attack heavily defended targets like the Ruhr. Though there had been few engagements with the Luftwaffe as yet, the British had had a foretaste of what was likely to happen when their Wellington bombers were severely mauled by German fighters in a daylight mission over the North Sea in December 1939. Night bombing seemed to be the obvious answer -- provided that it could be done effectively. As yet Britain lacked the means. Electronic aids for night navigation and bombing were not to be available for some time to come.

In the meantime, the leaflet raids had shown that, if Bomber Command were to switch to night attacks, the crews would have to develop greater skill in navigating at night, particularly in bad weather and when there was no moon. As for bombing accuracy, one of the first night raids the British attempted, in March 1940, when they bombed the German seaplane base on the island of Sylt in retaliation for a raid on Scapa Flow, was shown by photographic evidence to have been a dismal failure.

*Wheeler-Bennett, Chap. 4, especially pp. 475-497.

***Grand Strategy*, Vol. 2, p. 59.

These discouraging experiences taught the RAF lessons which had a lasting impact on the conduct of the air war. In daytime, the bombers were obviously too vulnerable to survive; at night they were safe from enemy fighters but the darkness which shielded them also protected the targets from being identified and hit. The only solution was to select targets that were conspicuous enough to be found at night, and large enough so as not to require a high degree of bombing accuracy. Thus the basis was laid for the future bombing policy of night attacks on area targets, long before British civilian or military leaders had made the mental transition to this form of warfare.

In the meantime, the British bombers continued their futile leaflet raids until the German invasion of Norway and Denmark, in April 1940, when they were employed in the vain Allied effort to repel the invaders. The aggression against the Scandinavian countries was a warning that the twilight war was about to end and that it would be the Allies' turn next. But the Air Ministry's plans for dealing with the imminent German offensive in the West were still completely unrealistic.

In April 1940 Bomber Command was given a new directive, to be used if unrestricted air action against Germany were authorized or if Holland and/or Belgium were invaded. The ambiguously worded directive put heavy emphasis on attacks against oil plants and other "self-illuminating objectives vulnerable to air attack." In case of an invasion of the Low Countries, the bombers were "to cause the maximum dislocation on the lines of communication of a German advance" through attacks on enemy troop concentrations and marshaling yards, but "the principal weight of attack should be directed against the oil plants."* It was not made clear how an attack on oil plants could help to stem a German advance.

In April, the last month before the storm, British leaders were preoccupied with their ill-starred operations in Norway. This may partly explain why they gave relatively little attention to the greater threat in the West. Another reason may have been that Britain was going through a crisis, as the ineptness of her leadership was being glaringly exposed by the bungled Norwegian campaign. The long-smouldering discontent with Britain's conduct of the war finally came to a head during the momentous debate in the Commons on May 7 and 8, when Mr. Amery used Cromwell's words to ask that Mr. Chamberlain resign.**

The Scandinavian episode is beyond the scope of this narrative, though it marked an important milestone in the war. It was important because it showed how Hitler's appetite for conquest had grown since the victory over Poland and how contemptuous he had become of public opinion in the West. His cynical claim that he was only giving "armed protection" to the neutrality of Norway and Denmark made a mockery of his promise to respect the neutrality of the Low Countries, whose turn would be next. The ruthless behavior of his troops against Norwegian

*_Air Offensive,_ Vol. 1, p. 142, and Vol. 4, App. 8 (i), pp. 109-111.

**"You have sat too long here for any good you have been doing. Depart, I say, and let us have done with you. In the name of God, go."

civilians and the bombing of undefended towns like Kristiansand and Elverum* were further reminders that the Nazis would not be restrained by moral scruples in their conduct of the war.

The Scandinavian campaign marked another important change: It was the first major operation of the war to be directed by Hitler himself through the thoroughly nazified officers of the OKW. In it, the Army High Command was reduced to a secondary role.** This meant that thenceforth the old-line German officers, who had upheld higher ethical standards of warfare, would have less and less to say about how the war was to be conducted. The significance of this change may not have been fully appreciated in the West at the time, but it was to become painfully evident later on.

The twilight war ended at dawn on May 10, 1940, when the Germans launched their offensive in the West. Mr. Chamberlain resigned that same day. In the evening, Winston Churchill had his audience with the King and assumed office.

*Spaight, p. 265.

**Greiner, pp. 75-88.

5

The Transition to Total War

The Gloves Come Off

THE DEFEAT of the Allied forces was accomplished in the incredibly short time of two weeks. By then, Holland had surrendered, parts of Belgium were occupied, the French armies had been routed, and the German forces had penetrated deeply into France and reached the Channel coast. On May 26 the British Cabinet ordered Lord Gort to begin the evacuation of his forces from the shrinking Dunkirk salient held by the British. The French armies, ineffectively led, and undermined by Communist anti-war propaganda,* were unable to halt the continuing German advance. On June 17 the new Pétain government sued for an armistice.

Blitzkrieg tactics had triumphed again, this time against an army which many Western observers had regarded as the finest in the world. Hitler, seeing Europe in his grasp, danced his famous victory jig.**

The Führer had reason to be elated. He had correctly predicted that the Allies would leave the initiative to him and do nothing to interfere with his timetable, allowing him to fight at times and places of his own choosing and to pick off his targets one by one. The only hostile action against the German homeland in eight months of warfare had been the leaflet raids.

As noted earlier, the British Air Staff had suggested air attacks on the essential Ruhr industries while the German forces were fighting in Poland, but the idea had

*It will be remembered that the Communist Party line prior to the German attack on Russia had required the faithful to demand peace and to obstruct the Allied war effort.

**Metaphorically he did, although the photograph may have been faked.

found no favor with the Chamberlain Government. There was to be no bombing of targets other than "strictly military objectives in the narrowest sense of the word," as promised in the Anglo-French Declaration. The promise was kept even though the Luftwaffe during the Polish campaign was thought to have violated a similar promise made by the Hitler government.

After the German victory in Poland it was to be expected that Hitler would turn against the West sooner or later, and the British Chiefs of Staff had wanted to know what the air policy would be in that event. Would the RAF be allowed to carry out air strikes against industrial targets in the densely inhabited Ruhr region, where civilian casualties were bound to be high? If the bombers were to assist in repelling an invasion of Belgium and the Netherlands, friendly civilians were certain to be killed even if the attacks were confined to strictly military objectives. The Chiefs of Staff pressed the Cabinet for a clear policy statement but got little satisfaction. In October 1939 the Cabinet discussed the subject and decided that

> ...while our air strength remained inferior to Germany's we should not be the first to "take the gloves off," but that if Germany initiated action against either ourselves or France which threatened to be "decisive" we must use our striking force in whatever way offered "decisive" results. . . . The Cabinet discussed how far an attack on the Ruhr would be an appropriate counter-stroke to an invasion of Belgium, but came to no decision except the negative one that an attack on the Ruhr or any but strictly military objectives would not be justified unless and until Germany either killed large numbers of civilians by air attack on one of the Allied countries or perpetrated a violation of Belgium.*

There was merit in the argument that British inferiority in the air made it undesirable for Britain to escalate the air war, though a leader more aggressive than Mr. Chamberlain might have argued differently. But the excuse that more provocation was needed before Britain could take the gloves off had a hollow ring. The Germans had already demonstrated their disregard for civilized conventions in Poland and through their naval warfare against merchant shipping. At least one member of the Cabinet felt that the Nazis had provided ample justification for treating them as international outlaws. In December 1939, when Winston Churchill was First Lord of the Admiralty, he proposed cutting off the important German traffic in Swedish iron ore through Narvik by laying mines in Norwegian territorial waters.** Though this would have been a clear violation of international law, Mr. Churchill considered it justified since Britain was acting under a higher law in its battle to defend Western civilization against the Nazi barbarians. His defense of the proposed action is significant, not least because it shows his rationale for

**Grand Strategy,* Vol. 2, p. 167.

**There was considerable support for Churchill's proposal, but both the British and French governments managed to drag out action until April of the following year, when the German invasion of Scandinavia was already under way. *Ibid.,* pp. 119-125.

some of the actions he was to take later, as Prime Minister, which often offended the British sense of decency:

> The effect of our action against Norway upon world opinion and upon our own reputation must be considered. We have taken up arms in accordance with the principles of the Covenant of the League [of Nations] in order to aid the victims of German aggression. No technical infringement of international law, so long as it is unaccompanied by inhumanity of any kind, can deprive us of the good wishes of neutral countries. . . .
>
> The final tribunal is our own conscience. We are fighting to re-establish the reign of law and to protect the liberties of small countries. Our defeat would mean an age of barbaric violence, and would be fatal, not only to ourselves, but to the independent life of every small country in Europe. Acting in the name of the Covenant, and as virtual mandatories of the League and all it stands for, we have a right, and indeed are bound in duty, to abrogate for a space some of the conventions of the very laws we seek to consolidate and reaffirm. Small nations must not tie our hands when we are fighting for their rights and freedom. The letter of the law must not in Supreme emergency obstruct those who are charged with its protection and enforcement. It would not be right or rational that the aggressor Power should gain one set of advantages by tearing up all laws, and another set by sheltering behind the innate respect for law of its opponents. Humanity, rather than legality, must be our guide.
>
> Of all this history must be the judge. We now face events.*

The events were soon to happen. But after May 10, 1940, Britain was facing them with a different man at the helm.

The immediate response to the German invasion was a public statement by the British Government, in association with the French, that the Allies reserved to themselves the right to take action which they considered "appropriate in the event of bombing by the enemy of civil populations, whether in the United Kingdom, France or in countries assisted by the United Kingdom."**

The time for the "appropriate action" -- meaning retaliatory air attack -- was soon to come. The violation of Belgian and Dutch neutrality alone was proof enough, if further proof was needed, that Hitler had "taken the gloves off"; the Low Countries had been scrupulous to the point of naiveté in preserving their status as neutrals and had even refused to hold staff conversations with Allied planners. More proof was added almost immediately when the Luftwaffe machine-gunned fleeing civilians on the roads in order to create panic and disrupt the movement of Allied forces.

*Winston S. Churchill, *The Second World War,* Vol. 1, *The Gathering Storm,* Houghton Mifflin Company, Boston, 1948, p. 547.

***Grand Strategy,* Vol. 2, p. 182.

The other stipulation that the Chamberlain Government had made before it would approve strategic air attacks -- that the Allies must be threatened with a decisive defeat -- was also met, three days after the start of the offensive, when the Germans crossed the Meuse river at Dinant and broke through the French defenses at Sedan. Nevertheless, it took another Nazi outrage before even the new Churchill Government steeled itself to take "appropriate action." The incident that triggered the British decision was the German bombing of Rotterdam on May 14. Dutch and neutral residents reported that large portions of the city had been destroyed, and that 30,000 civilian casualties had been inflicted.

The Western world was shocked by this latest example of Nazi ruthlessness. Few believed the excuse given by the Germans that the Luftwaffe attack on Rotterdam had been a legitimate, tactical operation against a fortified and defended city which had rejected a surrender appeal. The Nazis had only themselves to blame if their halfhearted protestations of innocence were dismissed as insincere. Hitler's past record, and his intemperate threats to destroy Rotterdam if it did not surrender, made it hard to believe that the mass bombing could have been intended as a "tactical operation." Nor is it likely that Hitler wanted his protestations to be believed; at that stage of the battle, he probably was more interested in exploiting his reputation for ruthlessness to demoralize his opponents than in undeceiving public opinion in the West. Once again, as with his propaganda film of the Polish campaign, he was hoist by his own petard.

On May 15, 1940, the day after the bombing of Rotterdam, the British Cabinet at last approved an air strike on industrial targets in the Ruhr. The decision was reached after prolonged debate, but, once made, it was carried out without delay. That same night, almost a hundred heavy bombers -- or what were then called heavy bombers -- took off to attack the German mainland for the first time with something more lethal than leaflets. The results of the bombing were negligible. But it was the beginning of the strategic air offensive against Germany.

It turned out to be a momentous decision, for it set in motion a chain of events which eventually, and perhaps inevitably, led to the all-out escalation of the war. Although its full implications were not recognized at the time, it was a drastic step for the British to have taken. Important decisions of this sort are rarely made for a single reason. In this case there were several compelling reasons for lifting the previous restrictions on Bomber Command, apart from the strong reaction in Britain to the Rotterdam "massacre." But official commentaries agree that it was this incident that triggered the British decision although it might have been made even if Rotterdam had not been bombed.

> The new British coalition Government formed by Mr. Churchill on 11th May was immediately confronted with the urgent demand that now at last Bomber Command, whose aircraft were already engaged in support of the land battle, should begin the strategic offensive against Germany. Four more days passed while the War Cabinet hesitated, and every day brought a still more critical

> situation. Any hopes that the Germans might apply a code of morals in the West different from that which Poland had experienced in the East were quickly shattered by the mass bombing of Rotterdam. This attack caused far less damage and death than was at the time reported, but it was obvious that the gloves were off.*

Another official source also notes the effect of the Rotterdam incident on the Cabinet's decision:

> On May 10 the Government announced publicly, in agreement with the French, that they reserved to themselves the right to take action which they considered "appropriate in the event of bombing by the enemy of civil populations, whether in the United Kingdom, France or in countries assisted by the United Kingdom." It was not, however, till May 15, the day after the Germans had bombed the city of Rotterdam, that after long discussions the Cabinet authorised an attack on the Ruhr and the Strategic Air Offensive began.**

We know, with the benefit of hindsight, that the facts of the case were somewhat different from what they were believed to be at the time and that they had been wrongly interpreted. To the British Cabinet, the apparently needless destruction of Rotterdam seemed to be a wanton act of Nazi barbarism, whose only meaning could be that Hitler had decided to cast all restraint to the winds and to fight the total war of extermination he had so often threatened. In bombing Rotterdam, the Germans were believed to have taken the first step toward unrestricted air warfare. Soon, it was thought, British cities would suffer the fate of Rotterdam, because Hitler, having decided to fight with the gloves off, would attempt the long-dreaded aerial knockout blow against Britain. In the circumstances, this was a reasonable conclusion, but it was based on a partial misunderstanding of the Rotterdam incident.

In the first place, the reports of the damage caused by the German attack on Rotterdam were greatly exaggerated. The actual number of civilians killed in the bombing was 980, not 30,000, as originally reported. Also, the postwar investigation has shown that there was some truth in the German claim that the attack had been originally intended as a tactical operation in support of the ground troops besieging the city. The ground commander was preparing an assault on the enemy positions and wanted to soften them up through an attack by Stuka dive bombers. But Hitler was getting impatient and gave the Dutch an ultimatum threatening complete destruction of Rotterdam unless it surrendered forthwith. There is little doubt that he would have made good his threat, and that Göring and Kesselring were only too eager to carry it out.

The German corps commander in charge of the siege, General Schmidt, when he thought that surrender was imminent, tried to call off the Stuka attack he himself

Air Offensive, Vol. 1, p. 144.

***Grand Strategy*, Vol. 2, p. 182.

had requested. An attack was launched nevertheless, and not by stukas but by the larger Heinkel bombers carrying heavier bomb loads. If Göring's and Kesselring's testimony is to be believed, they had gone ahead with the attack because they did not know that surrender negotiations were going on. They were probably lying. As the German bombers were seen approaching Rotterdam, General Schmidt tried to warn them off by firing red flares, but at least half the attackers either did not see the flares or did not heed them. General Schmidt, who had acted honorably throughout this sorry affair, personally expressed his regrets to the Dutch commander of Rotterdam.*

In weighing its course of action, the British Government had to go on the facts as they were perceived at the time, in the midst of a critical battle. In this particular case, its misconstruction of the enemy's intentions did not matter, because the British would have initiated strategic air warfare sooner or later in any case.

But the bombing of Rotterdam was an important event for another reason. It was one of several occasions during the war when both sides made far-reaching decisions on the basis of wrongly reported or erroneously interpreted facts. It may serve as a warning to those who like to believe that in a future war, because human survival itself will be at stake, decisions will be made more rationally than in the past, and with better knowledge of the facts.

The British bomber strikes against the Ruhr demonstrated the more aggressive spirit of the new Churchill Government and may have provided an emotional outlet. But they had little effect on the battle which was to decide the fate of France. The appalling news from the front kept piling up. Churchill flew to France, where he was shocked to hear from General Gamelin that the French *masse de maneuvre,* on which Churchill had been counting, did not exist. But it was not for lack of numbers that the battle was being lost. Even without a strategic reserve, the Allies had approximately the same number of divisions on the Western front as the Germans. What the French forces lacked was better morale, better organization, and better generals. Hitler had been right in insisting on a full-scale ground battle, in which the Germans would be able to exploit their superiority in the equipment, training, and leadership of ground forces.

The RAF could not redress the balance, though it did all it could to provide support for the ground forces. The medium bombers of the BAFF (British Air Forces in France) and the Hurricane fighters of the British Expeditionary Forces -- both operating from airfields in France -- as well as medium bombers and fighters based in Britain, all participated in the effort to stem the rout of the French forces. Even the heavy bombers were employed in tactical missions against marshaling yards and other LOC targets.

But the end was already in sight. On May 25, the British Chiefs of Staff submitted a review of the military situation that would confront Britain "in a certain

*This account is based on a study of the Air Ministry Historical Branch, reproduced in *Grand Strategy,* Vol. 2, App. 1, pp. 569-570.

eventuality" -- a euphemism for the imminent collapse of France.* Whether through self-delusion or in an effort to keep a stiff upper lip, they arrived at the surprising conclusion that "the defeat of Germany might be achieved by a combination of economic pressure, air attack on economic objectives in Germany and on German morale and the creation of widespread revolt in her conquered territories." What was more to the point was their recognition that Britain's chances for continuing the war alone depended on the air: "The crux of the matter is air superiority." The Germans would now be able to base their aircraft near the Belgian and French coasts for easier attacks on the RAF, and on the British aircraft industries on which it depended. Air strikes on industrial targets would inflict heavy casualties among the civilian population, whose morale would be severely tested. The Chiefs of Staff felt sure that the British people would meet the test.

The emphasis on the coming battle for air superiority over Britain was a change from the earlier belief that as soon as Hitler was ready to take the gloves off he would launch a knockout blow against British cities. It may have been because by this time the RAF had had some experience in trying to penetrate German defenses and had become less certain of the axiom that "the bomber always gets through." The British bombers of that time were no match for the enemy's modern fighters, and neither were the German bombers, as the Luftwaffe found out when it came up against the British Hurricanes and Spitfires.

Fighter Command had been greatly strengthened since the war began and could be expected to take a heavy toll of the Luftwaffe in daylight. Therefore, the Germans would have to concentrate on neutralizing the British fighters before attempting daylight attacks against cities in which they might lose more bombers than they could afford. They could, of course, avoid these losses by attacking at night, since night-fighter equipment and tactics were still in a rudimentary state, but it was not unreasonable to expect that the Luftwaffe would have as much trouble locating and hitting targets at night as the British were having in their own unsuccessful night attacks on Germany. These speculations, however, related to the future; Hitler was not yet ready to tackle Britain.

In his Directive No. 13 of May 24, 1940, the Führer promised the Luftwaffe that it would be given "unlimited freedom of action against the British homeland as soon as sufficient forces were available," when it would launch "a crushing attack in retaliation for the British raids on the Ruhr area."** But the Luftwaffe was still occupied in providing support for the ground forces in the concluding phase of the battle of France. Even after the French surrender on June 17, a great deal still had to be done to prepare air bases near the coast and to refit and redeploy the Luftwaffe for an attack on Britain.

More important, no decision had as yet been made on what to do about Britain in the inconceivable event that she should decide to continue to fight alone. German

Grand Strategy, Vol. 2, pp. 211*ff.*

***Ibid.*, p. 196.

planning had not gone beyond the defeat of the Allied forces on the Continent. In Hitler's Reich, only one man could make such decisions -- but after the defeat of France the Führer allowed his mind to dwell on more pleasant prospects.

Interlude

Hitler now abandoned himself to the enjoyment of his spectacular victory. He savored the sweet revenge of witnessing the surrender ceremonies in the Forest of Compiègne, where the Germans had capitulated after World War I. He was making plans for a great victory parade in Paris and paid a brief visit to the city while waiting for the formal end of hostilities.* Afterwards there were sentimental visits to the battlefields of the earlier war and a tour of the reconquered territory of Alsace.

Hitler's "groveling court" was infected by the Master's new mood of euphoria; the OKW diarist comments on the different atmosphere that began to prevail at the Führer's advanced headquarters in Brûly-de-Pesche.** There the talk was all of peace, for everybody was certain that the war was over and that Britain had no choice but to come to terms with the victor. Hitler even ordered a partial demobilization of the Army so as to release manpower for the civilian economy. He seemed to have lost all interest in the conduct of the war, although, so far as Britain was concerned, the war was far from over.

Between June 23 and July 11 Hitler remained inaccessible to his top Army and Navy leaders and even saw very little of Göring.*** He had dropped his role of the *Feldherr* and was occupying himself with the more congenial task of redrawing the map of a Europe of which he would be the ruler as well as the principal architect. His plans for the new Europe were still nebulous, and he kept them from his subordinates, but there were signs indicating the direction of his thoughts. The French civilians who fled from the battlefields north of the Somme were not allowed to return to their homes after the armistice. Northern France and Belgium were combined into a single military occupation zone under unified administration. A German source interpreted these moves as foreshadowing a plan to create a new "Greater Flanders," which would reach south as far as the Somme. France might lose additional territory in the East, where Hitler possibly was planning to carve out a new "Greater Burgundy" that would include Nancy and Belfort. The Briey ore basin probably would be incorporated in the new German Reich.****

*The plans for the Paris parade were canceled in favor of holding the victory celebration in Berlin. See below, p. 53.

**Greiner, p. 110.

***Telford Taylor, *The Breaking Wave: The Second World War in the Summer of 1940*, Simon and Schuster, New York, 1967, pp. 53 and 58.

****General Kurt von Tippelskirch, *Geschichte des zweiten Weltkriegs* (History of the Second World War), Athenäum-Verlag, Bonn, 1951, pp. 109-110.

During these halcyon days of June and July 1940 Hitler also dropped hints to his intimates of grandiose plans for building a new German city on Trondheim Fjord, transforming Norway with a network of *Autobahnen,* carving out a new German colonial empire in Africa, and, in general, changing the world in accordance with his visions. There would be a definite place for Britain in this world, provided only that she accepted the *fait accompli.* Hitler told Mussolini and Ciano in June that he had no wish to destroy the British Empire, since he considered it an important asset in helping to maintain the peace of the world. All he wanted from Britain was that she return the German colonies and acknowledge German hegemony on the Continent. His idea of an Anglo-German partnership was not new, for he had expounded it in *Mein Kampf.* He may have mentioned it to his Italian allies so that it would reach British ears, since he knew that anything he told the Italians always got to Britain.

It does not seem to have occurred to Hitler that his idea of sharing the mastery of the world might not appeal to Britain. His failure to take this possibility into account may explain why he was so certain after the defeat of France that Britain would come to terms with him as soon as her responsible leaders -- among whom he did not include Winston Churchill -- could prevail on their government to accept his irresistible offer.* It may also explain his temporary and uncharacteristic lack of belligerence toward Britain.

Hitler's famous order to halt the German armor in the final assault on Dunkirk is generally held responsible for permitting the successful evacuation of the British troops. Some historians have tried to explain this order as showing the Führer's desire to build a golden bridge for the retreating enemy and that, consciously or unconsciously, he wished the British to escape. But even if the order was given through incompetence, which seems more likely, Hitler was surprisingly unconcerned when the planned annihilation of the British forces did not succeed.** Another uncharacteristic behavior was his mild reaction to the British air attacks on German industrial targets. These sporadic attacks were carried out at night, with small forces, and did very little damage. In typical Nazi fashion, Göring wanted to exact fearful revenge by letting loose the Luftwaffe against Britain. But instead of working himself into one of his ungovernable rages in response to the British "provocation," Hitler casually brushed aside Göring's suggestion. He explained that the British must have become unnerved by the disaster in France and somebody had probably lost his head, or else that the RAF had undertaken the raids on its own, without Cabinet permission.***

*The Germans were persuaded of the existence of a "peace party" in Britain led by Lord Halifax and including such personages as the Duke of Windsor, who seems to have made a favorable impression on Hitler. See Hillgruber, p. 149.

**Telford Taylor suggests that "Hitler and the generals alike were bent on the destruction of French military power" and thus made the Dunkirk escape possible. *The Breaking Wave,* p. 20.

***Walter Ansel, *Hitler Confronts England,* Duke University Press, Durham, N.C., 1960, p. 113.

That Hitler was ambivalent in his feelings toward Britain is well known. He respected her as a Nordic sister nation and admired her achievements. He was probably sincere when he told his Italian allies that he had no wish to destroy Britain -- unlike his other enemies whom he always wanted to "smash" -- and that he would be willing to accept her as a partner in his schemes for the postwar world. What may be more to the point, however, is that there were urgent, tangible reasons for his desire to liquidate the war in the West.

Hitler's initial objective had been achieved with the defeat of France. For the moment he had no designs on Britain, provided she was willing to leave him alone so that he could digest his latest conquests and make preparations for the attack on his next objective. That objective was Russia -- huge, sprawling Russia, peopled by an inferior race and holding all the *Lebensraum* the German people would ever need. He had been dreaming about the war with Russia for many years, but now the time for it had come. The German Army had proved its mettle and had eliminated the French Army as a potential threat in the West. Hitler was ready to move East. We know that his plans for war with Russia had become sufficiently firm by the end of July 1940 for General Jodl to have passed them on officially to the top staff of OKW.*

Not only did Hitler see no reason why Britain should wish to continue the war in the West, but he did not see how she could. It was inconceivable to him that Britain, forced back onto her small island with the bedraggled remnants of her army, would try to hold out alone against the conqueror of Europe with his invincible armies. He was confirmed in his thinking by reports received from British and neutral sources that influential personages in Britain were trying to arrange an accommodation with him.

Hitler and his advisers did not appreciate the extent of the change that had come over Britain since Mr. Churchill became Prime Minister. They overrated the strength and influence of the remaining appeasers and mistakenly believed that the British desire for accommodation had been strengthened by the disaster in France, when just the opposite was true.

"SEA LION" Emerges

When the British showed no signs of being willing to give in, Hitler was confronted with the problem that no real planning had been done for that contingency. This was one of the many penalties he paid for his one-man style of government. In Hitler's Reich no important decision could be made, or carried out, unless he himself took an active interest in the matter. But so far, Hitler's thinking had not gone beyond the great offensive in the West which was to end the war with the Allies and leave him free to settle with Russia. He had spoken vaguely of forcing England to her knees by strangling her supplies but had given no serious thought to possible alternatives. One such alternative was a cross-Channel invasion of the island -- an

*Greiner, p. 288.

extremely uncongenial idea to an old infantry soldier like Hitler. Neither he nor his military advisers had seriously considered such a project, with the exception of the chief of the German Navy, *Grossadmiral* Raeder.

Earlier in the war, Raeder had ordered the staff of his Naval Operations Office* to prepare contingency plans for landing operations against the British Isles. This had been done more as a matter of prudence than of unusual foresight, but it proved useful to the Admiral when he thought the time had come to broach the subject to the Führer. He first did this on May 21, 1940, when victory in France seemed in sight. Unless Britain capitulated, plans for the further conduct of the war would soon have to be made. An invasion of Britain was one of the logical possibilities to be considered. If so, Raeder wanted to be prepared since the Navy would play a leading role in such a project. That this might also win him a share of the glory in which his victorious Army and Air Force colleagues were basking may not have been absent from his thoughts.

But the Admiral had misjudged his timing. Hitler had given no thought to an invasion which he, as well as his Army Supreme Commander, judged to be infeasible.** Raeder had to wait for another opportunity, which came in a conference with the Führer on June 20, shortly after the fall of France. This time Raeder was given a chance to describe his plans in greater detail. He was also able to get in a sly dig at his archenemy Göring by mentioning that operations against Britain were, of course, out of the question until the Luftwaffe had won air superiority over the RAF. But again he had misjudged his timing, for he had caught Hitler when his mood of euphoria was at its height. The Führer was interested in the military details of the proposed operation but was in no frame of mind to act on Raeder's recommendation.***

Nevertheless, after this meeting, and perhaps partly as a result of it, the Army did give a little more thought to the possibility that an invasion of England might be undertaken. Until then, OKH had always rejected Navy feelers on this subject with the argument that the large forces required for such an operation could not be transported or supplied, and that the necessary air superiority could not be gained. It is not certain what caused the Army to modify its position after the June meeting.**** Whatever it was seems to have had repercussions in Hitler's own OKW as well, for toward the end of June the OKW staff also began to occupy itself with plans for a possible invasion of Britain.

*The Naval Operations Office *(Seekriegsleitung)* kept a voluminous war diary which was captured intact and has provided a good source for historians, including those consulted for this narrative.

**Greiner, p. 111.

***Ansel, pp. 102*ff.*

****Ansel suggests that the Army Chief of Staff, General Halder, may have been influenced by the Foreign Minister, von Ribbentrop, who had a personal score to settle with Britain. Another factor may have been the partial demobilization of the Army which Hitler had ordered after the victory in France. The Army may have been looking for new tasks, since it had not yet been informed of Hitler's plans for war with Russia. *Ibid.,* pp. 106-110 and 115-116.

On July 2, OKW issued a directive which mentioned the subject of invasion for the first time. It had clearly been inspired by Army thinking, for it spoke of a "broad front landing by 25-40 divisions," whereas the Navy plans had always dismissed an operation on such a scale as impossible for the Navy to support. But, although the directive discussed the possibility of invasion, the words it used were so vague that it was difficult to tell what OKW really had in mind: ". . .the Führer has decided that a landing in England is possible, provided air superiority can be attained. . . ." The directive went on to order that invasion preparations be made, but without setting a date and with the understanding that this was "still only a plan and has not yet been decided on."* Not exactly the kind of language to inspire energetic action. It may be significant that the directive was signed by Keitel and not by Hitler.

The obvious reason for the vagueness was that Hitler had not yet decided what to do about Britain and was still hoping that she would spare him the need of doing anything at all. The last thing he wanted was to mount a cross-Channel invasion against strong opposition. But Hitler's wishful thinking that Britain would come to terms with him must have received a rude shock the day after the directive was issued. On July 3 occurred the incident at Mers-el-Kebir where the British took on the distasteful task of putting the French fleet out of action. After this demonstration of British resolve, even Hitler must have realized that he was facing a Britain very different from the one that had sued for "peace in our time" at Munich.

Perhaps it was this incident which prompted Hitler at last to give his personal attention to the possibility of invasion. He was still doubtful that the project was feasible, but he began to examine the practical problems involved. One result of this change was to force his planners out of the realm of fantasy in which the early invasion plans had been conceived.

On July 16 Hitler issued a new directive (No. 16), this time signed by himself, to replace the one signed by Keitel two weeks earlier.** The plan to invade Britain had been given more weight within the bureaucracy by being assigned a code name -- originally LION, soon changed to SEA LION -- and for the first time a tentative date was mentioned. Full preparations for the invasion were to be started at once and were to be completed by August 15. The actual invasion date would be decided later. The new directive was still vague on the crucial question of whether or not the invasion would take place. It listed a number of conditions that would have to be met *if* the operation were undertaken, chief among them the attainment of air superiority over the RAF: "The British Air Force must be morally and physically defeated to the extent that it will be unable to offer significant opposition to the passage of German forces."

A few days after issuing the directive, the Führer once more held out the olive branch to Britain in what he called his "last appeal to reason." The occasion was a

*Hinsley, pp. 65-66.

**Reproduced in *Dokumente zum Unternehmen "Seelöwe"* (Documents on Operation SEA LION), edited by Karl Klee (hereafter cited as *Dokumente)*, Musterschmidt Verlag, Göttingen, 1959, pp. 310-314.

gala Reichstag session at the Kroll Opera House on July 19 to celebrate the victory in France. Hitler rewarded a number of his top commanders by promoting them to the formerly rare rank of *Generalfeldmarschall.* A special honor was reserved for Göring, who was elevated to the newly-created top rank of *Reichsmarschall.* There was not much about peace in Hitler's harangue, beyond a few empty phrases to indicate that Germany had won her objectives and that there was no longer any reason for the war to go on. If it continued, the British would have to take the blame for the suffering that would result. This seemed to be the true purpose of Hitler's speech: to prepare the German people for continued hardship and to make sure that they would blame it on Britain. If he really hoped that his "last appeal" would be accepted, he had chosen a strange way of expressing it.

As might have been expected, the British Government curtly dismissed the Führer's so-called peace offer as a "summons to capitulate to his will." He may have been prepared for the rejection, because he told Count Ciano before the British response was known that he intended to take military action against Britain and that a decisive operation against her was being planned.* His reason for telling Ciano was probably to increase the pressure on Britain, for he could be sure that the news would quickly find its way to London.

At this stage, Hitler still hoped to be able to coerce Britain into a settlement instead of having to invade her. He would have preferred to attack Russia instead, and to do so as soon as possible, in 1940. He had explained to his senior commanders, who were staggered at the idea, that if he smashed Russia that year he would have solved the problem of Britain as well. His theory was that the only reason England had rejected his peace offers was that she was hoping for a Bolshevik attack on Germany which would relieve the pressure on Britain in the West. If Russia were knocked out as a potential menace, these hopes would collapse and Britain would have to seek terms.**

Hitler's military leaders finally convinced him that it was too late in the year to prepare and launch an enterprise of the scale of an attack on Soviet Russia. He reluctantly agreed to postpone Operation BARBAROSSA, as it later came to be known, until 1941. But this meant that Britain still remained to be tackled and that the preparations for the invasion had to proceed.

Yet it was clear to everybody concerned with Operation SEA LION that Hitler's heart was not in it. The only explanation for the confused and contradictory signals from the top was that Hitler was merely going through the motions and had not really made up his mind to launch the invasion.*** Most of his senior commanders

*Wheatley, p. 39.

***Grand Strategy*, Vol. 2, p. 536.

***"That Hitler's heart had not been in this project from the beginning was apparent even then [Summer 1940]. It was noticed all the way down to the operating commands that the preparations were being made without the driving force from the top that had always been present before. General Jodl, the Chief of Operations in OKW, regarded the invasion project as an act of desperation which was not justified by the general situation." Von Manstein, p. 165.

hoped that he would not go through with it. They were well aware of the risks, and the more deeply they got into the details of operational planning, the more they appreciated the enormous difficulties that would confront them.

The problems were aggravated by the lack of coordination among the services and by the basic disagreement between the Army and Navy on how such a project should be conducted. The Army, having had no experience with amphibious operations, thought of the invasion simply as an extended river crossing and had planned on landing a large force rapidly on a broad front. The Navy planners considered this scheme utterly unrealistic and wanted the operation scaled down to a more manageable size. The German Navy had never been designed for the support of amphibious operations and had suffered crippling losses in destroyers and other critical ships during the Scandinavian campaign. It lacked the capability to transport the forces required by the Army, let alone to protect them against the British Home Fleet.

So far as the Luftwaffe was concerned, it clearly had a critical part to play in an invasion, for both the Army and the Navy agreed -- one of the few points on which they did agree -- that it would be suicide to attempt a landing unless the Luftwaffe could win air superiority at least over the Channel and over the coastal areas selected for the invasion. But if Göring was making any plans for supporting SEA LION, he was keeping them to himself. His staff explained that the Luftwaffe was not concerned with the invasion because "Göring has passed the word nothing will come of it."*

There was nobody below the Führer himself who could iron out these interservice disagreements; OKW was a military secretariat, not a joint staff in the proper sense of the word. No unified commander had been appointed to be responsible either for the planning for SEA LION or for its execution.** After the war, General Warlimont, who had been Jodl's Deputy for Operations in OKW, commented:

> . . .a proposal to set up a special commander would certainly have been refuted by Hitler, also for the further reason that, as he saw it, political issues of the utmost importance were constantly involved in every step of the military preparations for this action.***

What he meant by the "political issues of the utmost importance" can be inferred from a remark Hitler is reported to have made to Field Marshal von Rundstedt in a rare burst of confidence:

> Three days later, after his Reichstag speech of July 19, Hitler conveyed to Generalfeldmarschall von Rundstedt, who had been slated to command the

*Ansel, p. 191.

**The lack of unified direction, and its effect on the project, have been discussed by several authors, e.g., Karl Klee, *Das Unternehmen "Seelöwe"* (Operation SEA LION), Musterschmidt Verlag, Göttingen, 1958, p. 77 and *passim.*

***Ansel, p. 149.

invasion army in his capacity as C.-in-C., Army Group "A", that in spite of his recently issued directive [No. 16] he considered the invasion preparations only as a deceptive maneuvre *(Scheinmanöver)* for the purpose of bringing psychological pressure on Britain.*

There is a great deal of evidence in the literature on SEA LION that the Führer, in common with most of his senior commanders, considered an *opposed* landing infeasible unless Britain's powers of resistance -- principally her air and naval forces -- had first been rendered ineffective in some (unspecified) manner. But if Britain could be made to believe that the invasion was really going to take place, the threat alone might bring her to her senses and make her agree to a settlement with Germany. The hope of being able to coerce Britain through psychological pressure alone, or pressure reinforced by military action, dominated Hitler's thinking throughout this period. It can be understood only if we remember that, ever since the fall of France, he had been so convinced of the hopelessness of Britain's position that he thought only the stubbornness of leaders like Churchill prevented her from acknowledging her defeat and coming to terms with the conqueror of Europe.

But if the invasion bluff was to work, the preparations for the landing had to be carried out as if for the real thing. Not only the British but the senior German commanders themselves had to be deceived into believing that the invasion would take place. Hitler's admission to von Rundstedt was therefore all the more remarkable and can perhaps be explained by the high regard in which he held the Field Marshal at that time. Hitler's distaste for SEA LION was, of course, no secret to his senior commanders,** but they could never be sure what was really in the mind of this unpredictable man. For all they knew, he might suddenly order the invasion to proceed in spite of all the reasons against it.

In the process of giving verisimilitude to the project, however, Hitler became a victim of his own deception. One of the problems that confronted him from the beginning was that his commanders, and especially Admiral Raeder, were pressing him for a firm decision on whether, and when, the invasion would take place, so that the necessary preparations could be set in motion. The earliest date by which the Navy would be ready and conditions for a landing would be suitable was September 15, but the irrevocable decision on whether to go ahead with it would have to be made at least ten days in advance. This did not leave much time for the Luftwaffe to win the air superiority which all had agreed was an essential prerequisite for the invasion.

Göring, to be sure, had bragged that it would take him no more than four days to smash British fighter defenses over southern England, and only two to four weeks to defeat the RAF altogether.*** But his Army and Navy rivals were skeptical of

*Hillgruber, p. 170. The Field Marshal reported the remark in a personal communication after the war. Hillgruber cites additional evidence in a footnote on the same page.

**See above, p. 53, third footnote.

***Ronald Wheatley, *Operation Sea Lion*, Clarendon Press, Oxford, 1958, p. 59.

Göring's boasts. They did not think that he could succeed in the short time remaining. If they turned out to be right, the project would have to be canceled or postponed tq the following year, and the blame would fall on Göring. This may have been what the Army and Navy leaders hoped.* They themselves lacked the courage to talk Hitler out of SEA LION even after they had received an authoritative appraisal by the Naval Staff that "its execution that year can not be responsibly considered" and that "its execution at any time appears extremely dubious. . .entirely apart from enemy action."**

Hitler, too, must have seen the proposed battle for air superiority as a solution to his own problems. It would give him an excuse for postponing a firm decision on SEA LION until the outcome of the battle was known. And, what was undoubtedly still more important in the Führer's eyes, the air attacks would add to the psychological pressure on Britain and perhaps make her more willing to come to terms with him. Another advantage would be that intensification of the war with Britain would enable him to retain his political-military initiative even if he could not attack Russia that year. By the latter part of July 1940, Hitler's Army commanders had finally convinced him that it was impossible to launch an offensive in the East that autumn, as he had originally hoped. The air assault against Britain would bridge the gap until next spring better than various diversionary actions he had considered, and rejected, against Gibraltar, in East Africa, or elsewhere. The air battle would be more spectacular and would awe the world with another demonstration of German might.

All these advantages would be gained even if the air battle failed in its real objective of coercing Britain into surrender. But Hitler seemed optimistic. As he saw it, Britain's spirit had been down, when "something must have happened in London" to lift her up again (presumably the hope that Russia would turn against the Nazis). The air attacks would demonstrate to Britain anew the hopelessness of her position.

These thoughts were voiced by Hitler, or could be inferred from his remarks, at an important Führer Conference on July 31, where the principal topics were SEA LION and the forthcoming air battle. Keitel, Jodl, Raeder, von Brauchitsch, and Halder were present. Göring was not, but evidently had had a private conversation with Hitler before the meeting. The upshot of the conference was a decision to launch the battle for air superiority as soon as the Luftwaffe could get ready for it, to continue preparations for SEA LION at full speed, and to set a tentative date of

*Ansel, p. 166.

**From the concluding remarks by the Navy Chief of Staff, Admiral Schniewind, in a *Memorandum on the Execution of Sea Lion* of July 29, 1940, by the Naval Operations Office. (In *Dokumente,* pp. 315-323.) The Memorandum presented factual evidence to back up its pessimistic conclusions regarding the chances of carrying out the landing and resupplying it in the face of the expected weather deterioration and enemy action. In his presentation to the Führer on July 31, Admiral Raeder omitted or watered down the most telling points in the Memorandum. (Hillgruber, p. 171.) The Army leaders who also attended the conference had read an advance copy of the document. (Ansel, pp. 169-170.)

September 15 for the invasion.* These decisions were incorporated in a new directive (No. 17), "For the Conduct of the Air and Naval War Against England," which Hitler signed on August 1.** The stated objective was intensification of aerial and naval warfare "in order to create the conditions for the final defeat of England." But almost the entire directive was devoted to the air offensive, except for a single sentence giving the Navy permission to step up naval warfare as well.

The Luftwaffe was directed to use all available resources to gain air superiority over Britain by engaging enemy aircraft in the air, by striking at the Fighter Command ground organization and supply system, and by attacking the aircraft industry. After local or temporary air superiority had been won, the attacks were to be shifted to British ports, especially those needed for supplying the island with food. Ports on the south coast were to be spared whenever possible, as they might be needed for contemplated German operations. The offensive was to be conducted in such a manner that the full capabilities of the Luftwaffe would be available when required to support SEA LION. (This was the only reference to the invasion itself.) The attacks were to begin as soon after August 5 as preparations could be completed and weather permitted.

The directive also contained the order, printed in block letters, that "Terror attacks in reprisal will be carried out only by my order." This did not mean that Hitler was opposed to such attacks, but it meant that he reserved the right to determine *when* they should take place. We know that he considered them primarily a weapon for psychological warfare; they were the *coup de grace,* the *Todesstoss,* that would cause an already defeated and demoralized opponent to give up. Hitler was confident that his infallible intuition and psychological insight would tell him when that moment had come. Therefore, he himself had to control the timing of the use of this weapon. It was not to be wasted prematurely.

In the case of Britain, the desired situation might be brought about by the defeat of the RAF. If Göring's promises were to be believed, his invincible Luftwaffe would inflict such damage that the demoralized British would be brought close to surrender. This would be the time to push them over the brink through terror attacks from the air, through an invasion, or by a combination of both. Hitler never made clear which method he favored for the *Todesstoss,* but we know that he thought of invasion only as a last resort.

Whatever his private thoughts may have been, the mission he had officially given to Göring was to gain air superiority in preparation for SEA LION. Nevertheless, Göring was sure, either because he knew or because he correctly guessed, that the Führer had no intention of risking a forced landing against strong opposition and

*Admiral Raeder's personal notes on what happened at the Führer Conference are reproduced in *Dokumente,* pp. 253-256. General Halder's are to be found in his *Kriegstagebuch* (War Diary), W. Kohlhammer Verlag, Stuttgart, Germany, 1962 (hereafter cited as *Halder Diary),* entry for July 31, 1940. For the background behind the Conference, I have drawn on the excellent accounts of Ansel (pp. 182-189) and Wheatley (pp. 38-51).

***Dokumente,* pp. 333-334.

that the plans for SEA LION which provided for such a landing would never be implemented. Göring therefore could not have looked on the air battle as a preparation for SEA LION, which he freely told his subordinates would never come off. For him it was the prelude to an all-out bombing campaign that by itself would force Britain to her knees.* By bombing the enemy into submission, he would not only please his master but win new glory for the Luftwaffe and for himself as well. This was Göring's war, and he threw himself into the preparations for it with his usual bombast. It was to be known as the *Adlerangriff* (Eagle Attack), and D-Day was christened *Adlertag* (Eagle Day). Toasts were drunk at Karin Hall to celebrate in advance the inevitable triumph of the Luftwaffe. Hitler would be on hand for the great day.

Events did not work out as Göring had hoped. The Battle of Britain he ushered in on *Adlertag* did indeed put an end to SEA LION, but not in the sense the *Reichsmarschall* had expected. Before turning to these events, however, we need to take a brief look at British air actions during the short respite between the middle of June and the middle of August.

Targets for Bomber Command

During June and July the British Air Staff issued to Bomber Command six different directives on bombardment policy. This was indicative of the understandable confusion into which British planners were plunged by the disastrous events in France. Until the middle of June the RAF had thrown all the resources it could spare into supporting the ground battle and protecting the evacuation of the British forces from the Continent. After the fall of France, four major objectives competed for the attention of the Air Staff.

The most important was to disrupt the German preparations for the forthcoming invasion, on which British Intelligence had provided a considerable amount of information. The British took SEA LION seriously and gave first priority to counterinvasion efforts. The task assigned to Bomber Command was to attack the shipping the Germans were assembling along the coast, to mine sea lanes, and to hit communications to the sally ports. Another, equally important objective was to weaken the Luftwaffe in anticipation of the expected air attacks on Britain. This objective was to be accomplished by the bombing of German aluminum plants, airframe assembly plants, and other targets connected with the aircraft industry. A third objective was to deplete Germany's precarious oil supplies by bombing oil plants and other "self-illuminating" industrial targets. A fourth objective, which could be achieved simultaneously with the third, was to lower German morale through strategic air attacks, which, according to "reliable sources," had proved a serious shock to the German public. Lest this last objective be taken too literally, Bomber

*Even one of the more partial German authors observed that "In view of Göring's reservations regarding a landing, it can be assumed that he had intended from the beginning to conduct the operations against England in terms of absolute [strategic] air war." See Klee, *Das Unternehmen "Seelöwe"*, p. 184.

Command was warned that "in no circumstances should night bombing be allowed to degenerate into mere indiscriminate action, which is contrary to the policy of His Majesty's Government."*

The Air Ministry eventually realized that the many tasks it was imposing on Bomber Command could not be carried out with the meager resources available. The effort only resulted in scattering ineffective attacks over a wide variety of targets without inflicting critical damage on any. On July 13 a new directive was issued, which listed ten first-priority targets connected with the German aircraft industry and five oil targets. But this directive was no more realistic than the earlier ones had been. Bomber Command did not have the capability to destroy these targets, and even if it could have destroyed them, their elimination would not have affected the strength of the Luftwaffe in time to make any difference in the imminent air battle.

Air Marshal Sir Charles Portal, who had been appointed Commander-in-Chief, Bomber Command, in April 1940, objected to the new directive on operational grounds as well. He wrote to the Air Ministry in July that he preferred a more flexible and more widely dispersed target system that would enable his crews to take advantage of favorable weather and visibility conditions and make it more difficult for the enemy defenses to anticipate British attacks. Another reason he gave was that a dispersed target system "largely increases the moral effect of our operations by the alarm and disturbance created over the wider area."** We shall encounter this argument throughout this narrative, for it was to have an increasing influence on British air policy throughout the war. At the time, however, the Air Staff, though concerned about Portal's criticism, still felt that the moral effect could not be decisive and that material destruction was to be regarded as the main object of the bombing.

During July and most of August, Bomber Command kept up its effort against the invasion ports, with telling effect. It also delivered small-scale strategic attacks on German industrial targets, but those were less effective. Their main value was to remind the German people that its homeland was no longer immune and to provide training for British bombardment crews. They had little impact on the German war potential or on the strength of the Luftwaffe.

*The Battle for Air Superiority ("ADLERANGRIFF")****

By the middle of July, the Luftwaffe had repaired the damages suffered in the Battle of France and had completed its deployment to the newly conquered bases

**Air Offensive*, Vol. 1, pp. 145*ff.*

***Ibid.*, p. 150.

***The factual details of the Battle of Britain mentioned in the following section are based mainly on the two authoritative accounts by Basil Collier: *The Battle of Britain*, The Macmillan Company, New York, 1962; and the more voluminous version in *The Defence of the United Kingdom*, in *History of the Second World War*, United Kingdom Military Series, Her Majesty's Stationery Office, London, 1957. For background, especially on the German side, I have relied primarily on the aforementioned works of Ansel, Telford Taylor, and Wheatley. Most of the German sources that were available to me on the Battle of Britain proved either inadequate or unreliable. For a discussion of this point, see Appendix A.

along the coasts of the Low Countries and France. The full-scale air offensive against Britain was still a few weeks off. Göring used the intervening time to step up air operations against British ports and against shipping in the English Channel. His main purpose was to wear down the British fighters who would be forced to defend the valuable convoys, and incidentally to give his flyers an opportunity to take the measure of their enemy. He also intended to compel the British to divert the convoys to West Coast ports, thus increasing their supply difficulties.

Göring was delighted with the results of the "Channel fighting," as it came to be called. The Luftwaffe succeeded in scattering two large convoys, sinking a good many merchant ships and a few British destroyers, and gaining temporary air superiority over the Channel. Göring claimed that hundreds of British fighters had been destroyed in the month prior to *Adlertag* and that the Luftwaffe had proved its superiority over the RAF.

The facts were that, between July 10 and August 12, the RAF lost 150 fighters while the Luftwaffe lost close to 300 aircraft. The British aircraft losses were more than offset by new production, which had turned out over 500 Hurricanes and Spitfires during the same period.* Fighter Command was therefore better off on *Adlertag* than it had been before the preliminary bouts began. What Göring did not know, because he did not want to know, was that his temporary success in gaining limited air superiority over the Channel had been made possible only because the British had decided to husband their fighter strength for the forthcoming Battle of Britain.

The *Reichsmarschall's* habit of exaggerating successes and underrating the strength and ability of the enemy -- a habit that was to cost him dearly when the real test came -- was well illustrated during a conference with his senior officers at The Hague on August 1. A Colonel Theo Osterkamp, who commanded a fighter unit in the Channel fighting and had been a flyer in World War I, dared to question the Luftwaffe intelligence figures on British fighters as too low. He himself recounts what happened:

> I wanted to say more, but Göring cut me off angrily: "This is nonsense, our information is excellent, and I am perfectly aware of the situation. Besides, the Messerschmitt is much better than the Spitfire, because as you yourself reported the British are too cowardly to engage your fighters!"
>
> "I shall permit myself to remark that I reported only that the British fighters were ordered to avoid battles with our fighters --" "That is the same thing," Hermann shouted; "if they were as strong and as good as you maintain, I would have to send my *Luftzeugmeister* [Udet, who was in charge of aircraft procurement] before the firing squad."**

This incident was unusual only in that Colonel Osterkamp, perhaps because he had been a World War I ace like Göring, had the courage to offer unpalatable

*Collier, *The Battle of Britain,* p. 75.

**Theo Osterkamp, cited in Telford Taylor, *The Breaking Wave,* p. 131.

information to his superior. But reactions like the above and like the disciplining of General Hellmuth Felmy* must have served as warnings to others, so that often information that was well known to the air crews themselves was not reported up to the higher echelons. The story goes, and may well be true, that Luftwaffe pilots suspected their "Knickebein" radio beams of being deflected by British electronic countermeasures but nobody dared to tell Göring.

There were other reasons, apart from Göring's personality, for the errors the Luftwaffe made in the Battle of Britain. But that these errors were not rectified, or not rectified in time, was due to the atmosphere that permeated the entire high command of the Luftwaffe. The air arm was the most nazified of the three services, and its leaders seem to have been chosen more for their subservience to Hitler and Göring than for their competence. Göring's staff of yes-men aped the groveling ways of Hitler's court and not only shielded the *Reichsmarschall* from unpleasant facts but discouraged staff activities that could have unearthed them. The Luftwaffe system of collecting and evaluating combat intelligence was notoriously poor.** Several authors have commented on the slipshod way in which operational planning and other important staff functions were exercised.*** This factor contributed to the growing disenchantment in the operating units of the Luftwaffe and to their more-than-normal hostility toward the upper echelons.

The directive of August 1 had presented the Luftwaffe with its most challenging task. But it allowed only a week for preparations, as Göring had scheduled *Adlertag* for August 8 and no serious planning had been done for the air war with Britain prior to the end of July. This did not bother the Commander-in-Chief, who was sure that he would defeat the RAF as he had defeated the Polish and French air forces. His grandiose ideas for achieving this feat were vague and unrealistic, with no attempt to consider the strengths and weaknesses of the opponent.

> Now, in historical perspective, the most extraordinary thing about the Battle of Britain is that the German attack -- the *Adlerangriff* -- was not the product of deliberation. There appears to have been no staff study, no high level conference at which the pros and cons were weighed.****

In Ansel's words, "the Luftwaffe literally stumbled into action." It had to improvise new plans and tactics while the battle was under way. In the circumstances, it is astounding that the Luftwaffe came as near to success as it did. For this it had to thank the bravery and determination of the air crews, not its leadership.

*General Felmy had had the bad taste to report the results of a map exercise that raised doubts about the possibility of destroying Britain in an all-out air war. He was reprimanded by Göring and the Chief of the Luftwaffe General Staff, General Hans Jeschonnek, and relieved from his command under a transparent pretext. Ansel, p. 191.

**Collier, *The Battle of Britain,* p. 57.

***Asher Lee, p. 17. See also Ansel and Telford Taylor, *passim.*

****Telford Taylor, p. 108.

Adlertag had to be postponed because of weather. It was rescheduled for August 13, when the Battle of Britain officially began.* The weather was still unfavorable, but Göring decided that the offensive could not be postponed any longer. On August 13, therefore, two German *Luftflotten* – No. 2 under Kesselring, and No. 3 under Sperrle -- launched a massive attack on Britain with approximately 500 bombers and 1000 fighter sorties. They were beaten back with the loss of 45 aircraft.

Although Fighter Command was the ostensible objective of the attack, the Luftwaffe scattered its bombs on many irrelevant targets, such as Army installations, Coastal Command airfields, Bomber Command facilities, and aircraft plants whose destruction could not affect British fighter strength in the near future. Some Fighter Command installations were also hit, but the attackers failed to concentrate on the fighter airfields, early warning radars, and the sector stations which were the defender's real Achilles heel. Basil Collier believes that Göring himself was to blame for this misdirected effort:

> The Luftwaffe High Command had a good knowledge of the disposition of Dowding's squadrons and understood the importance of the sector stations. It seems clear that the true explanation of their apparently random choice of targets was that Göring wanted to do too much in too short a time. Notoriously little interested in the invasion plans of the other services because he thought that they would never be put into effect, he believed that, by attacking a wide range of targets, the Luftwaffe could, at one and the same time, not only destroy Dowding's squadrons in the air but cause such havoc on the ground that the country would be brought to the verge of surrender, or beyond it, by the time the German army was ready to go ashore.**

The Germans followed up with three more full-scale attacks, all in the space of less than a week, repeating the mistakes made in their opening attack. Fighter Command suffered damage and lost valuable aircraft and pilots, but as yet the losses were not critical The Luftwaffe lost over twice as many aircraft as Fighter Command -- 236 against 95 -- and there were angry recriminations between bomber crews and their fighter escorts, and between the flyers and the staff officers who had done the planning for the missions.

At last Göring realized that he had to change his tactics. When the offensive was resumed, on August 24, after a week's suspension because of weather, the Luftwaffe was ordered to concentrate on the objective it should have been pursuing from the beginning, namely, the British fighters and their ground installations. In daytime, bombers were not to waste their bombs on irrelevant targets but were to single out the forward airfields and sector stations on which Fighter Command depended for the operation and control of its fighters. The ratio of fighters to bombers was increased, not only to reduce bomber losses but to seek out air-to-air combat

*Preliminary attacks had taken place on August 8 and 11.

**Collier, *The Battle of Britain,* pp. 78-79. (Air Chief Marshal Sir Hugh Dowding was Commander-in-Chief, Fighter Command.)

with the British fighters. Industrial targets were to be attacked only on night missions, when no fighter excort was required.

The period that began on August 24, when the Luftwaffe first used the new tactics, marked the most critical stage in the Battle of Britain. It was critical for both sides, for Hitler had vowed to make his final decision on SEA LION not later than two weeks from the beginning of the air offensive. The two weeks were almost up, and Göring had not yet come anywhere near to winning the air superiority without which the invasion could not be undertaken. Neither was there any sign that Britain was willing to come to terms. If the invasion was to take place at all that year, the decision would have to be made within a few days.

For Britain, survival itself was at stake. If the Luftwaffe did gain air superiority over southeastern England, it would undoubtedly attempt to deliver the dreaded knockout blow against British cities. The coming weeks would be crucial, for the new Luftwaffe policy of concentrating on the British fighters and knocking out their airfields and sector stations was proving extremely effective. In spite of heroic efforts by maintenance crews to repair bombed-out facilities, it was becoming increasingly difficult for Air Marshal Dowding to service and control his fighters. The better protection afforded to the German bombers by the increased ratio of escort fighters made it harder for the British fighters to get at the attacking bombers without being engaged by the German fighters -- a form of combat Air Marshal Dowding wished to avoid whenever possible in order to conserve British fighter strength. But he now had no choice in the matter if he was to protect his essential ground facilities from being knocked out by the German bombers. Aircraft losses on both sides were mounting, and the ratio was no longer as lopsided as it had been before Göring changed his tactics. However, British aircraft losses were partly made up from new production, which turned out more fighters during this critical period than had been estimated. One of the most serious threats to Fighter Command, apart from the destruction of ground facilities, was the loss of experienced pilots and the increasing strain on those who survived.* "The few," on whom so much depended, were taxed to the limit.

By the end of August, the Luftwaffe had achieved undeniable successes. But great as they were, they were only partial. Fighter Command could not yet be written off, nor had the Luftwaffe achieved air superiority even over southeastern England. It might have done so in a few more weeks if Göring had pressed home his advantage. But he failed to do so, partly because he exaggerated what had already been achieved, and partly because he was lured away by a more spectacular objective: the assault on London.

Commanders are always tempted to overestimate enemy losses, and the Luftwaffe leaders were certainly no exception. But it was not only a matter of overoptimism nor of inadequate combat intelligence; their estimates of enemy strength did not

*Britain had the advantage that her downed pilots were often recovered and could fly again, even on the same day. The German flyers brought down over Britain were of course permanently lost to the Luftwaffe.

even attempt to provide an objective assessment but were tailored to what their superior wanted to hear. On August 29, the head of Kesselring's fighter organization, General Kurt von Döring, claimed that "unlimited fighter superiority" (whatever that meant) had been won.* Yet the Luftwaffe had lost 800 aircraft in the two months since July 1. Kesselring's *Luftflotte* No. 2, which had carried the brunt of the daylight attacks, was down to 450 serviceable bombers and 530 short-range fighters (Me-109s).** On the day after General von Döring had made his extravagant claim, Fighter Command was so far from being defeated as to be able to put up for the first time more than 1000 sorties against the Luftwaffe.***

The empty boasts of their chief did not help the morale of the Luftwaffe crews, who knew the losses they were sustaining. Their own sortie rate declined after the end of August while the enemy maintained his. They saw no evidence of "unlimited fighter superiority" over an enemy who could fly more fighter sorties than they were able to: "By September 6 Dowding's squadrons were flying not only many more sorties than the German fighter force, but more than the German bomber and fighter forces put together."****

But Göring's boasts may have achieved their purpose of impressing Hitler. Though the Führer was alternately blowing hot and cold on SEA LION, the reports of the Luftwaffe's triumph over the RAF seem to have revived his interest in the invasion. After von Brauchitsch had met with Hitler on August 26, General Halder noted in his Diary: "SEA LION stays in. Interest in it seems to have increased."***** On August 30, when the two weeks from *Adlertag* were up, Hitler conceded that the prerequisites for SEA LION had not yet been fully met, and agreed to wait a few more days for good weather, presumably to give Göring a chance to "finish the job." The final decision on whether the invasion was to take place would be made on September 10, and the tentative invasion date would be September 21.******

The battle for air superiority continued during the first week in September with damaging attacks on Fighter Command installations in the London area. The Luftwaffe losses for that week were substantial (189 aircraft), but so were Fighter Command's (161 aircraft). Fortunately for Britain, the battle was broken off just in time, for Hitler and Göring already had set their minds on their new objective: the all-out air assault on London *(Grossangriff auf London)*. This was to be the knockout blow the British had been expecting for so long.

*Collier, *The Battle of Britain,* p. 108.

***Ibid.*, p. 122.

****Ibid.*, p. 168.

*****Ibid.*, p. 122.

******Halder Diary,* August 26, 1940.

*******OKW Diary* for August 30, 1940, in *Dokumente,* p. 49.

The Accidental Bombing of London

The momentous decision to destroy London was motivated by a complex mixture of factors, which will be examined presently.* But it may have been triggered, though it was not caused, by a chain of events that, as so often happens in wartime, began with an accident.

In the night of August 24, 1940, about a dozen German aircraft dropped bombs on Greater London. The City itself was hit for the first time since 1918, fires were started in several suburbs, and many homes were destroyed in Bethnal Green.** Inasmuch as Hitler had given strict orders against bombing London without his express permission, the crews must have done it unintentionally.

The incident occurred at the start of an intensified round-the-clock air offensive, during which the night bombers were to attack RAF installations and aircraft factories. The targets for that night included factories at Rochester and Kingston and oil tanks at Thameshaven, all in the vicinity of London. Some of the crews assigned to these targets may have made a navigating or bombing error -- not unusual in night operations -- and dropped their bombs on the city itself.***

Considering the importance of this incident, and its subsequent repercussions, it is remarkable that, with a single exception, none of the German sources consulted for this narrative even so much as mentions the first bombing of London.**** It is possible, of course, that the crews responsible for the error did not know what they had bombed, or that they were afraid to report it, though not if Bekker's informant was correct. It is also possible that the German records deliberately omitted the incident or, if they did describe it, that the records themselves were destroyed. None of this explains, however, why this crucial event is not mentioned by postwar German historians who have had access to the British sources that deal with the incident and who list these sources, including Basil Collier, in their scholarly bibliographies. Since the significance of the event could not have escaped a trained historian, one can only suspect that the omission was intentional.*****

*See below, pp. 71*ff.*

**Collier, *The Defence of the United Kingdom*, pp. 207-208.

***It would be ironic if, as a rumor among those in the know had it at the time, the error had been caused by Britain's electronic countermeasures against the "Knickebein" radio beam that the Germans used for night navigation. Churchill mentions that on August 23, a day earlier, the British still had "teething troubles" with their countermeasures. *Their Finest Hour*, p. 387.

****The exception is Cajus Bekker, *The Luftwaffe War Diaries*, Doubleday & Company, Inc., Garden City, N.Y., 1968, p. 172. Bekker reports a staff officer of a German bombardment wing as recalling a teletype from Göring to all units that flew over Britain that night. The guilty crews were to be instantly reported to him, and he, personally, would remuster their commanding officers to the infantry. The reliability of this journalistically written book is impossible to judge, since it contains no documentation.

*****This would be in keeping with the reticence of German authors on other events that reflected unfavorably on Germany's wartime actions. Why the accidental bombing of London should have called for such reticence is discussed below, in the section beginning on p. 71. The uneven reliability of the German sources is dealt with more fully in Appendix A.

At the time it happened, the British could not have known that the bombing of London was an accident; they must indeed have assumed that it was deliberate. Other port cities already had been bombed, and it was logical to expect London to be bombed as well, in preparation for the invasion which was expected momentarily. The time for restraint on Hitler's part was clearly past, and the British people were girding for the worst. But if they were to fight a desperate and lone battle for survival, they wanted at least the satisfaction of paying the enemy back in his own coin. Churchill reports:

> The War Cabinet were much in the mood to hit back, to raise the stakes, and to defy the enemy. I was sure they were right, and believed that nothing impressed or disturbed Hitler so much as his realisation of British wrath and will-power.*

On August 25, the day after London had been bombed, the British did hit back by attacking Berlin. For operational reasons, Bomber Command would have preferred an easier target, since the range of British bombers was too limited for an effective attack on so distant a target. The raid on Berlin did little damage. It did not "raise the stakes," as the War Cabinet had hoped to do, but it was a token of things to come. On August 28, a slightly more effective attack caused a few casualties in the center of Berlin; it was followed by two more raids on August 30 and 31.

The military effect of the attacks was negligible, but they seem to have had a considerable psychological impact on the inhabitants of Berlin.** They also enraged Hitler, who had left the Berghof for Berlin on August 29 to take personal charge of "reprisals" against Britain. The next day, Jodl informed his OKW colleagues that the Führer had given permission for an all-out air assault on London.*** A few days later, on September 4, Hitler addressed a mass rally and vowed "hundredfold vengeance" against England. "If they attack our cities," he shouted, "we will simply rub out theirs."

The preparations for doing so were enthusiastically set in motion by Göring in a series of hastily called conferences with his major commanders. Göring had been waiting for an opportunity to break off the unglamorous battle against Fighter Command, which he convinced himself had already been won, and to attack London instead; he was sure that the destruction of the capital would force Britain to her knees.

One slight obstacle to Göring's plans was Hitler's preference for confining the attacks, at least initially, to what German sources invariably refer to as "military and industrial targets" in London. The Führer wanted to save up for the

*_Their Finest Hour,_ p. 342.

**The American correspondent William L. Shirer reported from Berlin that the people were stunned by the attacks, and disillusioned that in spite of Göring's victory communiqués the "defeated" RAF should have been able to bomb their city. See Telford Taylor, p. 156.

***_OKW Diary_ for August 30, 1940, in _Dokumente,_ p. 49.

Todesstoss against Britain the deliberate destruction of residential areas "with the object of causing a mass panic." Göring was therefore ordered to concentrate on the dock areas and on public utilities. It was, of course, an unrealistic order.

> Like their counterparts in London, German ministers and officials were blissfully unaware that bomber crews on both sides had about as much chance of hitting precise objectives in a well-defended built-up area at night as a blind dart player has of throwing a double twenty. Except in daylight, it made no practical difference whether residential districts were included in the target list or not, because they were sure to be hit in any case.*

If ministers and officials did not understand night bombing, Göring should have. And if he did not, the professionals on his staff certainly did. They understood that, so long as they had permission to bomb London, it did not matter what targets they were supposed to hit. They would destroy the city, and they knew that was what Göring wanted.

The new phase of the Battle of Britain -- the London Blitz -- was ushered in on September 7 with a mass daylight attack on London. Another heavy raid followed that night. The assault was kept up for almost two months. It did not succeed in paralyzing London or in forcing Britain to her knees. But it aroused public opinion throughout the world and hardened the British resolve to pay the Nazis back in their own coin.

On September 7 the Germans sowed the wind of which they were to reap the whirlwind some years later. It was the start of indiscriminate air warfare -- the end of the road to total war.

*Collier, *The Battle of Britain*, p. 124.

6

Sowing the Wind

*The Assault on London**

THE GERMANS had reason to be pleased with the success of the opening blow in their all-out air offensive against London. The assault was launched by Kesselring's *Luftflotte* 2 on September 7 between 5 and 6 p.m., when the streets were crowded and panic was likely to be greatest. The attacking force consisted of approximately 300 bombers and 600 fighters -- all that Kesselring could scrape together after the heavy losses suffered in the preceding weeks' battle for air superiority. The primary target area, the London docks, suffered great destruction. In spite of excellent visibility, many bombs fell short and hit highly inflammable sections of town on both banks of the Thames. Extensive fires lit up the city long after darkness had set in.

The attack took the British Government by surprise. Though Hitler had threatened a few days earlier to exterminate British cities, his wild speeches were no longer taken seriously. On the two nights preceding the full-scale assault on London, the docks had been bombed and there had been minor daylight attacks on targets in the vicinity of the capital. An attack on the city itself had been made two weeks before, and further attacks could not be excluded. But the thought uppermost in the minds of British leaders during those anxious days was the long-heralded invasion, which was believed to be imminent. The German plans for SEA LION, of which the British had had "an inkling" since June,** were confirmed by the visual evidence

*Unless otherwise noted, the sources for this section are those mentioned on p. 59, footnote.

**Churchill, *Their Finest Hour,* p. 302.

of the mounting preparations across the Channel. Moon and tide conditions were favorable for a landing. In this atmosphere it was not surprising that on September 7, while the first German bombs were falling on London, an order by the Chiefs of Staff to put the defense forces on a higher alert resulted in the false rumor that the invasion had actually started.

Preoccupied as they were with the expected invasion, British defense planners naturally thought that the Luftwaffe would continue its damaging attacks on Fighter Command sector stations and airfields in southeast England in preparation for the forthcoming landing. The deployment of British fighter squadrons and the intricate dispositions for their reinforcement had been made with this threat in mind. Therefore, Fighter Command was caught in an unfavorable position when on September 7 the Luftwaffe unexpectedly switched to the assault on London. As misfortune would have it, Air Vice-Marshal K. R. Park, the experienced commander of No. 11 Group, which was responsible for the defense of the London area, was absent from his headquarters on this crucial day, having gone to confer with his chief at Stanmore. For these and other reasons, the defense of London against the first German onslaught was not effective. A number of enemy aircraft were shot down, but most of them had already dropped their bombs.

The daylight strike was followed after dark by 250 night bombers of Sperrle's *Luftflotte* 3. They were able to home on the huge fires still raging in London and made no attempt to hit specific targets. The Luftwaffe staff had divided the city into target areas "A" and "B." Area "A" comprised East London with the docks; "B" was described as "West London with the city's power plants and supply installations," and it also included the "City" and what the Germans called "the diplomatic quarter."*

The German bombers roamed freely over the city, since they met virtually no defense. The few British night fighters proved ineffective; antiaircraft defense in the London area was inadequate, and the gunners lacked experience. Enemy bombs and incendiaries fell all over the city, most of them within ten miles of Charing Cross. New conflagrations were added to those of the early evening, and great damage was inflicted. Victoria Station was blocked, the railroads out of London were cut in several places, and traffic was paralyzed. Approximately a thousand Londoners were killed in these first two attacks, and many more were maimed or rendered homeless.**

Thereafter, the Luftwaffe kept up the round-the-clock offensive against London whenever the weather permitted. Kesselring's second attack, on September 9, found the defenses better prepared and was beaten back with severe losses. The next two attacks were more successful, as the Germans changed their tactics to cope with

*Wheatley, p. 77.

**Total civilian casualties in the area of Greater London during the year 1940 – meaning the portion of the year beginning with the first attack on London on September 7 – were as follows: 13,596 killed; 18,378 hospitalized with severe injuries; 33,756 slightly injured. Titmuss, pp. 560-561.

the British defenses. By the end of the first week of the Blitz, London had suffered great damage. Yet the life of the city went on, and the population showed no sign of wishing to give up as Hitler and Göring had hoped. Though the strain on Fighter Command was beginning to tell, the Luftwaffe had lost over 200 aircraft between September 7 and 15, and was still a long way from having achieved the air superiority Göring had promised to win in four days.

Hitler himself had to admit this. Göring's fantastic victory communiques -- trumpeted over Goebbels' radio to the tune of the marching song *"Wir fahren gegen Engelland"** -- reported that London was in ruins and that countless British fighters had been destroyed. Yet it was evident that Fighter Command was still able to take a heavy toll of the Luftwaffe. Göring explained to the Führer that this was the last gasp of the nearly-defeated RAF and that only a few consecutive days of good weather were needed to finish the job. The weather, he said, had forced the Luftwaffe to space its attacks, which gave Fighter Command a chance to recuperate between raids.

Whether Hitler was convinced or not, he seemed glad of an excuse to postpone the date when he would make his "irrevocable" decision on SEA LION. On September 11 he promised to make it on the 14th; when the 14th came without as yet any indication that Fighter Command was defeated, the decision date was postponed to the 17th. This meant that the actual invasion could not take place before the 27th, which was the last possible date in September. Thereafter, moon and tide conditions would not again be suitable for a landing until October 8, by which time the weather was likely to be unfavorable.

The British, of course, did not know of these postponements and could not afford to relax their guard. The period of September 7 to 15, while the daylight assault on London was at its height, seemed particularly favorable for a landing. On September 11, Churchill solemnly warned the British people that the next few days would be critical and that an invasion could be expected momentarily. The RAF did its best to disrupt the continuing German invasion preparations by attacking the sally ports on the German-held coast; by destroying barges, landing craft, and other shipping, and by bombing troop concentrations and supply points in the vicinity of the invasion assembly areas. These attacks inflicted a good deal of damage, which might have proved critical if the invasion had gone off as scheduled.

Meanwhile the air battles over London continued. They reached their climax on September 15 -- the date that is celebrated in the United Kingdom as "Battle of Britain Day." It proved to be a crucial turning point in the war.

On that day, Kesselring threw all the resources of his *Luftflotte* 2 into two all-out daylight attacks on London, while Sperrle's *Luftflotte* 3 launched a diversionary

*"We are sailing against England." This song may have helped civilian morale in Germany but seems to have had the opposite effect on the combat forces that were preparing for the invasion, and especially on the Luftwaffe crews who were actually flying against England. See Ansel, pp. 1-6, and Adolf Galland, *The First and the Last,* Henry Holt and Company, New York, 1954, p. 38.

raid designed to draw off the British fighters. What happened is history. "The few" to whom Churchill paid his memorable tribute defeated the German escort fighters, scattered the enemy bombers, and destroyed 60 aircraft in a hard and close-fought battle. After this defeat, Göring was forced to change his tactics once again.

There was one more daylight attack on London a few days later, but only 70 bombers took part, and they met with stiff opposition. It marked the virtual end of the daylight bombing of London, except for minor raids, though for almost two more months the city continued to be bombed night after night. After that, the Luftwaffe shifted the weight of its night attacks to other British cities, such as Coventry and other manufacturing centers or ports. The German air offensive slackened off as the weather worsened, and stopped almost entirely in the spring of 1941, when a major portion of the Luftwaffe was redeployed to the East for the forthcoming offensive against Russia.

On September 17, 1940, two days after the great daylight attack on London, the War Diary of Raeder's Naval Staff noted that the Führer had "postponed SEA LION until further notice." The postponement, in effect, was a cancellation. Hitler ordered the preparations for the invasion to be kept up as a way of maintaining the psychological pressure on Britain, but for a number of reasons this did not prove feasible. The Navy was suffering from the British air attacks on the shipping that lay immobilized in the invasion ports, and the Army wished to shift troops and supplies to the East in advance of Operation BARBAROSSA. Hitler reluctantly had to agree to a partial stand-down of the invasion preparations. He waited until October 12, however, before he formally canceled SEA LION for that year.* To Mussolini he explained that the invasion had been prevented solely by the weather: "Only five consecutive fine days were needed" -- presumably to defeat the RAF -- "but they did not come." It was not the fault of Göring; the Luftwaffe had been on the verge of victory. Its bombing attacks had achieved great success and would continue, for "the British people cannot endure the hammering of the German air force indefinitely."**

Genesis of a Fateful Decision

The attempt to terrorize the British into surrender by destroying their capital had failed. The significance of this event in changing the course of the war -- and perhaps the fate of Western civilization -- is too well established to require comment. The aspect that concerns us here is that Hitler's decision to "rub out" British cities also marked the abandonment of his last restraint, and introduced a new level of violence, which was to be surpassed only in scale but not in kind. As the ultimate step in the process of escalation, it was comparable to what, in a future war, would be a

*The plans and some preparations for the invasion were kept up until March 1942, when the project was finally abandoned altogether. Wheatley, p. 98.

***Ibid.*, p. 95.

decision to launch intercontinental ballistic missiles against the opponent's capital. Its bearing on this inquiry is therefore obvious.

Even by Nazi standards, the all-out assault on London was not a routine act of war, Hitler's directive of August 1, 1940 -- the famous *Führerbefehl* -- had strictly forbidden "terror attacks" against cities without his express permission, which he had so far withheld. The earlier bombing of Warsaw and Rotterdam did not conflict with this order, because the Germans regarded these cities as defended enemy strongholds and therefore as legitimate military objectives. In August 1940, prior to the assault on London, the Luftwaffe did bomb British ports and armament centers, but these, too, were regarded as military targets.

When Hitler withdrew his prohibition and permitted, or ordered, Göring to destroy London as a functioning city, he was making a decision that could easily backfire. If the air assault did not succeed in knocking Britain out of the war, there would no longer be any hope that she would agree to a peaceful settlement. On the contrary, an enraged British people would demand revenge in kind, and indiscriminate air warfare was a weapon both sides had at their disposal.

In other words, if the war continued, it would be fought with no holds barred, by the British as well as by the Germans. In addition, Hitler would have to reckon with the repercussions elsewhere, especially in the United States. He may by then have ceased to care about public opinion abroad, and he had already reconciled himself to eventual American intervention, though he did not expect it to take place before 1941-1942.* But he must have been aware that the destruction of one of the greatest cities of the Western world, and the civilian casualties resulting from it, would further inflame anti-Nazi sentiment and could well hasten American intervention. Moreover, there was a good deal more that the United States could do to aid Britain short of direct participation in the war, once public opinion was sufficiently aroused.

Considering the penalties for failure, one would assume that the Führer was confident of success when he made his decision. As we shall see presently, this assumption may well be wrong. We shall never be certain, however, since, unfortunately, the background of this fateful decision remains obscure.**

There are records of numerous Führer conferences on the subject of SEA LION, but there is no similar record of any discussions Hitler may have had with his advisers on the decision to attack London. This would suggest that he made it on the spur of the moment, in one of his customary rages, after the British bombing of Berlin. He probably did. But decisions of such magnitude, although they may be made impulsively, seldom spring full-blown from a man's mind. The decision itself is only the last step, the culmination of a chain of thoughts and events that have gone before. By reconstructing this chain, therefore, we may hope to uncover,

*Hillgruber, p. 172.

**The lack of factual evidence on this point has been remarked by Andreas Hillgruber (p. 172) and Telford Taylor (pp. 79-82), who are among those most familiar with the documentary material for the period.

if not Hitler's own reasoning, at least some of the principal factors that may have entered into his decision.

The likelihood that London would be attacked sooner or later had always existed. One of the earliest OKW memoranda on the war against Britain, written by General Jodl on June 30, 1940, and unquestionably reflecting the Führer's own ideas, listed terror attacks on British population centers in second place, ahead of invasion, as among the preferred means for subduing Britain. Such attacks would take place after air superiority over southern England had been won, and would be combined with "siege operations" against Britain's supply system and armaments centers. General Jodl wrote:

> Combined with propaganda and *periodic terror attacks, proclaimed as reprisals,* this cumulative weakening of the English food supply system will paralyze and finally break the will to resist of the people and thereby force the Government to capitulate.*

The same memorandum also stated unequivocally that an invasion was not to be undertaken for the purpose of defeating Britain militarily -- that was to be accomplished by the Luftwaffe and the Navy -- but only, if necessary, to administer the *Todesstoss* to a country already paralyzed economically, whose air capability had been effectively eliminated.

An attack on London became an even stronger likelihood a month later, when Hitler ordered the *Adlerangriff* against Britain. Although the ostensible purpose was to pave the way for the invasion, there is no doubt that Göring's real objective was to subdue Britain through bombing alone after he had gained sufficient air superiority to attack her cities at will.** That he must have expected to include London among these cities as soon as he could convince Hitler that the time had come is shown by his subsequent actions; he even may have had the Führer's private reassurance on this point.

But the idea of bombing London was not Göring's alone, although he seems to have been its chief promoter. On August 13, 1940 -- *Adlertag* -- an OKW draft directive for SEA LION stated:

> Special effect is anticipated from a ruthless air attack on London, if possible on the day preceding the landing, as this would certainly cause countless numbers of people to stream out of the city in all directions, thereby blocking the roads and demoralizing the population. . . .***

*"Denkschrift des Generalmajors Jodl (Chef WFA) über die Weiterführung des Krieges gegen England" (Memorandum of Major General Jodl. . .on the Continuation of the War Against England), in *Dokumente,* p. 298. Italics mine. Note that it had been planned all along to announce these attacks as reprisals, *before* Britain had provided any occasions for reprisals.

**See above, p. 58.

***Wheatley, p. 71.

This proposal was in line with the tactics the Luftwaffe had so successfully employed in Flanders, when it machine-gunned fleeing civilians on the roads to create panic and block passage.

During the second half of August, further developments presented Hitler with such a Hobson's choice of evils as a result of his own mistakes that he probably would have been willing to resort to any measures, however brutal, to end his dilemma. There is good reason to believe that these developments alone made it virtually certain that London would be attacked, whatever additional reasons might be found to justify it.

One of Hitler's problems was the disappointing course of the air war. As already recounted, by the end of August it was clear that after more than two weeks the *Adlerangriff* had not succeeded in gaining air superiority or defeating the RAF, let alone in meeting the other conditions demanded by the Army and Navy as prerequisites for an invasion. Neither was there any evidence that Britain was ready to break under the strain.

When Hitler agreed, on August 30, to give Göring a few more days to finish the job, he obviously was not thinking of the kind of job that his Army and Navy commanders had in mind. They expected the Luftwaffe not only to eliminate the RAF as an effective force but to attack a long list of targets prior to the invasion, such as ports, naval installations, and British fleet units. In addition, air cover had to be provided for German mine-laying operations; during the crossing itself, the Luftwaffe had to have sufficient strength left to ward off the British Navy and such air attacks as the RAF might still be capable of, and also to provide fire support for the first waves of German troops. After the losses the Luftwaffe was suffering in the Battle of Britain, these tasks were clearly beyond its capability, even if it were given more time before the invasion, then scheduled for September 15. In short, in the eyes of the Army and Navy, the failure of the Luftwaffe to do its part had ruled out an opposed landing as originally contemplated.*

This was not the only reason, however, for their skepticism about the feasibility of an invasion. It was only in August, after the Führer Conference of July 31, that the Army and Navy first got together to try to reconcile their widely divergent ideas on some of the major features of the landing operation. But the Army's insistence on the need for a broad-front landing along some 235 miles of coastline could not be reconciled with the Navy's inability to provide shipping and protection for such a vast undertaking. Even a crossing in the narrow corridor proposed by the Navy -- which would have amounted to a front one-fourth the width of that demanded by the Army -- might have overtaxed Admiral Raeder's capabilities, which were being further depleted day by day as British bombing of shipping and sally ports took its

*The fact that the air war was not being conducted as a preparation for SEA LION was obvious to the military leaders of all three services at the time. Even Field Marshal Kesselring, the air commander most directly involved, admitted it in his postwar memoirs (*Soldat bis zum letzten Tag*, p. 92). Field Marshal von Manstein, whose Army corps was to provide the first wave of the assault, makes the point that the Luftwaffe would have been too depleted by the time it had won air superiority to provide the essential support for the invasion (*Verlorene Siege*, p. 167).

toll. For purely practical reasons, the decision had to be in favor of the narrow front. The Army's reaction was recorded in the *OKW Diary:*

> In this connection, Colonel Heusinger again emphasized the position of the Chief of Staff [General Halder] that an Army operation on the narrow front now ordered can not be carried out on the scale originally intended and that now it can only be a question of finishing off *(den Fangstoss zu geben)* an enemy who has already been defeated by the air war.*

As for the Navy's position, it was tersely summarized in the already cited memorandum on SEA LION that "its execution that year could not be responsibly considered."** Far from changing his position, Admiral Raeder became more apprehensive as the invasion date approached, and as his suspicion of Göring's intentions in the air battle became confirmed.

However guarded the Army and Navy leaders may have been with Hitler in their conversations about the invasion project, they must have managed to convey their apprehensions to him. But it mattered little whether they did or not, for every piece of available evidence points to the conclusion that he never had had any intention of going through with it in the form in which it was being planned: an invasion in force against a defended shore. Only the appearance of such a plan had to be kept up in order to frighten Britain into surrender.

What confused Hitler's listeners, and therefore some historians later on, was that the word invasion had two different meanings for him and that he used it sometimes in one sense and sometimes in the other. In discussions of the planning and operational aspects of SEA LION he wanted his reluctant commanders to believe that he was thinking of invasion in the same terms as they did, as a forced landing on a hostile shore. This was necessary if they were to carry out the preparations with the zeal and verisimilitude that would convince the British that such a landing was really going to take place. But it is clear from his frequent references to the *Todesstoss* idea that the kind of invasion he actually meant to undertake was an entirely different thing: a mopping-up operation of an essentially defeated and demoralized enemy, or even a bloodless occupation as in Czechoslovakia, with the full panoply of German armed might paraded to overawe the victim. His commanders, suspecting that the plans for a full-scale invasion were not intended to be carried out, tried to feel him out on this point. In the middle of August, the Naval Staff suggested to Jodl:

> If the Führer is inwardly resolved *not* to carry out Operation Sea Lion, but rather to maintain the *fiction* of an invasion, it is proposed that, in order to relieve the economy extensively, the retreat should be sounded for Sea Lion while secrecy is at the same time preserved.***

**OKW Diary* for August 30, 1940, in *Dokumente,* p. 49.

**See above, p. 56.

******Naval War Diary* for August 14, 1940, cited in Wheatley, p. 69, fn.

Failing to get the desired reassurance, however, the commanders had to act on the assumption that Hitler meant what he said when he spoke of SEA LION, namely an invasion in force as planned. The Naval Staff's suggestion had been naive in any case, though it was probably prompted less by fears for the economy than by concern about the invasion shipping and the supplies and troops that were being pounded by the British bombers. A cancellation of SEA LION could not have been kept secret, not even in Nazi Germany. Any slackening in the invasion preparations would have been noted in Britain and thus would have relieved the pressure on which Hitler was counting to bring his enemy to terms.

What Hitler did not realize was that in giving a spurious reality to the invasion project he was raising an incubus that was to become a source of greater pressure on him than on the British. Ordered to prepare for the most difficult combat operation of the war, the commanders concerned had to bury their private doubts, ignore the lack of firm direction or realistic planning, and allow the ponderous German war machine to grind into full gear. These massive preparations were of course watched all over the world, as Hitler had intended that they should be. During August, as barges, lighters, tugs, and other shipping were gathered together from all over occupied Europe and assembled in the invasion ports, and as troops and supplies were collected and embarkation maneuvers were held along the coasts of France, worldwide attention was centered on the forthcoming invasion, and every German move was watched for signs that it was about to start. When some barges capsized during landing exercises and the bodies of German soldiers were washed ashore, a rumor instantly sprang up that the invasion had already begun.

This was the effect Hitler had wanted, but there was also one that he had not planned for. As the invasion season neared its end and one suitable date after another passed without anything happening, doubts began to be voiced abroad as to whether the much-vaunted project would come off at all. Soon a note of scorn crept into these comments. A shop in occupied Brussels had the courage to advertise "bathing suits for Channel swimming." Hitler must have been stung especially by the taunting remarks in the British press and by the attitude of Churchill himself, who would have liked nothing better than to have the Nazis attempt a landing. Britain no longer was the virtually defenseless prey she had been in June; Churchill was sure that such an attempt would be a disastrous failure and would teach the Nazis a bloody lesson.

Ridicule was something the master of Europe could not tolerate. The comments in Britain and elsewhere must have wounded his vanity, for in his speech of September 4 at the *Sportspalast* he took note of them with a heavy-handed attempt at humor:

> And if people in England today are very curious and ask: "Yes, why doesn't he come then?" [the answer is] "Calm yourselves, he is coming."*

When Hitler made this remark, he already had found a way out of his problem. But he had found it only a few days earlier, and until then he had been facing one

*Wheatley, p. 75.

of the worst dilemmas of his career. Having made SEA LION the cynosure of world attention, he was threatened not only with ridicule but with a tremendous loss of prestige, his own and Germany's, if he quietly allowed the invasion season to pass without going through with the venture. Yet to risk it was also out of the question, unless, by some miracle, Göring could create the condition which the Führer had postulated in his own mind as the prerequisite for a landing: a Britain already defeated and on the verge of surrender so that she would only have to be nudged into acknowledging her defeat. At the end of August, when this dilemma became most acute, only a few days remained before September 10, when Hitler had promised to make his final decision on SEA LION. Even if he could believe Göring's boasts that the battle against Fighter Command had been virtually won and that only a few days of good weather were needed to finish the job, this did not necessarily mean that his private conditions for proceeding with the invasion would be met. The Luftwaffe might win air superiority over southeastern England, but would this change Britain's mood from one of angry defiance to one of surrender, and do it in only ten days?

This was the atmosphere in which Hitler approached the momentous decision whose genesis we are trying to reconstruct. The events that immediately preceded it already have been recounted and need only be recalled briefly.

On August 24 occurred the accidental bombing of London. During the following week the British carried out their feeble raids against Berlin, which did little damage but alarmed the German population and enraged Hitler. By August 30 he had returned to Berlin and had authorized an air assault against London, as tersely recorded in the *OKW Diary.*

There is no evidence on when, how, or why Hitler made the decision, except that it was made on or before August 30, 1940. It may have been in his mind since the Battle of Britain began, or it may have grown in him during the second half of August when he was faced with the SEA LION dilemma. It may have been brought to a head by the British raids against Berlin or by Göring's promises that he could end the war quickly if he were allowed to bomb London.

Hitler must have discussed the subject with Göring after his return to Berlin or even before, but there is no record of such discussions. What we do know is that Göring had some intimations of the forthcoming decision, or at least was hoping for it, on August 29, when he asked the Luftwaffe commanders to submit plans for the assault on London. He met with his *Luftflotten* commanders Kesselring and Sperrle at The Hague on September 3, by which time the decision was firm. On that day, a Dutch acquaintance of Göring's, Dr. Albert Plesman, having been told about the decision, tried to argue against it but was informed that the matter was out of Göring's hands, as the Führer had made up his mind.* The next day, September 4, Hitler made his *Sportspalast* speech, in which he threatened to "rub out" British

*Plesman, the founder of the KLM airline, had developed contacts with Nazi leaders as a result of his efforts to find a peaceful settlement of the war. See Ansel, p. 148.

cities. On the following two nights, preliminary attacks were launched against the London docks, and on September 7 the all-out, round-the-clock bombardment of London began in earnest.

Göring's reasons for favoring the assault on London are not difficult to imagine, although here, too, we are forced to rely mostly on circumstantial evidence. Always in favor of the bludgeon, he was sure that he could force Britain to give up if he were allowed to bomb her at will. That this had been his intention all along is admitted by German authors.* It was demonstrated also by the way he conducted the *Adlerangriff* in the beginning, before he realized the need for a more systematic battle for air superiority not only as preparation for SEA LION, which did not interest him, but also as a prerequisite for strategic bombing.

Deluded by his own optimistic victory communiqués, Göring apparently thought by the end of August that the time for wielding the bludgeon had come. As he saw it, Fighter Command was already defeated, or sufficiently so to permit him to finish off the remaining British fighters in the course of attacking his real objective, London. This would end Britain's will to resist and rid Hitler of the SEA LION incubus, since an invasion in force would be unnecessary. The Luftwaffe would have won the war singlehanded, to the dismay of Göring's service rivals, and brought new power and glory to its victorious commander.

The *Reichsmarschall* undoubtedly had argued his case for the bombing of London on earlier occasions, only to be stymied by Hitler's wish to reserve it for the *Todesstoss,* for which he judged the time had not yet come. But by August 29 or 30 the Führer had changed his mind, either on his own or because Göring persuaded him. There are three possible explanations for this change.

One -- the least plausible -- is that Hitler now believed, or was convinced by Göring, that Britain was so near defeat that it was time for the *coup de grace.* It is true that reports from unreliable German agents abroad constantly stressed what they thought Hitler wanted to hear: that British morale was tottering, that there were crippling food shortages, and that aircraft production was in a critical state.** But not until London was actually under bombardment, toward the middle of September, did these reports become so fanciful that they led Hitler to expect the outbreak of revolution in England. Before then, the reports, however exaggerated, could hardly have been accepted by Hitler as evidence that Britain was ready for the *Todesstoss.* On August 30, when Fighter Command flew over 1000 sorties and Hitler himself admitted that the prerequisites for SEA LION had not yet been met, there was little to indicate that Britain was on the verge of surrender.

Another explanation, favored by German authors, is that the assault on London was decided by Hitler in revenge for the British bombing of Berlin. It was an act of reprisal, the *Vergeltungsangriff* that it was proclaimed to be at the time.

*Cf. Klee, *Das Unternehmen "Seelöwe",* p. 184.

**Wheatley, p. 81.

There is no question that Hitler was thirsting for revenge. He was enraged by the raids on Berlin, not because of the damage they had done* but because of their impression on the German people and because they exposed his boasts that Britain was already defeated. An even stronger reason for Hitler's fury probably was that Britain had dared to spurn his peace offers and that her stubborn resistance in the face of all reason had upset his plans and confronted him with an intolerable dilemma. Whatever role Hitler's desire for revenge may have played in his decision to attack London, however, it is unlikely to have been the sole or even the principal motivation. We know that he found it convenient to use his rages for a purpose and that he rarely allowed them to conflict with what he considered expedient.

There are other reasons for not accepting the reprisal explanation as adequate. When Hitler vowed hundredfold vengeance at the *Sportspalast* on September 4, he was doing exactly what the Nazis had been planning all along: When the time came for terror attacks, they would label such attacks "reprisals."** That the British had given Hitler the semblance of an excuse by bombing Berlin was purely fortuitous; if they had not, he would have invented an act for which to exact a reprisal. The Germans had done this before, as in the case of the so-called "Freiburg Massacre." On the opening day of the offensive in the West, the Luftwaffe had accidentally -- some say, intentionally -- bombed the German city of Freiburg and caused civilian casualties. For years thereafter, the Goebbels propaganda machine used this incident to blame the British for having initiated indiscriminate air warfare with their *Kindermord in Freiburg* ("children's massacre in Freiburg").***

To label the assault on London a reprisal for the raids on Berlin was a distortion in another sense as well, for the raids had themselves been in retaliation for the accidental bombing of London on August 24. (This last fact may explain the conspiracy of silence in which German sources seem to be engaged regarding this bombing;**** they may be afraid that, if they admitted it, the reprisal theory would collapse.) Hitler himself surely was aware of what he was doing when he threatened "reprisals" for the raids on Berlin; it is inconceivable that he did not know that his own Luftwaffe had started the chain when it bombed London by mistake. Even if Göring had tried to conceal the Luftwaffe blunder, the bombing was reported in the foreign press, and the Führer would have demanded an investigation, as he had done in the case of the "Freiburg Massacre." If for no other reason, he would have done so merely to find out why his strict order had been disobeyed.

*It will be recalled that two months earlier the Führer had been quite casual in dismissing the equally ineffective RAF attacks on Ruhr targets. See above, p. 49.

**See above, p. 73.

***The incident is recounted by Telford Taylor (pp. 114-118), who quotes the British military historian Major General J. F. C. Fuller as saying as late as 1949: "There can be little doubt that the bombing of Freiburg and the subsequent attacks on German cities pushed him [Hitler] into his assault on Britain." Unfortunately, this is not the only occasion when Western apologists for the German side have swallowed the Goebbels propaganda. See also Appendix A, below.

****See above, pp. 65*ff.*

This leaves us with the third and most plausible explanation: the SEA LION dilemma. One way out of this dilemma would have been to find a quick means of defeating Britain or of breaking her morale so that a landing would meet no real opposition. But there was another solution, too attractive to have escaped Hitler's attention. It was to launch a spectacular military operation that would divert world attention from the much-advertised invasion project and permit him to cancel it without loss of prestige, letting the world believe that the invasion threat had only been a cover for the new operation. An attack on Russia would have served the purpose, if he had been able to mount it in the fall of 1940, as he had once planned. With that possibility ruled out, the ideal solution was the assault on London. It would rid him of SEA LION either by burying the incubus in the ruins of the city or even perhaps by removing the need for an invasion altogether.

Göring may have succeeded in convincing the Führer that his successes against the RAF had brought Britain so close to defeat that the assault on London would force her to give up. Although Hitler by then probably had his reservations about Göring's victory claims, and although, as we know, he had always been skeptical about the military value of terror attacks, they had never before been tried on the scale he was now contemplating. And if the military effect of the blow were to fall below expectations, there was the psychological impact, which would reinforce the pressures exerted on the British by the invasion threat. The combined effect might complete the demoralization of the people and destroy Britain's will to fight. When that happened, Hitler could stage the invasion as a formality enabling him to administer the *Todesstoss* and occupy the island, after which the Gestapo jackals would be let loose to work on the remains.*

But the beauty of the plan, and what must have been the clinching argument for Hitler, was that it would get him out of his dilemma even if the assault did not accomplish what Göring had promised. The destruction of a great city like London would be a spectacular act that would draw the attention of the world away from SEA LION and serve as an adequate substitute for an invasion even if it failed to bring victory. This is not a speculative reconstruction of Hitler's reasoning; for once there is evidence for what was in his mind. In Admiral Raeder's notes on the Führer Conference of September 14 the following passage occurs:

> If one is to avoid a loss of prestige, SEA LION must be cancelled only at the moment of maximum success in the air, giving as reason that SEA LION is no longer necessary. The Führer agrees, but will make his decision on September 17 with the tentative date again September 27.**

This is not to suggest that the decision to attack London was based on a single reason, compelling as it may have been. Hitler's desire to punish Britain was

*For an account of the Gestapo plans for the occupation of Britain, see Peter Fleming, *Operation Sea Lion,* Simon & Schuster, New York, 1957, Chap. 18; also Wheatley, pp. 122-124.

**Naval Operations Office *(Seekriegsleitung):* Record of Conferences of the Commander-in-Chief with the Führer, in *Dokumente,* pp. 263-264.

undoubtedly an additional motive. Even the hope that the destruction of London might cause Britain to give up may have been a factor in Hitler's thinking, although his views on strategic bombing are likely to have made him somewhat skeptical on this score. Major decisions are usually based on a mixture of good and bad reasons, emotion, and wishful thinking, and this was truer of the Führer than of most national leaders. The important point here is that among all the possible motives for the decision to bomb London there was one so compelling that it alone would have been sufficient: the fact that the assault on London would solve the urgent problem of SEA LION *regardless* of what else it might achieve. It might not bring victory, and it might turn out to be a costly and wasteful use of the Luftwaffe, but it would be a spectacular military operation in the eyes of the whole world and thereby alone fulfill Hitler's purpose. That it would bring great suffering upon innocent civilians and destroy a storied old city apparently did not concern the Führer and his Nazi leaders and probably did not even occur to them.

If the assault on London was the solution to Hitler's problems, it also rescued his Army and Navy commanders -- von Brauchitsch, Halder, and Raeder -- from a fate they must have viewed with the utmost apprehension. There is no evidence that the Führer consulted them on this decision, nor is there any record of what they thought of it at the time. General Halder saw Hitler on August 31, the day after the decision had been announced in OKW. Yet his *Diary,* in which he recorded far less important events, contains no reference to the bombing of London until September 14, when the subject was discussed at a Führer Conference. Admiral Raeder, too, spoke with Hitler on September 6, and again the record of this meeting mentions a variety of subjects, including SEA LION, but not the bombing of London.*

It is clear from the diary entries of Halder and Raeder that the plans and preparations for SEA LION were still the commanders' major preoccupation at the time and that Hitler kept them up to the mark by giving them the impression that he had warmed up to the project and might actually go through with it. Since we know what they thought of this prospect,** it is not difficult to imagine their own situation as they saw it. If the invasion turned out to be the disastrous failure they expected it to be, they would be held responsible and the fate that awaited them would make them wish they had died in the attempt.

Their plight must have been brought home to them on August 30, when Hitler announced that he was giving Göring a few more days to finish the job -- presumably the job of winning air superiority. They knew that Göring was not anywhere as close to it as he claimed. The worst that could happen to them would be for the Luftwaffe to continue its inconclusive battle with Fighter Command until the decision date of September 10 and to have Hitler declare, on the strength of Göring's boast, that air superiority had been won and the prerequisites for the invasion had thus been met; as the Army and Navy leaders knew, they could not have been met in the time available. Nor had Göring any intention of meeting them,

*In *Dokumente,* pp. 261-263.

**See above, pp. 74-75.

for even if the checkmating of Fighter Command could have been achieved, they involved a great deal more than that. And Göring himself freely admitted that he was not about to carry out the tasks assigned to the Luftwaffe in the invasion plans. In an OKW staff conference on September 5 it was reported that "the Reich Marshal is not interested in the preparations for Operation Sea Lion as he does not believe that the operation will ever take place."*

We may not know what the Army and Navy top leaders privately thought of the assault on London, but we know that it alarmed their staffs, to whom the invasion project was real and who may have been less hopeful than their superiors that the project would be canceled at the last moment. Their concern over the diversion of the Luftwaffe from the tasks assigned to it in the invasion plans was noted in the Naval War Diary on September 10:

> . . .the indispensable prerequisite for the undertaking (Sea Lion). . .has *not* been achieved, namely clear air command over the Channel. . .the shooting up of Boulogne of yesterday and today by destroyers shows the enemy is testing our defensive powers. Planned preparations for SEA LION would require the Luftwaffe now to concentrate less on London but more on Portsmouth and Dover and the (British) fleet forces. . . . However SKL [Naval Operations Office] does not hold it proper to come forward with such requirement to the Luftwaffe or to the Führer now since he regards the great assault on London as possibly decisive for the war and [feels] that the systematic and prolonged bombing of London can provoke an enemy attitude which might make SEA LION altogether unnecessary. . . .**

The diary entry two days later did not mince words:

> The air war is being conducted as an "absolute air war" without regard to the present requirements of the naval war, and outside the framework of operation "Sea Lion". In its present form the air war cannot assist preparations for "Sea Lion", which are predominantly in the hands of the Navy. In particular, one cannot discern any effort on the part of the Luftwaffe to engage the units of the British fleet, which are now able to operate almost unmolested in the Channel, and this will prove extremely dangerous to the transportation. Thus the main safeguard against British naval forces would have to be minefields, which, as repeatedly explained to the Supreme Command, cannot be regarded as reliable protection for shipping.
>
> The fact remains that up to now the intensified air war has not contributed towards the landing operation; hence for operational and military reasons the execution of the landing cannot yet be considered.***

*Wheatley, p. 60.

**Ansel, p. 252. Shorter extracts from this entry are given by Churchill (see below), and by Klee, *Das Unternehmen "Seelöwe"*, p. 175.

***Churchill, *Their Finest Hour,* pp. 328-329.

If Admiral Raeder shared his staff's concern, he gave little evidence of it at the Führer Conference of September 14, two days after the diary entry just quoted. On the contrary, he departed from his usual practice of sticking to strictly naval matters and spoke out in support of General Jeschonnek, the Chief of Staff of the Luftwaffe, who had urged that the air attacks on London be intensified and extended to residential areas.* Raeder's conduct on this occasion may have been simply the mark of a lickspittle personality that prompted him to say what he believed Hitler wanted to hear.** More likely, however, Raeder and his colleagues in the Army actually favored the diversion of the Luftwaffe to the attack on London. If they did, it was not because they shared Göring's belief that one could defeat a resolute enemy by destroying his capital. They had no faith in "absolute air war," as they called it, nor in Göring, for that matter. Unless their ideas about the military effectiveness of terror attacks had changed drastically in a single week, they did not expect the air assault on London to cause Britain to give up without an invasion. Nor were they likely to believe that it would so weaken Britain militarily as to make the invasion possible. What they may well have expected, however, was that it would make the invasion *impossible* by demonstrating that fact to the Führer. This would be their only salvation.

We must remember that the Army and Navy commanders could never be sure of Hitler's real intentions and therefore lived in constant dread of the possibility that he would order the invasion even in the face of impossible odds. The only thing they could be certain of was that he would not undertake a landing without air superiority, as he had affirmed over and over. He might disregard Göring's failure to accomplish other preinvasion tasks assigned to the Luftwaffe, but not his failure to win control of the air. If Göring wasted his bombs on London instead of keeping up the attack on Fighter Command's ground installations, they knew he would have to win air superiority the hard way by defeating the British fighters in the air. Even if he could do so (which the heavy Luftwaffe losses may have caused them to doubt), he was unlikely to succeed in the time available and with enough of his forces intact to be able to give adequate support to the landing itself. Therefore, if the campaign against London could be stretched out a few days longer, the last decision date on SEA LION would be passed and Hitler would be forced to cancel the project for that year.

If that was the way Army and Navy leaders reasoned -- and such thoughts must have occurred to them -- they were proved right. By September 13, less than a week after the assault on London had begun, Hitler, it seems, had privately decided to give up SEA LION,*** but he kept up appearances for a few days longer in the

*Klee, *Das Unternehmen "Seelöwe"*, p. 203.

**By comparison with Raeder's personality, as exhibited in his words and actions, his two Army colleagues emerge almost as upstanding characters. This is not saying too much. Although they did not descend to the level Raeder did, a contemporary observer noted: "Von Brauchitsch and Halder had lost all capacity of independent thought or action. Mentally and hierarchically, they had become mere understrappers to their *Führer.*" Ulrich von Hassell, quoted in Wheeler-Bennett, p. 512.

***Hillgruber, p. 176.

forlorn hope that the continued invasion threat combined with the destruction of London might still bring Britain around. On September 17, when he effectively cancelled the project for that year, his excuse was the weather that allegedly had prevented Göring from finishing the job.* This may have been the outcome that Army and Navy leaders had counted on, though they would have attributed Göring's failure not to the weather but to his ineptitude.

The decision to attack London thus promised to solve not only Hitler's problem but that of his Army and Navy commanders as well. It enabled the Führer to get out of SEA LION without loss of prestige and to strike a punishing blow at Britain into the bargain. It relieved the fears of his senior commanders that they might have to go through with a doomed project, which even Hitler would not risk without the air superiority Göring was unlikely to win by bombing London. They all stood to gain by the decision, whether Göring succeeded or failed, and perhaps even more if he failed. Göring alone would be the big loser if his gamble failed; but he was too sure of success to worry about this risk.

Once we recognize the problems that would be solved for the Nazi leaders by the assault on London, there can be few doubts as to why it was undertaken. Yet some of the postwar literature, especially by German authors, has raised just such doubts by advancing ingenious and fanciful explanations: that the assault was a justified reprisal for the British raids on Berlin; that it was not a terror attack at all but was aimed at legitimate economic and industrial objectives in the British capital; that it had the purely military objective of luring the remaining British fighters into battle.

These explanations will be discussed elsewhere** -- not because there is enough evidence for them to warrant such examination, but because they have been swallowed by some credulous historians and German apologists. Like certain historical myths that have been propagated for centuries, they are in danger of becoming accepted as the true story behind the decision to bomb London.

*See above, p. 71.

**See Appendix A.

7

*Ends and Means**

Another Debate Over Strategic Air Warfare

THE WEEKS between September 7 and the middle of November 1940, during which London was subjected to nightly bombardment, left more than physical scars. They hardened the determination of the British people to pay the Germans back in kind. Retribution was delayed, much to Churchill's dismay, partly because Britain still lacked the means to satisfy the popular clamor for reprisals, partly because some questioned that Britain had a moral right, even in the face of extreme provocation, to cast all restraint aside and resort to the indiscriminate air warfare the Germans had adopted.

It was almost two years before German cities were subjected to the kind of destruction London had suffered. And it took close to three years for the British bombing offensive to reach its height, if that is the word, in the frightful attacks on Hamburg that turned the city into a blazing inferno. By that time, the German air attacks on Britain had been reduced to the level of sporadic raids by relatively weak forces. Nevertheless, the desire to make the Germans suffer as Londoners had suffered was certainly a factor in Britain's allowing the air offensive against Germany to be conducted with less and less regard for civilian casualties. It was by no means the only factor, for there were other reasons why the British eventually resorted to their own version of total war. They will become apparent as we follow the developments on the British side with which the rest of this narrative is concerned.

As already recounted, the first British attack on Berlin was carried out the night after the accidental bombing of London on August 24. Though officially described

*The main source for this and the remaining sections of this narrative is Webster & Frankland, *The Strategic Air Offensive Against Germany, 1939-1945,* cited as *Air Offensive.*

as an attack on military objectives in the city, the raid on Berlin was an act of reprisal, pure and simple.

But it was a feeble reprisal that did not satisfy Mr. Churchill. He wanted Bomber Command to launch attacks on other German cities and to spread the bombs as widely as possible. His demand found a wider echo after the Germans had begun their systematic assault on London, two weeks later. The British people were now convinced that Hitler had cast all restraint aside and that there would be worse to come. "Our outlook at this time was that London, except for its strong, modern buildings would be gradually and soon reduced to a rubble heap."* The knockout blow, so long expected, had at last begun. The Londoners were willing to take it, but they demanded revenge. " 'Give it 'em back,' they cried. 'Let *them* have it too.' "**

On September 11, Sir Charles Portal, then Commander-in-Chief, Bomber Command, responded to the Prime Minister's request with a proposal that "twenty German towns should be warned by wireless and that each indiscriminate attack by the Luftwaffe on a British town should be followed by an indiscriminate Bomber Command attack on one of them."*** This was not quite what Churchill had had in mind. Portal's suggestion was aimed at deterring the enemy from further attacks on British cities, not at revenge for the attacks already made.

The Air Staff did not concur with the Portal proposal either, though for different reasons. They felt that "selective precision attacks" against military objectives would be more effective than the indiscriminate bombing of German cities. There also may have been a question in their minds, at least at first, whether the assault on London was really intended as a deliberate terror attack. The bombers could have aimed at docks and other military objectives in the port of London, and the destruction of residential areas and the heavy civilian casualties might have been unintentional. This, of course, was what German apologists were to say after the war.****

Their claim found surprising support in Basil Collier's official History:

> Although the plan adopted by the Luftwaffe early in September had mentioned attacks on the populations of large cities, detailed records of the raids made during the autumn and winter of 1940-1941 do not suggest that indiscriminate bombing of civilians was intended. The points of aim selected were largely factories and docks. Other objectives specifically allotted to bomber crews included the City of London and the government quarter round Whitehall.*****

Not having access to Mr. Collier's original sources, one can only suggest that he may have based his statement on the official Luftwaffe plans. These plans would

*Churchill, *Their Finest Hour,* p. 350.

***Ibid.*, p. 349.

****Air Offensive,* Vol. 1, p. 153.

****See Appendix A.

*****Collier, *The Defence of the United Kingdom,* p. 261.

have had to conform to Hitler's instruction that the bombing of London should be confined to military objectives within the city. What was actually done was of course a different matter, as has already been discussed.

Kesselring's daylight attacks between September 7 and 15 might have been intended against the port facilities and other military objectives, but the same could hardly be said of the concurrent night attacks by Sperrle's bombers. The charitable view of German intentions became even harder to maintain when the Luftwaffe started to drop parachute mines at night. Since these could not be aimed, their use removed the last pretense that the Germans were striking at military objectives. Churchill writes:

> About the same time the enemy began to drop by parachute numbers of naval mines of a weight and explosive power never carried by aircraft before. Many formidable explosions took place. To this there was no defence except reprisal. The abandonment by the Germans of all pretence of confining the air war to military objectives had also raised this question of retaliation. I was for it, but I encountered many conscientious scruples.*

The Prime Minister made numerous attempts to bring his military advisers around to his views. On September 19 he wrote a memorandum for the Chiefs of Staff in which he linked the German use of parachute mines with the proposal he had received from Sir Charles Portal:

> 1. It was not solely on moral grounds that we decided against retaliation upon Germany. It pays us better to concentrate upon limited high-class military objectives. Moreover, in the indiscriminate warfare the enemy's lack of skill in navigation, etc., does not tell against him so much.
>
> 2. However, the dropping of large mines by parachute proclaims the enemy's entire abandonment of all pretence of aiming at military objectives. At five thousand feet he cannot have the slightest idea what he is going to hit. This, therefore, proves the "act-of-terror" intention against the civil population. We must consider whether his morale would stand up to this as well as ours. Here is a simple war thought.
>
> 3. My inclination is to say that we will drop a heavy parachute mine on German cities for everyone he drops on ours; and it might be an intriguing idea to mention a list of cities that would be blacklisted for this purpose. I do not think they would like it, and there is no reason why they should not have a period of suspense.
>
> . . . .
>
> 5. I wish to know by Saturday night what is the worst form of proportionate retaliation, i.e., *equal* retaliation, that we can inflict upon ordinary German cities for what they are now doing to us by means of the parachute mine. . . .

*Churchill, *Their Finest Hour*, p. 363.

It seems that even Mr. Churchill's fabled powers of persuasion proved unequal to the task: "A month later, I was still pressing for retaliation, but one objection after another, moral and technical, obstructed it."*

The Prime Minister's desire to strike back at Germany reflected the prevailing sentiment of the British people. But there were other reasons as well why Churchill deemed it imperative to take some offensive action against the enemy at this stage of the war. Britain's forces had been driven from the Continent, she had lost her ally, her capital was under devastating attack, and the island itself was threatened with invasion. Throughout the world, Britain was in danger of being written off as a lost cause. The doubters had to be shown that she would stay her course, despite all the reverses she had suffered. They had to be convinced that the appeasement spirit of the Chamberlain period was dead, that Britain would make no deals with the dictator and would fight on alone, if necessary, "until, in God's good time, the New World, with all its power and might, steps forth to the rescue and the liberation of the Old."**

It was especially important that the American public be convinced of the British resolution to continue the war. Britain was in desperate need of war materials from the United States. President Roosevelt was doing all he could to maintain the flow of weapons and supplies to Britain, but he was faced by a growing demand that they be retained at home for America's own rearmament program. The President's hand would be strengthened if the British showed through aggressive conduct of the war that they were making good use of the matériel supplied by the United States to fight the common foe.

Direct action against the German homeland was needed also to impress upon the German people that the war was not yet over for them, that it would be fought on their own soil, and that it would subject them to hardships and suffering that they may have hoped to escape by virtue of their early triumphs. This was considered an important objective, for the British Government believed -- wrongly, as it turned out -- that the German people were restive under Hitler's yoke, and that the restiveness might be turned into active revolt if they could be shown what their rulers had let them in for.

For all these reasons it was important for Britain to seize the initiative by striking at Germany proper. Bomber Command was the only force available at the time that could be employed in direct military action against the German homeland. While invasion seemed imminent, even that force had to be used defensively, to disrupt the enemy's preparations for SEA LION. Toward the end of September, however, when the invasion danger had passed or greatly lessened -- and when the clamor for retaliation against Germany was loudest -- Bomber Command was once again available for use in an offensive role.

The temptation was great to use it for attacks on German cities in retaliation for what the Luftwaffe was doing to London and other British cities. But the war was

*Ibid., pp. 364-365.

**Ibid., p. 118.

at too critical a stage, and Bomber Command too precious a resource, to allow its use to be governed by emotion. As Mr. Churchill had said earlier, before he himself had yielded to emotion, "The Navy can lose us the war, but only the Air Force can win it." Bomber Command might not win the war, but it had to be employed in consonance with a larger strategic plan for the conduct of the war. What plans there were all envisaged a strategic air offensive against Germany that would constantly grow in volume and effectiveness as new and better aircraft and more trained crews became available. This meant, however, that Bomber Command had to husband its resources, which were essential for the contemplated expansion. It followed that air attacks on Germany could be carried out only at night, since daytime bombing would lead to prohibitive losses. Moreover, Bomber Command could not afford to scatter its efforts over a wide variety of targets with little or no effect on any one. It had to concentrate on the most valuable target system, preferably one small enough to be destroyed or seriously damaged with the small force available for such attacks.

The target system that had always been the first choice of British air planners because it seemed to meet these specifications was German oil production. It was regarded by the Ministry of Economic Warfare as the Achilles heel of the German economy. Lord Hankey* and other influential civilians believed that destruction of the seventeen synthetic oil plants could cripple the German war machine, and had urged the British Government to concentrate all its efforts against this target system.

There was general agreement that, if the strategic air offensive were to be aimed at the German economy, oil would be the logical target. The disagreement was over whether it should be aimed at the economy or at civilian morale. This had already been an issue in the Trenchard debate of the twenties.** It had never been resolved, since there was no basis for assessing the relative importance of the two objectives. The earlier debate had been beclouded by emotion on one side of the argument, on the part of those who as a matter of moral principle objected to making war on civilians. In the autumn of 1940 there was emotion on both sides of the argument, for as well as against city bombing. Military men in Britain still abhorred this form of warfare and shrank from the idea of matching the enemy's brutalities. But they would not have been human if they could have witnessed the senseless destruction of London night after night without a desire to pay the Germans back in kind.

Few British leaders were as honest with themselves as Mr. Churchill, who frankly admitted that he was out for revenge; most of them found it easier to defend their preference on logical grounds. Those who were for outright city bombing -- at that time, a minority -- believed that civilian morale in Germany was already shaky, that it was the most vulnerable point of the entire Nazi edifice, and that it was likely to collapse under strategic bombing. There was no solid evidence to support these beliefs.

*Then Chancellor of the Duchy of Lancaster and Chairman of the Committee on German Oil.
**See above, pp. 9-13.

The majority, who opposed making war on civilians, in turn found a way of reconciling their moral scruples with a desire for retaliation by recommending that air attacks be directed at military or economic objectives in a city without bombing of the city itself. There was no reason to believe that this could be done at night or that it would keep down the number of civilian casualties, and there was much evidence to the contrary. But the proponents of this solution either minimized the inevitable civilian casualties, or actually welcomed them provided they were a by-product of the bombing and not its main objective.

This argument with all its self-deception and curiously scholastic flavor was not confined to ignorant laymen. It formed the basis of the disagreement between the Air Staff and Bomber Command over the objectives of the strategic air offensive:

> Though the limitations in the accuracy of night bombing were still far from fully realised, it was obvious that the Germans, even if they wished to, could not execute an attack on Battersea power station without endangering numbers of civilians living in that area. Equally it was impossible for Bomber Command to attack the marshalling yards at Hamm without running the same risk. If there was to be any strategic bombing at all, civilians would be killed; hospitals, churches and cultural monuments would be hit. The Air Staff, as represented by its Vice-Chief, Sir Richard Peirse, believed that what was inevitable was also desirable only in so far as it remained a by-product of the primary intention to hit a military target in the sense of a power station, a marshalling yard or an oil plant. Bomber Command, as represented by its Commander-in-Chief, Sir Charles Portal, now [September 1940] believed that this by-product should become an end-product. He believed that this course had been justified by previous German action and that it would be justified as a strategy in the outcome.*

When the next official bomber directive was written, in October 1940, it turned out, not surprisingly, to be a compromise between the two conflicting views.** As is often the case with compromised solutions, it was phrased in vague language that permitted conflicting interpretations. Both oil *and* civilian morale were to be the primary target systems. The oil targets were to have priority "when favourable conditions obtain." At other times "concentrated attacks should be made on objectives*** in large towns and centres of industry, with the primary aim of causing very heavy material destruction which will demonstrate to the enemy the power and severity of air bombardment and the hardship and dislocation which will result from it." Berlin was to be the first choice whenever deep penetrations were

**Air Offensive,* Vol. 1, p. 154. A few weeks after the time to which this passage refers, Sir Charles Portal became Chief of the Air Staff, and Sir Richard Peirse took his place as Commander-in-Chief, Bomber Command. After the switch each man began to swing around toward the views he had opposed in his former capacity.

**The directive is reproduced in *Air Offensive,* Vol. 4, App. 8 (xi).

***The draft version had specified "military" objectives, but the word "military" was crossed out, and did not appear in the final version. *Air Offensive,* Vol. 1, p. 156.

practicable; otherwise attacks were to be directed against cities in central and western Germany. Regarding these attacks, the directive was unusually specific: It instructed Bomber Command to employ a high proportion of incendiaries and to "focus their attacks to a large extent on the fires with a view to preventing the fire fighting services from dealing with them and giving the fires every opportunity to spread."

The directive thus contained something to please each side. The order to attack specific objectives in the cities, unrealistic though it was, served to allay moral scruples against making war on civilians. Those who did not have such scruples, or were more interested in getting back at the Germans, could find satisfaction in the detailed instructions on how to raise fires in German cities. If the Air Staff was still reluctant to come out openly in favor of attacking civilians, at least it was willing to adopt the German tactics that had proved so successful in killing civilians in British cities. According to Webster and Frankland,

> Thus, the fiction that the bombers were attacking "military objectives" in the towns was officially abandoned. This was the technique which was to become known as area bombing.*

This interpretation is in error on an important point. The bombing directive of October 1940 did outline a procedure which, in effect, amounted to area bombing. But the fiction that the purpose of the attacks was to hit specific objectives in the cities was not abandoned, officially or otherwise, until much later. Subsequent bombing directives continued to specify factories, oil plants, marshaling yards, and other industrial objectives that were to be hit in the attacks on cities, and the cities themselves were chosen on the ground that they contained such targets. The official communiques reported bombing results in terms of the specific objectives allegedly destroyed or damaged. Civilian damage inflicted in the course of these attacks continued to be regarded as an incidental, though not unwelcome, by-product of the bombing. In short, the rationale behind the bombing offensive was still based on the fiction that it was possible to single out specific objectives in a city at night, and that there was a difference between inflicting civilian casualties as a by-product and doing so as the end-product of strategic bombing.

Though the fiction became more and more transparent as time went on, it was maintained at least until the spring of 1942, a year-and-a-half later, when the "Thousand Bomber" raids against Cologne and other German cities made it clear that the by-product had become the end-product. How could the fiction have been kept alive for so long?

One important factor, which will be discussed presently, was that the British leaders simply did not know what the bombers were actually accomplishing and that they believed the exaggerated reports brought back by the pilots. But this was not the only reason. They wanted to believe that it was possible to hit precision targets at night, because the only alternative was area bombing, which many found morally reprehensible. Their "conscientious scruples" were sincere; else they would not

**Ibid.*, p. 157.

have devoted time and attention to the moral aspects of strategic bombing at a time of greatest peril, when they were hard-pressed on every side. They were reluctant to subordinate their notions of decency to the demands of fighting a dirty war. It was this moral dilemma that encouraged their wishful thinking and caused them to cling to a fiction that they maintained to deceive not others but themselves. It also led them to the kind of halfhearted compromises reflected in the bombing directive of October 1940 -- as though, if compelled to fight dirty, it would be less dishonorable to do so inefficiently.

If it was difficult for British leaders to make the mental transition to unrestrained warfare, the physical transition came naturally and almost without volition. Bomber Command drifted into area bombing because it was the only kind of bombing that could be done at night and not because it had been chosen as the preferred strategy. When that choice was finally made, in the spring of 1942, it merely ratified a practice that had already been developing over a year-and-a-half. Operational considerations, not moral sentiments or strategic objectives, governed what was actually done as the strategic bombing offensive developed. The Cabinet, the Chiefs of Staff, and the Air Staff could engage in lengthy debates over the strategic value or moral acceptability of different target systems, but their conclusions were irrelevant if Bomber Command could not find or hit the targets they had selected. As Sir Charles Portal was to point out later in connection with the oil targets, ". . .the most suitable object from the economic point of view is not worth pursuing if it is not tactically attainable."* Cities were easier to find and hit than isolated oil plants.

To appreciate what could and could not be accomplished at the time, we must keep in mind that the Bomber Command of 1940 was a puny force compared to what it was to become later in the war. It was severely limited in the quality and quantity of crews and aircraft, it lacked electronic equipment for night navigation and bombing, and it had yet to develop the tactics that would compensate for these deficiencies. The bombing directives had to make allowance for these operational difficulties by granting Bomber Command discretion to attack alternate targets when bombing of the primary precision targets was precluded by tactical considerations. Since this was much of the time, the alternate targets -- euphemistically described as "industrial areas" -- often became the primary targets. One of the joint authors of the British History of the bombing offensive, Dr. Noble Frankland, stated the case succinctly in his Lees Knowles Lectures of 1963:

> It therefore becomes clear that the decision to confine Bomber Command mainly to night action, which was taken in April 1940, resulted inevitably in a policy of attack upon whole German towns, the policy of area bombing. All the arguments based on strategic and economic reasons which have gone on since and, surprisingly, still go on, about the alternatives of this or that kind of attack are wholly groundless for operational reasons alone. The alternative to area bombing was either no strategic bombing or daylight bombing. In the

**Air Offensive,* Vol. 1, p. 168.

circumstances of the time, the idea of abandoning strategic bombing was scarcely a practicable proposition though there were those who presently claimed that it might have been.*

The fact that it was not a policy decision but operational reasons that caused Britain to drift into a form of warfare which many of her leaders considered morally repugnant and strategically worthless has far-reaching implications. The events surrounding the gradual transition toward unrestrained war have so far been discussed here as if they had been the result of strategic and policy decisions made by the two sides. This is an oversimplification. As the war unfolded, the decisionmakers became as much the prisoners as they were directors of the forces they had unleashed. On the German side this was certainly the case from the time that the air attack against Britain was launched. On the British side, it began when Britain, in turn, carried the air war into Germany.

The evolution of the strategic air offensive against Germany was shaped by operational considerations which often vitiated the strategic decisions that were supposed to govern it. As the war dragged on, decisionmakers may have sensed their impotence, for some of their decisions seemed almost to be a mere formality, designed to ratify a course of action that had been forced upon them by operational necessity. Since it was so often the means that shaped the ends, we must now consider some of the operational problems with which Bomber Command was confronted in the air offensive against Germany.

Bombing in the Dark

The continuing debate over suitable target systems for the strategic air offensive was carried on in a vacuum of information, since nobody really knew what air power could actually accomplish or how its effectiveness would change under different tactical conditions and against different targets. All peacetime experience had been gained in daylight bombing under ideal conditions, whereas now the RAF was engaged in night bombing over unknown terrain under combat conditions. That this would make a vast difference in the navigating accuracy and bombing error of the crews was slow to be appreciated. In the early part of 1941, most RAF planners were still unaware that on dark nights the crews often could not find even a large city and would drop their bombs in open country, miles away from their target.

The troubles that the Luftwaffe was having in trying to hit British targets at night should have served as a salutary check on excessive optimism as to what could be accomplished with nighttime bombing. But with a few exceptions, the Air Staff was content to accept at face value the pilots' glowing reports of the damage they claimed to have inflicted on their targets. According to a typical report of an attack on Berlin in October 1940, the crews had allegedly identified and hit such precision targets as power stations, marshaling yards, and even individual buildings such as the

*Frankland, *The Bombing Offensive Against Germany*, pp. 61-62.

Berlin Chancery and the War Office -- all this in bombing a distant and heavily defended target on a night when there was only partial moonlight. Similar success was reported in attacks on the synthetic oil plants at Gelsenkirchen, on aircraft factories, and on other difficult targets. The official British History notes the false optimism engendered by the pilots' claims:

> These reports, which were typical of those made on operations throughout the year, made complete nonsense of the doubts and anxieties which had been expressed from time to time about night bombing. If they were reliable, it was clear that Bomber Command had achieved not only an astonishing standard of navigating accuracy but also an ability to distinguish a wealth of detail about its precision targets. It was very rarely that these reports indicated that there had been any difficulty in reaching and locating the target, whether it was an oil plant, a marshalling yard, an aircraft factory or even an individual building in a city.*

The reports might have met with some skepticism if they had not been confirmed by the spurious intelligence received from sources inside Germany. Agents reported excellent results of the bombing attacks and embroidered them with sufficient quantitative detail to make them sound convincing. In October 1940, when British raids had barely made a dent in German production, reports from "well informed industrialists" alleged that "some twenty-five percent of 'the total productive capacity of Germany' had been affected by the bombing."** Reports such as these made pleasant reading and confirmed what British leaders believed or wanted to believe. They caused Air Vice-Marshal Harris*** to complain bitterly about the "half-witted" public relations people in the Air Ministry who did not have sense enough to publicize these achievements in the manner he thought they deserved.

The uncritical acceptance of these reports is easier to understand if we remember that, apart from the unreliable intelligence reports out of Germany, there was no means of checking on the claims made by bomber crews. Occasionally, strike pictures were taken by the bomber crews themselves or by other aircraft, but only in isolated instances and with inconclusive results. The crews resented the use of cameras as an attempt to spy on their performance, and usually put the blame on the camera when the picture did not bear out their own claims.

There was no systematic effort at photographic bomb-damage assessment until November 1940, when the first Spitfire photo reconnaissance flight was formed. The pictures brought back by the new unit immediately showed a startling contrast between what the crews had reported and what had actually been achieved. But it was many months before enough evidence had been accumulated to gain acceptance for the new method of bomb-damage assessment and to change the prevailing ideas of the over-all effectiveness of the bombing.

**Air Offensive,* Vol. 1, p. 219.

***Ibid.,* p. 220.

***Then Air Officer Commanding, No. 5 Group, Bomber Command.

This explains why bombing directives issued prior to 1942 continued to be based on the fiction of precision bombing, although the photographs that already were available showed that what was actually taking place was in fact, if not in intent, area bombing. Ironically, the first serious doubts about the effectiveness of night precision bombing began to arise on one of the rare occasions when Bomber Command was specifically directed by the War Cabinet to undertake an area attack, the raid against the city of Mannheim, on December 16, 1940. It was probably intended as retaliation for the devastation of Coventry in the previous month, for its announced purpose was "to concentrate the maximum amount of damage in the centre of the town." A pathfinder force of experienced crews was to mark the aiming points with incendiary bombs, and the aircraft following were to aim on the fires raised in the initial attack. The raid was carried out under conditions of full moonlight.* The crews brought back their usual glowing reports. The majority of the bombs had fallen in the target area, and the center of the city had been left in flames. The Commander-in-Chief, Bomber Command, congratulated all concerned on the "successful operations."

But this was December 1940, and now at last a means for making an independent check of the results was available. A Spitfire aircraft of the newly formed Photographic Reconnaissance Unit obtained a daylight photograph of Mannheim. It showed that, although some damage had been done to the city, the attack had been widely dispersed and many bombs had fallen outside the target area. As the chief of Bomber Command himself had to admit, the attack had "failed in its primary object."

This was a sobering lesson. It provided "the first of any real evidence we have had as to the general standard of bombing accuracy which characterises our present night operations."** If it was so difficult to hit the center of a city in full moonlight, how could the bomber crews hit an isolated oil plant, a much smaller target and more difficult to find in the first place?

Since German oil production was the target system favored by the Air Staff and by many influential civilians, the Mannheim evidence should have given the planners pause. It did in fact raise doubts in the minds of a few experienced RAF officers, but not enough to dispel the deep-seated illusions about bombing effectiveness. More evidence was provided on December 28, when the strike photographs obtained on two large attacks against synthetic oil plants at Gelsenkirchen showed that neither of the two plants had suffered major damage, although the crews, as usual, had reported excellent results.

Nevertheless, the German oil plants continued to be regarded as the most suitable target system. In its Fifth Report to the War Cabinet on the German oil situation, the Lloyd Committee had made a "conservative" estimate that so far the British bombing offensive had already achieved a 15 percent reduction in the German

**Air Offensive,* Vol. 1, pp. 163, 215, and 226.

***Ibid.*, p. 227.

output of synthetic oil.* Largely on the strength of this report, the Chiefs of Staff recommended in January 1941 that the attacks on oil should be continued as a matter of first priority, because "the destruction of Germany's synthetic oil plants will reduce Germany to such a shortage of oil within the next six months that there will be widespread effects on German industry and communications."** The Chiefs of Staff made this recommendation in spite of the evidence provided by the Mannheim and Gelsenkirchen photographs. What is even more difficult to explain is that Sir Charles Portal could still assure the Prime Minister that the Air Staff's estimate of the number of sorties required to destroy the synthetic oil plants was based on "actual experience of night operations."***

Mr. Churchill was skeptical of the oil plan. He may not have appreciated the significance of the new photographic evidence any better than his military advisers did, but he had an instinctive distrust of "cut-and-dried" solutions for winning the war. Also, he was still trying -- so far without success -- to get the Cabinet to adopt a more ruthless policy of bombing German cities in retaliation for the Luftwaffe attacks on Britain. The Cabinet, however, approved the oil plan which the Chiefs of Staff had recommended. An unusually explicit directive for its implementation was issued to Bomber Command on January 15, 1941. Sir Richard Peirse was to consider destruction of the synthetic oil plants as his "sole primary aim." Other targets were to be attacked only when "tactical or weather conditions" precluded strikes against the oil plants.****

As it turned out, the weather was so bad during the two months the directive was in force that only relatively few sorties could be flown against the oil targets. The results were negligible. By spring, even such a staunch proponent of the oil plan as Sir Charles Portal had lost his enthusiasm for it.

This was not the reason, however, why the oil directive was canceled in March 1941. The Battle of the Atlantic was then at a crucial stage, and Bomber Command was needed to assist the hard-pressed Admiralty. A new directive ordered Bomber Command to devote its major effort in the next four months to helping to combat the German naval and air forces that were threatening to cut Britain's lifeline to the West. The Air Staff was unhappy about this latest diversion from the strategic bombing offensive. But it may have come at an opportune time, "for if Bomber Command had, at this stage, been left free to carry out the oil plan it would probably have done a great deal more damage to its prestige than to its targets."*****

Even without wasting itself on the difficult oil targets, Bomber Command did not succeed in arresting the decline in its prestige. Its contribution to the Battle

*This interagency committee headed by Mr. Geoffrey Lloyd had been set up especially to advise Lord Hankey's Cabinet Committee and the Joint Intelligence Committee on the status of German oil supplies.

***Air Offensive*, Vol. 4, App. 9.

****Ibid.*, Vol. 1, p. 163.

*****Ibid.*, Vol. 4, App. 8 (xiii).

******Ibid.*, Vol. 1, pp. 165-166.

of the Atlantic consisted to a large extent of attacks on coastal cities containing German naval installations and factories connected with the production of long-range aircraft -- much the same kind of targets that might have been attacked if the Battle of the Atlantic directive had never been issued. Bomber Command had little more success in destroying specific objectives in these cities than it had had on previous occasions. Churchill, the "former Naval Person," was particularly incensed that the bombers were unable to sink the German battle cruisers GNEISENAU and SCHARNHORST, which were holed up in French Atlantic ports and by their mere presence immobilized a sizable portion of the British fleet. Much of the criticism that was being leveled at Bomber Command was undoubtedly unjust, but it may have reflected the disappointment of British leaders as the limitations of the weapon for which they had held such high hopes gradually were revealed to them.

By the spring of 1941 the Photographic Reconnaissance Unit had hit its stride and was providing more and more evidence of a kind that could not be disregarded. Responsible officers were now less inclined to rely on crew reports or on the dubious intelligence received from within Germany, and instead turned to the photographs to see what was really happening. They found that even under perfect moonlight conditions bombing accuracy was nowhere near the 300-yard aiming error they had been assuming. After a bombing attack on the Focke-Wulf aircraft factory in Bremen, in March 1941, the photographs showed that only one-third of the bombs had fallen within 600 yards of the target and fewer than 10 percent had hit the factory. The attack was carried out on a brightly moonlit night, and there was no problem of navigation, as the factory was near the coast.*

On dark nights, and in attacks against inland targets, navigation was so difficult that the bombing error often became irrelevant. On some occasions, crews who had relied blindly on meteorological wind forecasts were shown to have made navigation errors of as much as 100 miles. In the absence of electronic aids to navigation, which were not to become available until 1942, there were undoubtedly many more occasions when crews had similarly missed their target, but no photographs were there to prove it.

Cherished ideas die hard, and they rarely die a clean death. The fiction that night precision bombing was feasible persisted, at least in some quarters, through a good part of the year 1941, the gathering evidence to the contrary notwithstanding. Sir Richard Peirse was still hopeful that the bombing offensive against the oil targets could be resumed, and some of the commanders of his operational groups agreed with him. But, gradually, even the advocates of precision bombing began to make concessions to reality by selecting objectives situated in large towns, so that the bombs that missed their targets would not be wasted but would at least produce an effect on civilian morale. Inflicting civilian damage thus came to be more widely accepted as a desirable objective in itself, whether as the "by-product" or as the "end-product" of strategic bombing.

Ibid., p. 246.

In the early summer of 1941 Bomber Command was released from its commitment to the Battle of the Atlantic. As this permitted the bombing offensive to be resumed, a new survey of the military situation was made with a view to defining the strategy that the offensive was to serve. The Air Staff was not yet ready to accept area bombing as an avowed policy, but had begun to think about a target system that would be easier to attack than oil and would show better results for the effort expended on it. Specifically, it was looking for targets in populated areas, where bombing would produce a "bonus effect" on civilian morale.

The target system that seemed to fit in best with the new and more realistic attitude of the Air Staff was German transportation. Marshaling yards were large targets, reasonably easy to find, and usually located in populated industrial areas. They had often served as alternate targets when crews could not reach their primary target.

Transportation was favored as a target system on strategic grounds as well. The Chiefs of Staff had considered it as a possible alternative to the oil plan in their January Report on Air Bombardment Policy, but at that time had recommended against it for practical reasons. They felt that Bomber Command would not be capable of the heavy, sustained effort required to produce a decisive effect on such a large target system. In their view, the attack on transportation should be left to a later stage, when more and better aircraft were available for the job.

The strategic reasons in favor of attacking German transport had become more compelling by early summer, when the bombing policy was under review. The German armies were on the march again all over Southern and Eastern Europe as well as in Africa. In February 1941 the German Africa Corps had embarked for Libya, where the Italian armies were hopelessly bogged down. In April Hitler rounded out his conquest of the Balkans by moving against Greece and Yugoslavia. And in June he finally launched the blow that was to clinch his mastery of the world: the attack on the Soviet Union. British planners reasoned that the German transport system would be strained to the utmost in trying to supply the armies that were heavily engaged on such widely dispersed fronts, and that it might even surpass oil as "one of the weakest links in the German economic chain."*

The objection that German transport was too large a target system to be effectively interdicted was still valid. The numerical strength of Bomber Command -- an average of 500 operational aircraft -- had not changed since January, although some of the new four-engine Stirlings and Halifaxes were beginning to replace the older aircraft in the inventory. But the Air Staff argued that it was not necessary to attack the entire German transport system. They believed that the system could be crippled if one destroyed its links with the essential Ruhr area. The effect would be similar to cutting Britain's lifeline to the West across the Atlantic.

Bomber Command thereupon prepared another of its detailed estimates, based on hopeful assumptions about weather and bombing accuracy, in which it specified the number of sorties and the length of time it would take to "destroy" the transport

*Ibid., p. 171.

targets in the Ruhr. The proposal found no more favor with the skeptical Prime Minister than had the estimates prepared earlier in connection with the oil plan. Apart from the doubtful validity of the figures, Mr. Churchill regarded concentration on any single target system as "a very bleak and restricted policy" -- another of the "cut-and-dried" solutions he always mistrusted.

Another target system, which competed with transport for serious consideration as a primary objective for the bombing offensive, was civilian morale. The idea of attacking civilian morale by hitting cities pleased the British public and was favored by leaders who had become disenchanted with the results of precision bombing. Also, German civilian morale was being pictured as an extremely vulnerable objective in the stream of reports coming from inside Germany and in the advice received from real and self-appointed experts in the West.* According to these sources, German morale was tottering, and the people of Germany were exhausted by the war effort, terrified of British bombing, and ready to revolt against their leaders.

Among the influential British personages who urged an all-out attack on German morale was Sir Robert Vansittart, whose recommendation was backed up by a memorandum from another "German expert," and Lord Trenchard, who did not need any backing to get a respectful hearing.

Lord Trenchard's recommendations on bombing policy were put in the form of a memorandum to the Prime Minister, which the latter circulated to the Chiefs of Staff for comment. It reached them at a critical moment, in May 1941, when they had become disillusioned with the results of precision bombing and were searching for a more effective bombing policy. The memorandum proposed essentially the same bombing strategy that Trenchard had recommended back in 1928. It pointed out that if the strategic bombing offensive were to be effective it would have to be pursued with a singleness of purpose that had so far been lacking. The single purpose should be to concentrate on civilian morale through persistent and daily attacks on German cities, regardless of losses. The losses might be high, but should be accepted even if they amounted to 70 percent of the operational aircraft per month. Bomber Command should be built up with an overriding priority that would permit it to maintain a 400 or even 500 percent reserve of aircraft. Trenchard also urged that only towns in Germany proper, not in the occupied countries, be selected for attack. His reasoning was that, since 99 percent of the bombs were likely to miss hitting a military objective, they would at least "kill, damage, frighten or interfere with Germans in Germany and the whole 100 per cent. of the bomber organisation is doing useful work, and not merely 1 per cent. of it."** He warned that the policy he was recommending could succeed only if it were relentlessly pursued and if no long-range bombers were diverted from the single task of bombing objectives in German cities.

*Among the unlikely sources who contributed to this picture was President Roosevelt, whose knowledge of the German people was acquired when he studied in Imperial Germany during his youth.

***Air Offensive,* Vol. 4, App. 10.

Lord Trenchard's views differed only in degree and emphasis from those that were coming to be held within the Air Staff. Sir Charles Portal and his senior officers had already developed a preference for targets located in populated areas, where the inevitable bomb misses would produce an "incidental" effect on civilian morale.

The Chiefs of Staff agreed that civilian morale was the most important and the most vulnerable objective for strategic attack but they had reservations about giving Bomber Command the overriding priority Lord Trenchard was demanding. They felt that, if the Trenchard proposal were taken literally, it would result in depriving other arms of the RAF of the aircraft needed for support of the Army and Navy in their part of the war effort. Even the Chief of the Air Staff thought that the absolute priority for building up Bomber Command should be postponed until the essential requirement for other types of aircraft had been met.

The consensus of the Chiefs of Staff, as expressed in the comment of the CIGS and subsequently incorporated in a formal Minute to the Prime Minister, was that

> As a *short-term* policy, transportation should be our primary target, with morale the secondary one.
>
> As a *long-term* policy, we should attack morale as a primary target as soon as our bomber force is large enough to have decisive effect.*

This was not quite what Lord Trenchard had suggested, but it appealed to the military leaders as a sensible solution that would achieve something worthwhile without compromising the rest of the war effort. The attack on transport would help to whittle down German morale -- though without crippling it -- and make it that much more vulnerable to the planned all-out attack later on. It would be striking at a weak link in the German economy while allowing Bomber Command to be gradually built up in an orderly fashion and with the help of the United States.

Mr. Churchill reluctantly went along with the recommendation of the Chiefs of Staff, though he would have preferred a less rigid bombing policy that would permit the attack to be switched quickly to different target systems as new opportunities presented themselves. The plan for the offensive against transport was incorporated in a new directive, sent to Bomber Command on July 9, 1941. By that time the German assault on Russia was already in full swing. This may have influenced the Prime Minister, who was anxious to aid Britain's new and difficult ally. The disruption of German transport might gain a breathing space for the hard-pressed Russian armies. The directive instructed Bomber Command to concentrate on the Ruhr-Rhineland railway system, and appended a list of specific targets that were to be attacked on moonlit nights. The intent behind the new policy could not be mistaken:

> 5. Most of the railway centres listed in Appendix "A" lie in congested industrial areas and near concentrations of workers' dwellings. These objectives are therefore to be considered as suitably located for obtaining incidental effect on the morale of the industrial population. . . .**

**Ibid.*

***Ibid.*, App. 8 (xvi), p. 136.

On moonless nights, the bombers were to strike at communication centers, such as Cologne, Düsseldorf, and Duisburg. As secondary targets, the directive specified German cities outside the Ruhr area, notably Hamburg, Bremen, Hanover, Frankfurt, Mannheim, and Stuttgart.

It is clear that the new bombing policy, whatever its ostensible objective, was only one small step removed from the unrestricted area bombing of cities. The difference lay more in concept than in execution. Some RAF leaders still clung to the illusion that on moonlit nights the accuracy needed to destroy marshaling yards could be attained. (In practice, most crews were fortunate if they hit an industrial area in the vicinity of a marshaling yard.) That illusion had to be destroyed before the final step toward outright area bombing could be taken.

Photographic evidence produced by the Reconnaissance Spitfires had done a good deal to dispel the myth of precision bombing but not until the "Butt Report" was published, in August 1941, were the implications of the evidence spelled out in a form that could be readily understood. The author of the report was a member of the War Cabinet secretariat whom Lord Cherwell had asked to undertake a systematic analysis of bombing effectiveness. Mr. Butt's analysis covered Bomber Command's operations during the months of June and July, using photographs, operational summaries, and other available records. His conclusions:

1. Of those aircraft recorded as attacking their target, only one in three got within five miles.
2. Over the French ports, the proportion was two in three; over Germany as a whole, the proportion was one in four; over the Ruhr, it was only one in ten.
3. In the Full Moon, the proportion was two in five; in the new moon it was only one in fifteen.
4. In the absence of haze, the proportion is over one half, whereas over thick haze it is only one in fifteen.
5. An increase in the intensity of A.A. fire reduces the number of aircraft getting within 5 miles of their target in the ratio three to two.
6. All these figures relate only to aircraft recorded as *attacking* the target; the proportion of the *total sorties* which reached within five miles is less by one third.

Thus, for example, of the total sorties only one in five get within five miles of the target, i.e. with[in] the 75 square miles surrounding the target.*

Bomber Command found it hard to credit these startling conclusions. But they were taken seriously by Lord Cherwell and by the Prime Minister, who asked Sir Charles Portal to give the Butt Report his "most urgent attention."

**Ibid.*, App. 13.

The report had far-reaching repercussions. Coming when it did, it crystallized ideas that had been gradually taking shape and converted vague doubts into certainty. The stark facts revealed in the report forced government leaders to act. It was no longer possible to let Bomber Command continue as it had been doing to waste itself in fruitless attacks against targets it could not find or hit.

One of the important contributions of the Butt Report was that it focused attention on the crucial role played by navigation in the success or failure of strategic bombing. There had been evidence before that crews occasionally missed their target by a wide margin, but the implications had not been appreciated. Bomber Command had always been more concerned with bombing accuracy in the narrow sense. Yet a navigating error measured in miles made it unimportant whether the bombing error was 300 or 1000 yards. As a result of the Butt Report, the problems of night navigation received far more attention than they had in the past. The development of electronic navigation aids was pushed with a new sense of urgency, though it was not to bear fruit until the following year.

Another development in the wake of the Butt Report was the creation of an Operational Research Section in Bomber Command. The job of the new section was to make a systematic analysis of the operational results of every bombing attack and to provide periodic reports. This gave Bomber Command an essential tool for evaluating and improving its performance, and also provided British leaders with a better basis for making decisions on bombing strategy.

In view of the findings of the Butt Report, it was obvious that the strategy reflected in the last directive to Bomber Command -- the attack on transport targets in the Ruhr -- would have to be abandoned. There was no point in wasting crews and aircraft over an area where only one in ten succeeded in getting within five miles of the target. Improvements in navigation sufficient to permit attacking specific objectives, even objectives as large as marshaling yards, could not be expected for many months. This left only a single alternative: area bombing of cities.

The Chiefs of Staff were agreed that the bombing offensive must go on. It was the only means available for creating the conditions that would eventually permit British forces to return to the Continent. Britain had come a long way in the year since Dunkirk, and she was no longer fighting alone. The prospect of wresting control of Europe away from the Nazis was not the forlorn hope it had once been. British and Commonwealth forces had fought creditably against the Germans in Greece and Crete and were forcing Hitler to commit more and more men and supplies to North Africa. The new ally, Russia, might not last through the winter, but in the meantime German armies and air forces were being used up in the East. The United States had declared an "Unlimited National Emergency" in May, and Churchill was increasingly hopeful that America would become an active belligerent by the time British forces were ready to reenter Europe. But before this could come to pass, the Chiefs of Staff believed,

> We must first destroy the foundations upon which the [German] war machine rests -- the economy which feeds it, the morale which sustains it, the supplies

> which nourish it and the hopes of victory which inspire it. Then only shall we be able to return to the continent and occupy and control portions of his territory and impose our will upon the enemy. . . . It is in bombing, on a scale undreamt of in the last war, that we find the new weapon on which we must principally depend for the destruction of German economic life and morale.*

This was written after Russia had been invaded but before publication of the Butt Report. Considering the meager results that British bombers had achieved so far (as revealed later by that report), the "destruction of German economic life and morale" was going to be a difficult task. Strategic bombing was still the only instrument available for the job, but it would have to be used in a new fashion.

The preference for precision bombing had been partly dictated by the fact that Bomber Command was too small to do anything else. Area bombing required much larger forces, not only because the target was spread out but because a high concentration of force in space and time was necessary to produce a decisive effect. The experience of the last few months had shown that area attacks with small forces were ineffective, even if the crews found their target, and that the damage could be quickly repaired. Severe and lasting damage was achieved only in attacks on the scale of the Luftwaffe raid on Coventry, where a high concentration of force had been attained and self-sustaining fires had been started. The force requirement for area attacks was the same whether the purpose was to destroy a specific objective, which the bombers could reach only by devastating the entire area in which it was located, or to undermine civilian morale by forcing evacuation of a densely inhabited district. In both cases, extensive as well as intensive damage was necessary to produce the desired effect, and this in turn called for employment of a large bomber force.

If Bomber Command was to operate thenceforth as a "bludgeon, not a rapier," it would have to be built up along the lines urged by Lord Trenchard. The Air Staff was already working on plans to that effect; the figure of 4000 heavy bombers -- an eight-fold increase in operational strength -- was being mentioned. These plans were brought to a head when the revelations of the Butt Report convinced British leaders that the policy of precision bombing was no longer tenable and that Bomber Command would have to be converted into an instrument for area attack. Bomber Command responded with another of its familiar estimates showing that, with an average operational strength of 4000 first-line aircraft, it would be possible to destroy forty-three selected German towns with a total population of around fifteen million people. According to Sir Charles Portal, who passed this proposal on to the Prime Minister on September 25, 1941, a bombing offensive on this scale would "break Germany in six months."

This was clearly the wrong way to approach Mr. Churchill. He not only mistrusted estimates of this sort, but he had become increasingly suspicious of the claims made

*Chiefs of Staff Memorandum, July 31, 1941, quoted in *Air Offensive,* Vol. 1, pp. 180-181.

by airmen. The Butt Report had further disillusioned him and caused him to lose faith in the effectiveness of strategic bombing in general. In replying to Sir Charles Portal, the Prime Minister plainly showed his discouragement by arguing that "it is very disputable whether bombing by itself will be a decisive factor in the present war." He pointed out that British morale had improved under bombing and prophetically warned that German progress in ground defenses and night fighters could overtake the attack. Finally, in the unkindest cut of all, Mr. Churchill reminded the Chief of the Air Staff that only one-fourth of the bombs hit their targets and that therefore an improvement in bombing accuracy to 100 percent "would in fact raise our bombing force to four times its strength."*

In a subsequent Minute of October 7, the Prime Minister softened his language, though it was clear that he still objected to the exaggerated claims made for strategic bombing. He assured Sir Charles Portal that everything was being done to create the largest possible bombing force and that there was no intention of changing this policy. "I deprecate, however, placing unbounded confidence in this means of attack, and still more expressing that confidence in terms of arithmetic."** The Minute is important primarily in showing that Mr. Churchill, who had been among the strongest proponents of city bombing, now considered it a second best. He would have preferred "heavy accurate daylight bombing of factories," though he realized that this could not be done without fighter protection, which at the time was not available on attacks against inland targets.

As it turned out, Mr. Churchill's lack of enthusiasm for city bombing was temporary; it was rekindled the following summer when the "Thousand Bomber" raids against German cities showed what the bombing offensive could accomplish. But enthusiasm or no, there was no alternative to city bombing in any case. Mr. Churchill, the War Cabinet, and the Chiefs of Staff were now all in agreement on that. The only question was how fast Bomber Command could be built up to the size required to make city bombing really effective.

The problem was what to do in the meantime. Should Bomber Command be allowed to continue its costly attacks on German cities? Results on moonless nights and during poor weather were extremely disappointing. Navigation was so bad that on one occasion, when the bombers had been directed to attack Karlsruhe and Stuttgart, they were reported over twenty-seven cities other than the ones they had been told to hit. At the same time, the losses were mounting and out of all proportion to the results achieved. In October and November, losses as high as 10, 12 and 13 percent were sustained in single attacks, and in one case -- an attack on the Ruhr -- 21 percent of the aircraft failed to return.

Greatly concerned over these losses, Mr. Churchill insisted that Bomber Command adopt a policy of conserving its resources during the months of bad weather lest it destroy the nucleus around which the future buildup must take place. Sir

**Air Offensive,* Vol. 1, p. 182.

***Ibid.*, p. 184.

Richard Peirse pointed out that such a policy would have an adverse effect on the morale of the crews, but the War Cabinet agreed with the Prime Minister, partly because they shared the growing disillusionment with the performance of Bomber Command. Thus, on November 13, 1941, a new directive was issued, instructing Bomber Command to conserve its resources "in order to build up a strong force to be available by the spring of next year." Webster and Frankland felt that this directive "was no less than a formal expression of the belief that the results which Bomber Command was achieving were not worth the casualties it was suffering. . . . 1941 had, indeed, brought Bomber Command to the nadir of its fortunes, but its prospects were by no means extinguished."*

**Ibid.*, pp. 186-187.

8

The Whirlwind

Bomber Command on Trial

THE YEAR 1941 had been one of great disappointments for Bomber Command. The greatest was the realization that precision bombing, at night, and with the means then available, was too ineffective to justify the cost. Except under unusually favorable circumstances, and until new equipment or new techniques became available, the strategic air offensive against Germany would have to consist largely of area attacks against cities.

This was a bitter pill to swallow for those who objected to this form of warfare because of moral scruples. It was frustrating on other grounds as well, for it meant that bombing policy had to accommodate itself to the operational limitations of the weapon, instead of being governed by strategy, as had been envisaged before the war.

It was particularly galling to Mr. Churchill. He wanted a flexible bombing policy so as to be able to exploit the opportunities opened up by the vast changes that had occurred in the strategic situation during the latter half of 1941. The Germans had planned on a six-week campaign against Russia, but the Blitzkrieg had not worked out as expected, and six months later the German armies were stalled in the bitter Russian winter. The danger that Hitler would revive SEA LION after a lightning conquest of Russia was thus averted, at least until the next spring, by which time Britain would be infinitely better prepared against such an attempt than she had been in the fall of 1940. In Africa, British and Commonwealth forces were on the offensive against Rommel, and Mr. Churchill had far-reaching plans for exploiting the hoped-for victory in Libya. Most important of all, the Prime Minister's fondest dream had become reality when the Japanese attack on Pearl Harbor brought the United States into the war as a full belligerent.

These and other events presented opportunities for offensive action against the enemy in addition to, or in the place of, strategic bombing. Bomber Command no longer held the unique position it did a few months earlier, when the Chiefs of Staff, in their memorandum of July 31, 1941, had said: "After meeting the needs of our own security, therefore, we give the heavy bomber first priority in production, for only the heavy bomber can produce the conditions under which other offensive forces can be employed."* In early 1942 the rival claims of other arms for production priority were receiving greater consideration, even if this meant that the promised buildup of Bomber Command to the strength needed for effective area bombing might have to be delayed.

The debate over priorities even reached the House of Commons. On February 25, 1942, the new Lord Privy Seal, Sir Stafford Cripps, made a statement that was known to reflect the Prime Minister's own views at the time:

> . . .if I may, I would remind the House that this policy [the buildup of Bomber Command] was initiated at a time when we were fighting alone against the combined forces of Germany and Italy and it then seemed that it was the most effective way in which we, acting alone, could take the initiative against the enemy. Since that time we have had an enormous access of support from the Russian Armies, who, according to the latest news, have had yet another victory over the Germans, and also from the great potential strength of the United States of America. Naturally, in such circumstances, the original policy has come under review. I can assure the House that the Government are fully aware of the other uses to which our resources could be put, and the moment they arrive at a decision that the circumstances warrant a change, a change in policy will be made.**

Aside from the question of whether Bomber Command should continue to enjoy its high priority for future production, there was the quandary over how best to employ its existing capabilities. Strategic bombing had never been its only task, though Bomber Command itself had always regarded its other missions as diversions from its proper employment. But the demand for such diversions was constantly increasing. In the winter of 1941-1942 Bomber Command was under pressure to send long-range aircraft to North Africa for support of the Army; to assist the Navy in its efforts against Axis shipping in the Mediterranean; to make more aircraft available to Coastal Command; to participate more actively in the critical Battle of the Atlantic; to attack German naval installations and warships in Atlantic ports. During the winter months over a third of Bomber Command's effort was expended in a fruitless attempt to disable the German battle cruisers in Brest before they made good their escape through the Channel.

The pressure on Bomber Command to undertake tasks not connected with the strategic air offensive against Germany was partly stimulated by disappointment

**Ibid.*, p. 181.

***Ibid.*, pp. 328-329.

over the results of that offensive during 1941. Bomber Command was caught in a vicious circle. The extravagant claims made for strategic bombing had not been substantiated. As a result, confidence had been withdrawn from Bomber Command just at a time when it was ready to profit from past mistakes and to demonstrate its potential through improved performance. But it might never get a chance to do so if lack of confidence denied it the resources needed to make strategic bombing effective, or if it were continually diverted to tasks it could not perform effectively.

The first step toward breaking out of this vicious circle was taken on January 8, 1942, when Sir Richard Peirse was relieved as Air Officer Commanding-in-Chief, Bomber Command. Though he was not to blame for all the mistakes made during the inevitable learning period, a new and more vigorous leader was needed if Bomber Command was to regain the prestige it had formerly enjoyed. Fortunately, a man with unusual qualifications for leadership was found in Air Chief Marshal Sir Arthur Harris, who assumed the post on February 22, 1942, and retained it to the end of the war. His record as well as his personality, with its virtues and its shortcomings, made him one of the outstanding commanders of the time. Also, Air Marshal Harris had the good fortune of being able to establish a close relationship with the Prime Minister, which gave him direct access to the most important source of power in wartime Britain.

It was only a few weeks after the hard-driving new commander had taken over that Bomber Command achieved the kind of success it needed to demonstrate its potential and to restore faith in its future. In March and April Bomber Command scored impressive results in attacks on the Renault plant near Paris and on the cities of Lübeck and Rostock -- results which gained a breathing space for Air Marshal Harris and enabled him to mount the spectacular "Thousand Bomber" raids that ushered in a new era of strategic bombing.

The stage was set for resumption of the strategic air offensive in early February 1942, when the Secretary of State for Air, Sir Archibald Sinclair, pleaded with the Defence Committee to release Bomber Command from its commitment to assist the Navy in the Battle of the Atlantic. He knew that he would have to make a strong case in view of the general disillusionment with strategic bombing, and of the innumerable other tasks in which long-range aircraft could be employed to good advantage. In the preceding two months, beginning with Pearl Harbor, the Allies had suffered a series of unmitigated disasters in the Pacific, in the Atlantic, and in Africa, and the end was not yet in sight. In a few days the Japanese were to cap their triumphant march across the Pacific with the conquest of the "impenetrable" fortress of Singapore, whose loss Mr. Churchill considered "the greatest disaster in our history." Sir Archibald Sinclair expected strong opposition to his proposal from the Navy, which was particularly hard-pressed after the loss of its two proud capital ships off Malaya. As the First Sea Lord quite reasonably pointed out, "If we lose the war at sea, we lose the war."*

**Ibid.*, p. 327.

Sir Archibald Sinclair based his argument for the strategic air offensive primarily on two factors. One was that heavy air attacks on Germany would "enhearten and support the Russians" while at the same time depressing German morale, which had already been weakened by the unexpected Russian successes. The other important point was that the RAF expected dramatic improvements in bombing effectiveness through the introduction of a new electronic navigation aid, called GEE, which was about to become operational.* Sinclair recommended resuming the air offensive as soon as weather conditions permitted so as to take full advantage of GEE, whose operational life was expected to be short. GEE could be jammed, and British scientists estimated -- correctly, as it turned out -- that this would happen in less than six months.

One reason against releasing Bomber Command from its commitment to help the Navy had been the presence of the German battle cruisers in Brest. But on February 12, three days after the Defence Committee meeting, this problem had, in Mr. Churchill's words, "settled itself by the escape of the enemy." The Prime Minister was now in favor of resuming the full air offensive against Germany. This was enough for the Air Staff, which promptly issued a new directive to Bomber Command without waiting for formal approval from the Chiefs of Staff or the Defence Committee.**

The directive ordering resumption of the strategic air offensive was dated February 14, 1942, the day before the fall of Singapore. It canceled the conservation order that had been issued the previous November and authorized Bomber Command to employ its force "without restriction," though not in disregard of unfavorable weather or extreme hazard to aircraft. The substance of the directive was contained in the sentence: ". . .the primary object of your operations should now be focussed on the morale of the enemy civil population and in particular, of the industrial workers. With this aim in view, a list of selected area targets. . .is attached. . . ."

The primary targets listed were four important industrial cities in the Ruhr-Rhineland area: Essen, Duisburg, Düsseldorf, and Cologne. The alternates were the coastal cities of Bremen, Wilhelmshaven, and Emden. All were within range of GEE. In order to permit Bomber Command to disperse its operations and thereby prevent the enemy from concentrating his defenses, the directive specified a number of additional cities, including Berlin, which were beyond GEE range but could be attacked when conditions were favorable. Clearly, this was to be no halfhearted effort. Bomber Command was instructed that ". . .the cardinal principle which should govern your employment of TR.1335 [GEE] from the outset, should be the complete concentration on one target until the effort estimated to be required for its destruction has been achieved."***

*GEE, also referred to under its code name "Tr. 1335," employed a principle similar to that used in LORAN. In contrast to the latter, however, its range was only 300-400 miles. For a description of GEE and of two subsequently introduced electronic navigation and bombing aids called OBOE and H2S, see *Air Offensive,* Vol. 4, Annex 1.

***Air Offensive,* Vol. 1, p. 330, fn. 2.

****Ibid.,* Vol. 4, App. 8 (xxii).

There could be little question that the intent was to launch a concentrated air offensive against German cities. But the directive was written so ambiguously as to lend itself to misinterpretation. For example, the appendix contained an additional list of industrial objectives, not area targets, against which precision attacks could be launched if conditions were especially favorable or if experience with the as yet untested GEE showed that effective attacks against such targets were feasible. Also, the list of area targets identified the principal industries associated with each of the cities to be attacked. The reason for this is not clear. It may have been intended as a hint to the bomber crews that they should single out those particular objectives within the cities for special attention. Or it may have been merely to permit the interpretation that the cities were to be attacked because they contained "military objectives." At any rate, the Chief of the Air Staff wanted no misunderstanding on whether the air offensive was to be directed against cities or against specific objectives. He penciled an explanatory note for the guidance of the new chief of Bomber Command, who was to take command the following week:

> Ref the new bombing directive: I suppose it is clear that the aiming points are to be built-up areas, *not*, for instance, the dockyards or aircraft factories where these are mentioned in Appendix A. This must be made clear if it is not already understood.*

There was little danger that Air Marshal Harris would misread the intent of the directive, for it accorded with his own preference.

Webster and Frankland refer to February 14, 1942, when the directive was issued, as "a pregnant date in air history."** It was indeed, for it ushered in an onslaught on Germany that made the Luftwaffe attacks on London seem puny by comparison. For the first time a bombing directive had singled out civilian morale as the primary objective. Except for the inevitable diversions, it was to remain the primary objective for Bomber Command, not only during the period of approximately one year that the February directive was in effect, but throughout most of the remaining years of the war.

The far-reaching implications of the directive aroused surprisingly little opposition from those whose "conscientious scruples" had led them to protest against city bombing when it was first urged by Churchill during the Battle of Britain.*** This time controversy arose not over the issue of area bombing as against precision attacks, but over alternative tasks for Bomber Command in support of the other services, over its role in the over-all strategy of the war, and over what priority should be given to the buildup of its forces. In spite of the improvements in bombing

**Ibid.*, Vol. 1, p. 324.

***Ibid.*, p. 325.

***A possible explanation is that, when the military leaders first voiced these scruples, in the fall of 1940, they still thought that it was not necessary to bomb cities, and that it would be both more humane and more effective to attack quasimilitary objectives. A year-and-a-half later, most of them had come to understand that, if there was to be a strategic air offensive, it would have to be directed against urban areas. And by that time the brutalizing effect of the war may have diminished their scruples.

accuracy that were expected from the new navigation aid, many still doubted that the results obtainable by strategic bombing justified the resources already invested in it, let alone the additional buildup needed to mount bombing attacks on a scale that could be decisive.

Debate over these matters did not end when the directive for resumption of the bombing offensive was issued to Bomber Command. It went on after the bombing of German cities was well under way. In one form or another, it continued throughout the war, though it was temporarily muted in the elation over the successes Air Marshal Harris was able to achieve in the first months.

Toward the end of March 1942, advocates of the all-out bombing offensive against Germany received powerful support from a new source when the Scientific Advisor, Lord Cherwell, sent the Prime Minister a Minute on what he thought the projected offensive could accomplish. He estimated that, given certain assumptions as to bombing accuracy and damage effect, the planned output of 10,000 heavy bombers during the coming year would yield a force that could create enough destruction in 58 German towns of over 100,000 population to deprive approximately one-third of the German people of their housing. Lord Cherwell felt that being turned out of one's home was even more damaging to morale than seeing one's friends or relatives killed. "There seems little doubt," he wrote, "that this would break the spirit of the people."*

Lord Cherwell's paper with its optimistic conclusions was reminiscent of the Bomber Command estimates for the oil plan and the transport attack -- offering, as it did, the kind of "cut-and-dried" solutions for winning the war which always annoyed the Prime Minister. It rested on a set of assumptions that were necessarily speculative. They were promptly challenged by such a respected scientist as Sir Henry Tizard, who, while in general agreement with the bombing policy, tried to discourage overly optimistic expectations of what could be achieved. In his rebuttal to Lord Cherwell's paper, Sir Henry pointed out that for the next two years Bomber Command could not reach the strength needed to produce "decisive" results against civilian morale; "so if we try to carry out the policy with a much smaller force it will not be decisive, and we may lose the war in other ways."**

The Prime Minister, however, had great faith in his Scientific Advisor and apparently was influenced by his Minute in spite of Tizard's arguments. At any rate, he allowed the bombing offensive to proceed as planned.

Another factor in favor of proceeding with the offensive was that at this crucial time the nèw chief of Bomber Command began to provide impressive evidence of what strategic bombing could accomplish. On March 3, while the debate over the bombing offensive was still going on in Parliament, Sir Arthur Harris executed an extremely successful night precision attack on the Renault factory near Paris, which was producing armaments for Germany. GEE had not yet become operational, but a new flare technique for target illumination was used to good effect. On the basis

**Air Offensive*, Vol. 1, pp. 331-332.

***Ibid.*, p. 335.

of photographic evidence, "it was estimated that forty per cent of the Renault machine tools had been destroyed" and that "very few buildings had escaped damage."* This outstanding success after a discouraging year boosted morale in Bomber Command and duly impressed government leaders.

On March 28 Bomber Command achieved another, more spectacular victory in a test of saturation incendiary tactics against the Hanseatic city of Lübeck. This time a number of GEE-equipped aircraft were employed, though the city itself was beyond the range of GEE. The attack was carried out under ideal conditions, and the ancient city with its many medieval structures presented a highly inflammable target. Photographs showed that almost half the city was destroyed, including the main railway station, the central electric power plant, public buildings, factories, and an estimated two thousand houses.

A month later, Bomber Command followed up with a series of four consecutive night attacks against the city of Rostock, where the Heinkel long-range bombers were manufactured. Again Air Marshal Harris experimented with new tactics, involving a combination of area attack against the city itself and a precision attack on the Heinkel factory. On the first two nights the results were modest. But in the next two attacks excellent concentration in time and space was achieved, bombing accuracy was high, and most of the attacking aircraft hit their targets, including the Heinkel factory. Photographic evidence confirmed that Bomber Command had scored another impressive victory. These successes acted as a tonic in Britain after the long string of Allied military defeats in the preceding few months. But, as Sir Arthur Harris well realized, they did not settle the future of Bomber Command and of strategic bombing.

In another attempt to solve the problem by analytical methods, the Government once again called on Mr. Justice Singleton to lend his talents to the investigation of a controversial issue.** In April 1942 it asked him to conduct an inquiry into the results likely to be achieved by an all-out strategic air offensive against Germany. Not surprisingly, for he had been given an impossible task, Mr. Justice Singleton failed to arrive at firm conclusions and was forced to resort to vague statements that only added to the existing confusion.

It was clear, to Air Marshal Harris at least, that only actual results would bring an end to the debate over strategic bombing. The Government had drifted into the decision to resume the air offensive against Germany because it was the course of least resistance at a time when British leaders were preoccupied with other, world-shaking events. Their qualified approval of the February bombing directive by no means represented a policy decision to adopt strategic bombing as the primary strategy in the war with Germany. It did not mean that henceforth the military

*_Ibid._, p. 388.

**In early 1941 Mr. Justice Singleton had conducted a successful inquiry into German aircraft production in an attempt to resolve a dispute among several government departments as to the strength of the German Air Force. See Winston S. Churchill, _The Second World War_, Vol. 3, _The Grand Alliance_, Houghton Mifflin Company, Boston, 1950, p. 41.

conduct of the war and the production effort would be oriented to such a strategy. The bombing directive was subject to being revoked whenever the Government should decide that Bomber Command could be more usefully employed in support of a different strategy, in which the other services would play the leading role. In such a case, the resources needed for building up the bombardment force were likely to be reallocated to other needs.

Strategic Bombing Proves Itself

As matters stood in early 1942, Sir Arthur Harris was still caught in the same vicious circle as before: To obtain the resources he needed to make strategic bombing effective, he had to demonstrate results which could not be obtained with the inadequate force available to him. As he was to reflect after the war,

> My own opinion is that we should never have had a real bomber offensive if it had not been for the 1000 bomber attack on Cologne, an irrefutable demonstration of the power of what was to all intents and purposes a new and untried weapon.*

The results Sir Arthur Harris sought in order to prove the value of strategic bombing were different from those envisaged by the Air Staff. The February directive had singled out German civilian morale as the primary objective. Harris agreed that strategic bombing might have an effect on civilian morale but thought that, to be decisive, the bombing would have to be on a scale that was out of the question for a long time to come. Even then, he was not sure how important civilian morale was in a police state. Wholesale bombing might shatter the morale of German civilians, but would it affect their *conduct* so long as there was a Gestapo to control their behavior?

These thoughts may have been formulated after the event. Even at the time, however, Harris seems to have regarded civilian morale as an imponderable whose effect on the German war effort was too uncertain for it to be made the main target of the bombing offensive. He believed that the primary objective should be to disrupt the enemy's industrial activity wherever it was conducted, which was normally in cities or larger towns. If the area bombing of cities also happened to affect civilian morale, and if low morale slowed up the war effort, this was to be regarded as a bonus effect.

Before taking over Bomber Command, Sir Arthur Harris had made a careful study of the German air attacks on Britain. He had concluded that the most effective form of attack was the kind the Luftwaffe had conducted against Coventry -- a highly concentrated mass attack against the city as a whole rather than against specific objectives within the city. He recorded his impressions as follows:

*Sir Arthur Harris, *Bomber Offensive,* Collins, London, 1947, p. 113. I have drawn on various sections of this book, especially Chaps. 4 and 5, in paraphrasing Harris' views on strategic bombing and on the related matters discussed in the following pages. Page references have been omitted except where direct quotations are used.

> Coventry was a large and important town, with the great majority of its inhabitants engaged in war industries; the light engineering industries of Coventry were almost indispensable to the production of a great range of weapons and war equipment. On the day after this attack production in all the war factories of the town was one-third of what it had been before. Some damage had been done to the factories themselves, but it was very slight compared with non-industrial damage. The loss of production was almost entirely due to the interruption of public utilities, the dislocation of transport, and absenteeism caused by the destruction of houses, and many other causes. There was very heavy damage, for example, to sewers, water supply pipes. electric cables, gas pipes and so forth, and this had an immediate effect on production. Output was back to normal again in about two months, but there were special circumstances which led us to believe that production would not recover so quickly in Germany as in England.*

It was this general disruption of industrial activity within a city that Harris thought should be the aim of strategic bombing. He believed that the effect of such bombing on Germany would be greater than that of similar attacks on Britain, for he shared the mistaken opinion that the German economy was more tightly stretched than the British. As it turned out later, there still was a good deal of slack in the German economy. But this was not realized at the time, perhaps because it was tacitly assumed that the inventors of total war would have mobilized the entire economy for a total effort. This erroneous idea led British economic experts to urge that strategic bombing be directed at what they considered to be critical bottlenecks in an already overburdened economy, such as oil and ball bearings. These targets remained high on the list of the Ministry of Economic Warfare long after area bombing had become the operative policy. They were also the kind of targets that appealed to certain members of the Air Staff who, for different reasons, had remained in favor of precision bombing and regarded area bombing as a necessary but, they hoped, temporary expedient.

Air Marshal Harris did not agree with either their preferences or their reasoning. Though he, too, had selected German industry as his target, he was strongly opposed to what he called "panacea targets," whose elimination was supposed to paralyze the German war machine. Since Germany had gained access to the resources of most of Europe, he did not believe that there were bottlenecks in the German economy; if there were, he did not think that they could be correctly identified or that they should be made the primary target for attack. Like his friend Winston Churchill, he disliked cut-and-dried solutions. Harris thought that Britain's best way to win the war was to disrupt the enemy's over-all industrial and economic activity by inflicting widespread and general, rather than selective, damage.

Operational considerations undoubtedly influenced his preference. He still did not possess the means for launching effective precision attacks, except under unusually

*Harris, pp. 86-87.

favorable conditions. When such conditions presented themselves, he was not averse to combining selective with general destruction, as he had done in the combination area-and-precision attack on Rostock. But he refused to limit himself to a few selected high-priority targets, since to do so would have meant permitting the enemy to concentrate his defenses and exact heavier losses. He did not wish Bomber Command to be constrained in its freedom to vary its targets, its routes, and its methods of attack.

The major difficulty Sir Arthur Harris foresaw in his plan to inflict widespread destruction on the enemy's industrial cities was that it required a much larger force than he possessed at the time. On the day he took over command, he had 378 serviceable aircraft, of which 69 were what were then called "heavy" bombers. But only two-thirds could be considered operational, since some squadrons were in the process of converting to new types of aircraft, and new squadrons were being formed.* This force was too small to inflict the kind of destruction Air Marshal Harris considered necessary against an important area target. Yet he could not wait for the promised buildup of Bomber Command, which, he knew, might not materialize unless the effectiveness of strategic bombing could be demonstrated through actual results. This meant that the force needed had somehow to be scraped together from existing resources. Thus the plan for the "Thousand Bomber" raid was born.

The apparently hopeless task of assembling a force almost three times the operational strength of Bomber Command required one of the most daring decisions Sir Arthur Harris ever had to make: He had to stake the future of his command on this single venture by committing all his reserves and by stripping the training units of all the aircraft they could muster. Even then, he would have to levy on Coastal Command and on other RAF commands for a major contribution of aircraft -- an expectation in which he was largely disappointed.

Assembling the force was not the only problem the Commander-in-Chief had to solve. Methods had to be devised for controlling the force in combat so as to achieve the high concentration in time and space needed to maximize destruction and to afford the bombers protection against the growing enemy defenses. Routes to and from, and over, the target had to be worked out, pathfinder and targetmarking tactics had to be developed, and innumerable other details ironed out. The lessons learned in the successful attacks on Lübeck and Rostock as well as in the unsuccessful attacks against Ruhr cities were useful, but they did not cover all the problems that would be encountered in managing a force of such unprecedented size, twice as large as the Germans had ever employed in a single attack.

By the middle of May 1942, Sir Arthur Harris was ready to put his plan before the Chief of the Air Staff and the Prime Minister. He saw Mr. Churchill at Chequers late one night and got his approval for a plan that was novel and daring enough to please the old warrior. Harris drove home from the meeting humming to himself *"Malbrouck s'en va-t'en guerre."***

*Harris, pp. 73 and 101.

**Harris, p. 110.

The Harris plan reached the Government at an opportune moment. The country was incensed over the "Baedeker raids" against England's historic cities, which had begun with the German bombing of Exeter on April 23, 1942. The raids on these largely undefended cities, most of which contained no conceivable military objective, were terror attacks pure and simple, and were so described in Hitler's directive.* They were in retaliation for the British bombing of Lübeck, which had "caused such resentment in Germany and seems to have made a deep impression on the Führer."**

Fortunately for Britain, the remnant of the Luftwaffe that could be spared for the Baedeker raids was low in quality as well as quantity, and had to be assembled from aircraft normally engaged in antishipping and minelaying operations. But even small-scale attacks with incendiaries could do a good deal of irreparable damage in such old cities as Norwich, York, Bath, Exeter, Chester, and Canterbury. Coming as they did almost a year after the attacks on Britain had virtually ceased with the withdrawal of the German bombers to the East, the Baedeker raids served to rekindle the memories of the London Blitz and to bring new demands for revenge.

The plan for the Thousand Bomber raid was therefore welcomed for a number of reasons apart from its strategic importance. A heavy blow against Germany would lift morale in Britain just when it was most needed. In spite of the fact that Britain was no longer fighting alone, the Allied cause had recently suffered a series of disastrous defeats. The long-awaited entry of the United States into the war had failed to bring the immediate relief that many had expected, and on top of everything the British people were faced with the resumption of German terror attacks against their storied cities.

But before the Harris plan could be put into effect, new problems arose as the expected contribution of aircraft from other commands failed to materialize. The Admiralty had vetoed the diversion of aircraft from Coastal Command, and most of the aircraft volunteered by other commands turned out to be unsuitable for operational reasons. Yet Air Marshal Harris was insistent on reaching the magic figure of one thousand bombers which gave the plan its special flavor. And reach it he did. To do so he relied almost entirely on Bomber Command's own resources, by committing every available aircraft. This made the stakes enormous, for if the venture failed the training and conversion program would be wrecked, perhaps irremediably, and Bomber Command might never recover from the loss.

The force was ready at the beginning of the moon period toward the end of May 1942. Hamburg was the first target choice if weather permitted; otherwise the target was to be Cologne. The weather was troublesome, as usual, and the attack had to be postponed for several days; Sir Arthur Harris was determined to cancel the operation rather than risk his force under unfavorable conditions. Finally, on May 30, the weather forecast held out hope that conditions over Cologne might be acceptable for the attack.

*Collier, *The Defence of the United Kingdom,* p. 512.

***Ibid.*, p. 305.

The Commander-in-Chief decided to take the gamble, and that night launched an unprecedented force of 1046 bombers against Cologne. "The greatest attack yet made in aerial warfare was now under way, but it still remained to be seen whether the disaster would fall upon Germany or upon Bomber Command."* It fell on Germany, and it was indeed a disaster. Overnight, Cologne became a blazing ruin. The pall of smoke hanging over the city the following morning was still so dense that no reconnaissance photographs could be taken.

The attack had been well planned and executed, and it was favored by good weather over the target. It showed what strategic bombing could accomplish if the force was large enough and if the right tactics and equipment were employed. The single Thousand Bomber raid did more damage than all the previous seventy attacks on Cologne put together, although the total tonnage dropped in the earlier attacks had been greater.

The new raid devastated six hundred acres, half of them in the center of the city. The marshaling yards were wrecked, many factories destroyed or severely damaged, and public utilities put out of commission. Civilians suffered severely: Over 3000 houses were destroyed, more than 9000 damaged, and 45,000 people rendered homeless. Casualties were close to 500 killed and 5000 injured, with over 500 of the injured requiring hospital treatment.**

The great cathedral of Cologne was damaged in the raid.

The whirlwind had struck.

*_Air Offensive,_ Vol. 1, p. 406.

**_Ibid.,_ pp. 485-486.

9

Epilogue

WITH THE FIRST Thousand Bomber raid on Cologne in May 1942, the air offensive against Germany had entered its all-out phase. Under Air Marshal Harris' vigorous leadership, Bomber Command grew into an instrument of awesome destruction as new and better equipment became available and the tactics of area bombing were perfected.

Though the number of operational aircraft did not increase substantially until 1943,* their quality improved as the obsolete twin-engined bombers were replaced with the heavier Halifax and Lancaster bombers, and as the invaluable Mosquito light bombers were added to the inventory. Toward the end of 1942 the new radar bombing and navigation aids OBOE and H2S became operational. They made it possible to undertake successful attacks on the Ruhr cities, where the ever-present haze had frustrated all earlier attempts at visual bombing.

New target-marking techniques by selected Pathfinder crews equipped with special marker bombs greatly improved the effectiveness of night attacks. Other tactical innovations were introduced to assure better concentration in time and space over the target and to frustrate enemy defenses. Bigger and more effective high explosives and incendiaries were substituted for the inadequate ordnance carried on earlier missions, thus multiplying the weight of attack delivered by the same number of sorties. Crew shortages were gradually remedied with the help of the Commonwealth training scheme.

*It will be remembered that more than half the aircraft used in the Cologne raid were borrowed for the purpose. The average daily availability of bombers with crews did not approach the one-thousand mark until March 1944.

By the end of 1942, Bomber Command, though still inadequate for the job that its chief envisaged for it, had become a force capable of inflicting enormous damage on German cities. Better prepared than in 1942, Sir Arthur Harris now was ready to launch his great air assault of 1943. That year saw the Battle of the Ruhr, in which Essen with its Krupp works and several other cities suffered heavy destruction; it saw the beginning of the long-drawn-out Battle of Berlin, in which Bomber Command pitted itself against one of the most difficult and most heavily defended targets of the campaign; it also saw the unimaginable horrors of the fire raids on Hamburg which caused such devastation that the German Minister of Armament and Production, Albert Speer, feared that a continuation of these attacks might bring the war to a rapid end.*

Yet more, much more, was still to come. In 1943, the American Air Force joined in the assault on Germany itself with daylight precision attacks on industrial objectives.** As the two air forces increased in size and capability, the combined bomber offensive gained in tempo and reached a crescendo during the last year of the war. Of all the bomb tonnage released on Germany during the war, 85 percent was dropped *after* January 1, 1944. During the single month of March 1945, German targets received a weight of bombs almost equal to that dropped by Bomber Command during the entire year 1943.

In the dark days of the London Blitz, Winston Churchill had promised the British people that he would "let *them* have it too."

> . . .and this promise was certainly kept. The debt was repaid tenfold, twentyfold, in the frightful routine bombardment of German cities, which grew in intensity as our air power developed, as the bombs became far heavier and the explosives more powerful. Certainly the enemy got it all back in good measure, pressed down and running over. Alas for poor humanity!***

* * *

This narrative has been concerned with the escalation to unrestrained air warfare. On the German side the change was ushered in abruptly when the Luftwaffe switched to the attack on London in September 1940. In Britain it was a gradual transition; there was no clear beginning although certain milestones can be identified along the way. One was the bombing directive of October 1940, in which the British went part way toward adopting the policy of indiscriminate air attacks that the Germans had initiated with their assault on London.**** The transition had clearly begun. Another milestone was the "transport directive" of July 1941. This

*See the Interrogation of Albert Speer, reproduced in *Air Offensive,* Vol. 4, App. 37 (ii).

**During 1942 the initial American bomber effort had been confined to France and other occupied countries.

***Churchill, *Their Finest Hour,* p. 349.

****See above, p. 90.

went a good deal further toward unrestricted air warfare, as it singled out targets in heavily built-up areas.* The transition appeared complete by February 1942, when a new bombing directive gave first priority to the attack on German cities and specified civilian morale as the primary objective.**

But even after the February directive had been issued, strategic bombing policy continued to be debated within the Government and in Parliament. The outcome of the debate was by no means a foregone conclusion. If it had not been for Sir Arthur Harris' successful attacks on urban areas, the bombing offensive might well have been curtailed or suspended so that Bomber Command might be freed for the many other tasks for which the Army and Navy were always clamoring. It was the Thousand Bomber raid on Cologne in May 1942 which completed the British transition to unrestrained warfare. After that raid, continuation of the strategic bombing offensive along similar lines was no longer in doubt.

How long it would remain the official British policy, however, was not at all certain. Urban-area bombing had become the operative strategy because it had proved successful and because at the time it was the only effective way of striking directly at Germany. But it was not the result of a considered decision to adopt a policy of all-out warfare. Though this was, in fact, what British leaders had approved when they issued the new bombing directive, they had approved it reluctantly and were ambivalent about it. Most of them still had conscientious scruples against making war on civilians and hoped to return to a more civilized form of warfare as soon as it became possible. Their ambivalence was reflected in the vague language of the directive, which left a great deal of leeway to the man charged with executing it, the man in charge of Bomber Command.

> Nor had the February [1942] directive, and more particularly the memorandum in which Sir Archibald Sinclair had prepared the way for it, closed the door on a resumption of precision bombing. There were, after all, those who accepted the policy of area bombing only as a temporary and an operational expedient. To these, the idea of returning to precision attack as soon as the means, tactical and technical, justified the attempt was ever present. In the course of 1942 some of those means were created and others were soon to follow.
>
> Thus, the February directive, to some extent inevitably, had not clearly defined the objects of the bombing offensive. It had established certain emphases, dictated by the operational circumstances of the time, but it had mentioned many possibilities. Above all, it had shown, more clearly than any previous directive, how bombing policy had to be decided primarily on the grounds of its operational feasibility and secondarily on those of its strategic desirability. *The decision, therefore, necessarily and to a large extent, devolved upon the officer charged with the execution of the offensive; upon*

*See above, p. 100.

**See above, pp. 109-110.

> *the officer whose judgment of what could, and what could not, be done was most weighty; upon Sir Arthur Harris.*
>
> It is now possible to see how the Commander-in-Chief, Bomber Command, though theoretically only responsible for carrying out a policy decided by his superiors, was, in practice, in a very strong position to influence the making of that policy. If he had convictions of his own, he could always, or nearly always, rule out competing ideas on the ground that they were impossible. All the more would this be so if the direction from above was weak or uncertain.*

Sir Arthur Harris did, indeed, have convictions of his own.** Until the end of 1943 his views usually prevailed and he was able to conduct the air offensive pretty much as he wished, limited only by the capability of his force and the growing strength of German air and ground defenses. His objective being the general disruption of life in Germany, he continued his single-minded policy of launching mass attacks against large cities, where a given tonnage of bombs would produce the greatest amount of destruction and affect the largest number of people. Within this general policy, his target choice usually was governed by tactical considerations.

This was not quite what the authors of the February directive had intended.*** They had gone along with the general area offensive in the hope -- which was not shared by Sir Arthur Harris -- that it would break German morale. But they thought that this should be the "main aim," not the sole aim of the bombing campaign. The Air Ministry was under constant pressure from British and American leaders to launch attacks against specific targets that were deemed important to the German war effort. By that time it was understood that Bomber Command could not carry out night precision attacks, but the Air Staff thought that Air Marshal Harris should modify his general area offensive at least to the extent of occasionally launching selective area attacks against towns associated with some particular industrial activity.

The Commander-in-Chief was strongly opposed to this idea. As we know, he thought that the value of what he called "panacea targets" was overrated and that he lacked the operational capability for successful attacks on them. Also, these targets were often in small towns that were not only hard to find at night but too small to permit the British to obtain full effect from the bomb spillage. What Harris objected to most strongly, however, was that a systematic campaign against a single target system, such as the oil plants, would make his attacks predictable and thus enable the enemy to concentrate his defenses. He was willing to use them as alternate targets when appropriate, but he wanted to be free to select his own primary targets to suit the weather and other tactical conditions, including enemy defense measures.

**Air Offensive,* Vol. 1, p. 345. Italics mine.

**See above, pp. 113*ff.*

***This discussion is based on *Air Offensive,* Vol. 1, pp. 337-352 and *passim.*

Sir Arthur Harris had no doubt that, taking all factors into account, the most suitable use for Bomber Command was in the general area offensive, to which he continued to devote the major portion of his effort.

The Air Staff, reluctant to quarrel with success, did not press the issue for the time being. But later it became the subject of major and enduring controversy within the British Government and between the British and the American members of the Combined Chiefs of Staff.

The American Air Force was doctrinally and operationally geared to daylight precision bombing, just as the Royal Air Force had been before the war. By the end of 1942, however, Bomber Command had become as fully committed to night area bombing as the U.S. Army Air Force was to daylight precision bombing. Neither could have switched to the opposite technique without major changes in equipment, trianing, and tactics that would have taken long to accomplish. This was recognized by both sides. The real issue, therefore, was not the method of bombing but the objective to be pursued by the different methods:

> The issue did not concern simply the operational distinction between day precision and night area bombing, though that was to some extent involved. It arose from the strategic difference between selective and general attack. Selective bombing was based upon the principle that "it is better to cause a high degree of destruction in a few really essential industries than to cause a small degree of destruction in many industries." It could be pursued by precision bombing, which would strike at individual factories and plants in the particular key industries which had been selected, and by area bombing, which would strike at particular towns associated with those industries. The principle of general attack was based upon the belief that there really were no key points in the German war economy whose destruction could not be remedied by dispersal, the use of stocks or the provision of substitute materials. It postulated the theory that the only effective policy was that which, by cumulative results, produced such a general degree of devastation in all the major towns that organised industrial activity would cease owing to a combination of material and moral effects.*

The issue was raised at the Casablanca Conference, in January 1943, where an abortive attempt was made to reconcile the divergent viewpoints and to agree on a common objective for the Anglo-American Combined Bomber Offensive. The controversy was not solely between the British representatives on the one hand and the Americans on the other; there were disagreements between the British Air Staff and Bomber Command, and among other service leaders of both countries. What emerged from these deliberations was a vague directive that straddled the main issue of how the Combined Bomber Offensive was to be conducted.

The dispute over the issue of selective versus general area attack continued until almost the end of the war. But it was carried on at the policy level and had little

Air Offensive, Vol. 2, p. 5.

impact on the operations. After the Casablanca directive had been issued, each bomber force proceeded in accordance with its own preference: The Americans launched daylight precision attacks against selected targets, while Bomber Command continued its general area offensive with night attacks on German cities that were chosen mainly because of their size and accessibility. The result was that "for most of 1943 there was no combined offensive, but, on the contrary, a bombing competition."*

To follow the developments in this dispute, important though they were, would carry us beyond the scope of this narrative. The dispute is relevant here only because it has often been represented as a conflict between proponents and opponents of unrestrained warfare, between the vengeful advocates of the indiscriminate bombing of cities and the more humane advocates of selective attack on military objectives. For example:

> It is not surprising that proposals for all-out attacks on Berlin, the Ruhr, or other critical areas of Germany always seemed to come from the British, who had undergone the German air raids of 1940-41 and were now enduring the punishment of V-1's and V-2's. All proposals frankly aimed at breaking the morale of the German people met the consistent opposition of General Spaatz, who repeatedly raised the moral issue involved, and AAF Headquarters in Washington strongly supported him on the ground that such operations were contrary to air force policy and national ideals. . . .**

Urban area bombing was not as foreign to American Air Force thinking as this passage may lead one to believe. Attacks on civilian morale had been a definite part of official American air doctrine, though reserved for the closing phase of a war. They were to be the *coup de grace* that would force an enemy to surrender after his will to resist had been undermined by military defeat and selective damage to his economy.***

This was still the official doctrine in August 1941, when the air annex to the American Joint War Plan (AWPD/1) was prepared in anticipation of the United States' entry into the war. The Plan provided for a campaign of daylight precision bombing of key target systems, such as the enemy aircraft industry, power plants, transportation, and oil, to be followed by attacks on civilian morale.

> Some of the objectives listed were already under night attack by the RAF, but to AWPD they appeared as precision targets to be destroyed by approved AAF

Ibid.

**Wesley F. Craven and James L. Cate (eds.), *The Army Air Forces in World War II,* Vol. 3, *Europe: Argument to V-E Day (January 1944 to May 1945),* The University of Chicago Press, Chicago, Ill., 1951, p. 638.

***USAF Historical Division, *The Development of Air Doctrine in the Army Air Arm 1917-1941,* "USAF Historical Studies" No. 89, The Research Studies Institute, Air University, September 1955.

methods. *Only when the industrial fabric of Germany began to crack should the AAF turn to area bombing of cities for morale purposes.* *

Apart from any preference for using force in a discriminating fashion, there were practical reasons why American Air Force doctrine gave priority to selective attacks. Daylight precision bombing required command of the air if losses were to be held to acceptable levels. The first step, therefore, had to be a campaign for air superiority through an attack on the enemy's existing fighter force in the air and on the ground, combined with selective attacks on the production facilities that were the sources for its replenishment.

At the time of the Casablanca Conference, the American Air Force had not yet attempted deep inland penetrations against Germany proper, and thought that its "self-defending" formations of heavily-armed and armored Flying Fortresses would be able to hold their own against the German fighters. When it turned out a few months later that this was not the case, the problem of gaining air superiority became a pressing issue, and there were urgent demands that Bomber Command join the air superiority campaign of the Eighth Air Force by launching selective area attacks on targets associated with the German fighter aircraft industry, particularly targets against which daylight attacks would be too costly.

Senior RAF officers, with the notable exception of Sir Arthur Harris, agreed with their American colleagues that selective attacks were desirable -- not only against German fighter production but also against other key targets which British economic experts had recommended for destruction. Most of the officers favored selective attack as a matter of principle; the RAF had always preferred the rapier to the bludgeon and disliked killing civilians as much as the USAAF did. If the British had turned to the bludgeon it was not because they were more bloodthirsty than the Americans, or because they believed in unrestrained warfare, but because they had found selective attacks too costly in daytime and ineffective at night. They differed with the Americans, therefore, not over whether selective attacks were desirable but over whether they were feasible.

The British knew from their experience in bombing Germany that daylight attacks against strongly defended targets would result in an attrition rate for the attacker that even the USAAF would not be able to sustain. They were proved right, especially after Hitler, spurred on by the devastating attacks on German cities, made an all-out effort to increase fighter output and to strengthen antiaircraft defenses. After the Americans suffered disastrous losses in their attack on Schweinfurt in October 1943, daylight attacks involving deep penetrations against inland targets had to be virtually suspended until long-range fighter escorts became available. Bad weather during the winter months forced bombing operations against central Europe to be curtailed in any case. By the time they were resumed in full force, in the early part of 1944, the P-51s (Mustangs) and other long-range fighters

*Craven and Cate, Vol. 1, *Plans and Early Operations (January 1939 to August 1942)*, p. 599. Italics mine.

had become operational, and the USAAF was able to go back to daylight bombing of precision targets without danger of incurring the prohibitive losses that had been the main reason for the British objections to this form of attack.

At this stage of the war, the bombing of the enemy's fighter production facilities, which required precision attack, had become a matter of the greatest urgency. The Allies had to win command of the air before the invasion of Europe, which was only a few months away. The British Air Staff was also concerned over the growing rate of losses in night-bombing operations, as the Germans had developed an effective night-fighter capability which was threatening to make Bomber Command's night attacks as prohibitively costly as the daytime attacks had been. The only way to whittle down German strength in night fighters was to attack them at the source and destroy their command and control system on the ground.

The reasons in favor of selective attacks were reinforced by the growing disillusionment of the Air Staff with the results of the general area offensive against German morale. Sir Arthur Harris picked the wrong time when he wrote to the Air Ministry, in December 1943, that he could "produce in Germany by April 1st 1944, a state of devastation in which surrender is inevitable."* Though the general area offensive of 1942 and 1943 had inflicted vast suffering on Germany, there was no indication that civilian morale was cracking or that the German war effort was seriously affected. The Air Staff could see no reason why three more months of bombing would produce a result that a year-and-a-half of devastating attacks had failed to achieve.

The Deputy Chief of the Air Staff, Air Marshal Bottomley, pointed this out in an official reply to Sir Arthur Harris. The letter was unusual both for its content and its firm tone. It reminded the Commander-in-Chief that his principal task was to complement the efforts of the USAAF to win air superiority through selective attacks against towns associated with the German fighter-aircraft industry and the ball-bearing industry. He was not to allow his general area offensive to prejudice accomplishment of this task, to which the Combined Chiefs of Staff had assigned the highest priority. This rebuke to a successful commander, whom his superiors had always handled with kid gloves, showed that a matter of basic policy was involved.

> These doubts about the efficacy of the general area offensive, though they had been growing for some time, had never been officially expressed by the Air Staff since the initiation of the policy in 1941. Air Marshal Bottomley's words, therefore, had an extraordinary significance which amounted to nothing less than the disavowal of the long established "main aim" of Bomber Command.**

A strategy is rarely disavowed until an alternative becomes available. There had been none when civilian morale was selected as the "main aim" of the general area

*_Air Offensive,_ Vol. 2, p. 56.

**_Ibid.,_ pp. 59_ff._

of the general area offensive. Indeed, some would say that it had not been selected so much as dictated by the fact that Bomber Command was capable only of attacking large cities and that a strategy had to be invented to justify such attacks. But in the closing days of 1943, when the Air Staff voiced its disenchantment with the general area offensive, an alternative was in sight. Bomber Command had become a more efficient and more flexible instrument. In the course of 1943 it had occasionally shown its ability to deliver selective area attacks on smaller towns with considerable accuracy, and even to carry out precision attacks at night against such difficult targets as the V-weapon establishment at Peenemünde and the Möhne and Eder dams. Bomber Command's capability for selective attack was further developed in the period between April and September 1944, when the Combined Bomber Offensive was severely curtailed and the strategic air forces of both nations under General Eisenhower's direction were used instead against specific objectives in support of OVERLORD.

When they had been released from this last task and were able to resume the bombing offensive, in October 1944, the strategic situation had drastically changed in favor of the Allies. The reconquest of France had deprived the enemy of a vital portion of his early-warning network, while the British and American bomber forces, on the other hand, had increased tremendously in quantity and quality and were now enjoying the protection of escort fighters in large numbers. The Luftwaffe was handicapped by a shortage of well-trained fighter pilots, partly because lack of oil had forced curtailment of training, and partly because of the attrition suffered in air-to-air combat. The Allies thus were within sight of their goal of achieving command of the air both in daylight and at night. Weather permitting, the strategic air forces of both nations were now able to engage in either precision or area bombing, by day or by night, depending only on the preference of their commanders and the strategic direction of the Allied High Command. Not unnaturally, each commander continued to favor the bombing technique in which his force had become specialized and which was more compatible with its equipment and training.

Air Marshal Harris' preference was to put even greater effort into the general area offensive against German cities, now that the enemy was so near defeat. Though he was allowed to persist in this campaign, his nominal superiors prevailed on him -- they were still reluctant to compel him -- to devote a portion of Bomber Command's effort to selective attacks on preferred target systems, such as German oil production and communications. That they were at least partially successful is shown by the fact that in October 1944, when the full strategic air offensive was resumed, approximately one-fourth of Bomber Command's operational sorties were flown against selected targets, mostly in daylight precision attacks. By then, however, the size of the force was such that in the same month Sir Arthur Harris was also able to launch almost 12,000 sorties against urban area targets.*

While Harris was reluctantly accommodating himself to the demand for selective attacks, the Commander of the U.S. Strategic Air Forces, General Spaatz, was making

Ibid., Vol. 3, pp. 66-67.

an equally reluctant accommodation to the desire of Allied leaders for American participation in urban area bombings. The Eighth Air Force now began to launch massive attacks on German cities, including a "Thousand Bomber" raid of its own on Berlin on February 3, 1945. It was estimated that 25,000 civilians were killed in this last attack alone, with many more injured.* Later in February, the Americans joined Bomber Command in an all-out assault on Dresden that was among the most devastating raids of the war. The deaths inflicted among the civilian population, swollen as it was by refugees from the East, could not even be estimated because of the terrible destruction caused in the city. The casualties were undoubtedly several times those inflicted in the bombing of Berlin.

These attacks had widespread repercussions after an Associated Press correspondent reported that they had been the result of a "long awaited decision to adopt deliberate terror bombing of German population centres as a ruthless expedient to hastening Hitler's doom."** The report caused consternation among Allied leaders. When General Spaatz was asked by his superiors whether he was now engaging in indiscriminate attacks on cities, he replied that.

> what had occurred was not a change in priority but a shift in emphasis. The Americans were not bombing cities indiscriminately, but attacking transportation facilities inside cities in missions which the Russians had requested and seemed to appreciate.***

General "Hap" Arnold, the Commanding General of the U.S. Army Air Forces, nevertheless wanted to know "whether there was any significant distinction between morale bombing and radar attacks on transportation targets in urban areas." General Spaatz reassured him that he "had not departed from the historic American policy in Europe, even in the case of Berlin. . . ."****

If General Spaatz saw a distinction, it was presumably that he regarded the civilian casualties in American attacks as an unintentional and regrettable by-product of bombs aimed at military objectives in the cities, whereas the avowed purpose of Sir Arthur Harris' area bombing was to destroy the city itself, without regard to civilian casualties. Such a distinction -- of no comfort to the victims -- would have been reminiscent of the argument between Sir Richard Peirse and Sir Charles Portal over the moral difference of killing civilians as the "by-product" as against the "end-product" of strategic bombing.***** But that had been in 1940, before it was understood that in a mass attack on a city it made little difference to the civilians what the bombers were aiming for.

General Spaatz was undoubtedly sincere and can be faulted only for his lack of realism in failing to acknowledge that American policy was indeed changing.

*Craven and Cate, Vol. 3, p. 726.

***Air Offensive,* Vol. 3, p. 113.

***Craven and Cate, Vol. 3, p. 726.

****_Ibid._, p. 727.

*****See above, p. 90.

> That opposition in the AAF to area bombardment had actually weakened, the exchange of communications on the question in February 1945 notwithstanding, is indicated not only by the almost simultaneous launching of sustained B-29 attacks on Japanese cities but by proposals for the use of robot-controlled B-17's in Europe.*

Ironically, the American proposal to use radio-controlled drone bombers, which could only be employed for inaccurate area attacks, was vetoed by the British, who feared retaliation in kind. But, if further proof was needed that the American Air Force had become converted to area bombing, it was furnished by the B-29 forces engaged in the war with Japan. In March 1945 their recently appointed commander, General Curtis LeMay, inauguarated a campaign of systematic area attacks on Japanese cities with an incendiary raid on Tokyo that killed more civilians, and caused more extensive destruction, than the atomic bomb later dropped on Hiroshima. General LeMay's general area offensive against Japan had the same objective as Sir Arthur Harris' offensive against Germany, and was undertaken for the same reason, namely, that selective attacks against military objectives had proved ineffective owing to operational limitations.

Much has been made of the Anglo-American controversy over strategic bombing. But it was not a matter of conflicting philosophies. The differences between the British and American air forces resulted from the fact that at the beginning of the Combined Bomber Offensive they had different capabilities and their strategic choices had to be geared to these capabilities. Morality had little part in it.

> It might appear, and it has often been suggested, that a great moral issue was involved in this situation, but the moral issue was not really an operative factor. The choice between precision and area bombing was not conditioned by abstract theories of right and wrong, nor by interpretations of international law. It was ruled by operational possibilities and strategic intentions. Though these matters have been much confused by propaganda, the Germans, the British and the Americans, too, adopted the policy of area attack when they considered that precision bombing was either impossible or unprofitable.**

Throughout the period with which most of this narrative has been concerned, the controversy over the moral aspects of urban area bombing was academic, as operational limitations left the British no other choice. The issue ceased to be academic, however, during the last six months of the war, when these limitations had been largely overcome and the Allies were free to choose a bombing strategy that suited their strategic objectives and moral preference. Why, then, were the attacks on German cities continued although both air forces were now capable of waging a more restrained form of warfare? The remaining pages of this account will attempt to answer this difficult question.

*Craven and Cate, Vol. 3, p. 727.

***Air Offensive*, Vol. 2, p. 22.

Historians trying to find an easy explanation have been tempted to put the blame on Sir Arthur Harris -- "Bomber Harris," as he came to be labeled -- whom they picture as the ruthless, stubborn, singleminded commander whose sole objective was to crush the enemy at whatever cost to German civilians. Yet the Allied leaders who disapproved of Sir Arthur Harris' urban-area offensive were themselves advocates of attacks on German cities, though under a different guise. If there is to be blame for these attacks, it must be shared by others.

In September 1944, when the joint Anglo-American directive for resumption of the strategic air offensive was written, a number of target systems competed for attention. Chief among them was the petroleum industry, which was given highest priority. Others were the German transportation and communications network, munitions plants, "policing" of the German aircraft industry, and strikes in direct support of Allied land and naval operations. These were specified as targets for precision attack, with this added provision:

> When weather or tactical conditions are unsuitable for operations against specific primary objectives, attacks should be delivered on important industrial areas, using blind bombing technique as necessary.*

The weather over Germany in late autumn and winter being what it is, this last provision allowed for a generous number of attacks on "important industrial areas." Given the inaccuracy of radar bombing, these attacks usually caused the same kind of indiscriminate destruction that might have been expected if they had not been aimed at any particular target within the city. The important change in the new directive, however, was one of intent. The "main aim" of the bombing offensive from now on was to be not morale bombing but selective attacks on military objectives.

Yet some of these objectives themselves invited, even dictated, urban area attacks. It was not only when weather or tactical conditions prevented selective bombing that cities could be hit; they had to be hit in the course of attacks on marshaling yards, railroad stations, and other transportation targets, which had been given a high priority in the new directive. Attempts to bomb such targets inevitably resulted in much damage to the part of the city in which they were located.

The principal sponsor of the bombing offensive against German transport -- and therefore, in effect, against urban areas -- was Air Chief Marshal Sir Arthur Tedder. As General Eisenhower's deputy, he had retained an important voice in selecting objectives for strategic bombing that were important to the ground commanders. And most Allied leaders concerned with the land offensive, including General George C. Marshall, agreed that the general disruption of the German transport system through systematic air attack should have high priority.

In addition, the ground commanders favored concentrated interdiction attacks on strategic areas on which the defending forces depended for support. As the

**Ibid.*, Vol. 4, App. 8 (xl).

Allied armies approached the Rhine, they requested a massive air assault on the entire Ruhr area, which served as a communications hub for the German forces. This was tantamount to an attack on urban areas, though its purpose was interdiction. The Ruhr cities, which had already suffered heavily in earlier Bomber Command attacks, were further devastated in this new, Anglo-American assault, which was known as Operation BUGLE. (Sir Arthur Harris objected that his bombs were "merely stirring up the rubble"; he would have preferred to continue his general area offensive against cities that were still relatively intact.) Similar interdiction attacks were launched against other German transport and communications centers of concern to the Allied ground commanders. As their armies advanced further toward the heart of Germany from East and West, the line between urban area attacks and selective attacks in tactical support of the ground forces became increasingly blurred.

This was demonstrated most clearly in the East. Prior to the Yalta Conference of February 1945, the British and American leaders asked for air attacks against transport centers in the eastern part of Germany to support the advance of the Russian armies. The Russians were expected to be even more difficult than usual at Yalta; they were constantly complaining that the Anglo-American allies were concerned only with their own offensive in the West and were doing nothing to help their allies in the East. Mr. Churchill wanted to be armed against this charge. Strongly urged by him, the Allied military leaders -- including General Spaatz -- agreed that, while first priority for air attack would continue to go to German synthetic oil plants, second priority was to be given to the bombing of Berlin, Leipzig, Dresden, "and associated cities where heavy attack will cause confusion in civilian evacuation from the East and hamper movement of reinforcements from other fronts."* It was this directive that resulted in the devastating attacks on Berlin and Dresden mentioned earlier.

There was still another reason that Allied leaders, apart from Sir Arthur Harris, favored urban area attacks. At various times in the last year of the war they had discussed the idea of concentrating all available air effort on a catastrophic blow against a single target, such as Berlin or some other major city. One of the earlier versions of the plan -- THUNDERCLAP -- envisaged that the combined Allied air forces could deliver something like 20,000 tons of bombs in the space of four days and three nights, which should be sufficient "to suspend all ordinary life in Berlin."**

The purpose of such an attack, according to Webster and Frankland, was to deal "a *coup de grace* to German morale."*** "The idea was, in fact, conceived, not as a means of bringing about the defeat of Germany, but of inducing an organized surrender after that had occurred." It is noteworthy that the idea originated not in Bomber Command but in the British Chiefs of Staff, and that it was endorsed by

**Air Offensive,* Vol. 3, p. 104. For Mr. Churchill's role in the bombing of Dresden, see *ibid.*, pp. 101-104 and 112-113.

***Ibid.,* p. 54.

****Ibid.,* p. 98.

Sir Charles Portal and the Air Staff. Evidently, the notion of using air power to give the *Todesstoss* to a nearly defeated enemy was not confined to the Germans alone. Not only was it part of the official American Air Force doctrine, but it came to play a role in British thinking as well.

THUNDERCLAP was never carried out in its original form, but the idea of delivering a tremendous aerial attack that would break the will to resist of the German leaders continued to exert an influence on Allied planning. In later plans based on the same idea, the objective of breaking German morale was usually combined with that of achieving at the same time a decisive military effect against transport and communications facilities. In one version -- HURRICANE I -- the plan was for 2500 heavy bombers to drop 12,000 tons of bombs on the Ruhr in the short space of one or two hours, with the dual objective of assisting the Allied ground offensive and "influencing the war-will of the German High Command."* The plan had to be modified for operational reasons, but in Operation BUGLE a tremendous blow was in fact delivered against the Ruhr area.

The combined Anglo-American attacks on Berlin were another modified application of the *Todesstoss* idea. The nearest the Allies ever came to executing the original conception of THUNDERCLAP was in the assault on Dresden, which happened to be a target that Sir Arthur Harris had long picked on his own for an awesome demonstration of Allied air power.

It must be clear from the foregoing that the differences between Sir Arthur Harris and other Allied leaders could not have been over the principle of attacking cities. In the closing period of the war, when operational capabilities had become such as to permit a relatively free choice of bombing objectives, the Combined Chiefs of Staff, and indeed their civilian superiors themselves, ordered cities attacked for strategic reasons. Their reasons varied: Some favored urban area attacks to break civilian morale; others hoped to undermine the war-will of the German High Command, or to disrupt the transport system, or to deny the German war machine some vital resources. Sir Arthur Harris happened to think that the general area offensive was the most effective way of breaking the enemy's ability to resist. But these were disagreements over strategy, not over principle. And so far as civilian casualties were concerned it made little difference whether a city was attacked to eliminate it as a transport center or as part of the general area offensive. Why, then, was Sir Arthur Harris singled out as if he alone had selected cities as his objective? Why did Mr. Churchill turn away from him in the closing months of the war, after a close and intimate working relationship that had lasted almost three years?

Sir Arthur Harris' difficult personality and his acrimonious relations with his nominal superiors were undoubtedly a factor. But this was nothing new. He had long given the Government reason for losing patience with him and he was not the only successful Allied commander who was difficult to get along with. That the break seems to have occurred after the assault on Dresden is the more puzzling as the

**Ibid.*, p. 72.

assault had been demanded by Mr. Churchill himself. Moreover, it had resulted from a joint Allied decision, and the American Air Force had participated in the bombing.

A possible explanation may lie in the widespread moral revulsion against city bombing which set in after the horrors of the Dresden attack had become public. Since Sir Arthur Harris had long been identified with this form of warfare, he was a logical target on which population indignation could vent itself. People in the West were war-weary and tired of killing. Whatever desire for revenge had existed in Britain earlier in the war must have been sated by the terrible havoc already inflicted on Germany. The public, unlike the military professionals, considered the enemy already defeated and saw no need for piling more devastation on the destruction already caused, which the Allies would have to help rebuild after the war.

Mr. Churchill himself may have been caught up in this mood. It almost seems as if, after the attack on Dresden, he wished to dissociate himself from this act and from the entire strategic air offensive of which he had been one of the principal architects. We are forced to resort to speculation here, because neither Mr. Churchill's own History of the Second World War nor Sir Arthur Harris' account of the Bomber Offensive discusses this matter, and even the painstaking history of Webster and Frankland offers only sparse clues.

We do know that at the end of March 1945 the Prime Minister ordered a review of the policy of urban attacks "from the point of view of our own interests," lest the Allied occupation forces find themselves deprived of accommodations in a ruined country.* But this does not explain his change of attitude toward his Commander-in-Chief, who was executing a policy Churchill himself had established. Nor can that change be explained on moral grounds, for such scruples had not troubled the Prime Minister when Hamburg and other cities suffered a fate similar to that of Dresden.

The full story of what happened in the closing months of the war to turn Mr. Churchill against his own brain-child probably still waits to be written. But we know that he did turn against it. Sir Arthur Harris and the heroes of the strategic air campaign** received scant reward from a government that was lavish in its bestowal of praise on other successful commanders and on the forces under them:

> When victory over Germany was celebrated but little was said of the part played in it by the strategic air offensive. The Prime Minister did, it is true, pay a tribute to Bomber Command in a special message to Sir Arthur Harris, in which he spoke of their "decisive contribution to Germany's final defeat" and praised the "fiery gallant spirit" of their crews. But no tribute was paid to that campaign in the Prime Minister's victory broadcast of 13th May except for a cryptic reference to the attack on V-weapons, and no campaign medal was struck to distinguish those who took part in the strategic air offensive. The Prime Minister and others in authority seemed to turn away from the

**Air Offensive*, Vol. 3, pp. 112 and 117.

**They included 57,143 dead in Bomber Command alone. See Frankland, *The Bombing Offensive*, p. 91.

> subject as though it were distasteful to them and as though they had forgotten their own recent efforts to initiate and maintain the offensive.*

It is easy to understand why Sir Arthur Harris was unpopular in the government. We can also see how a fickle public would turn against its former hero as the symbol of a form of warfare which violated its moral instincts -- after people could permit themselves the luxury of indulging these instincts once again.

What is difficult to explain is why other Allied leaders, though equally responsible for this form of warfare, should have escaped censure and why all the blame should have fallen on Sir Arthur Harris. Was it because they carried out their task with reluctance while the Air Marshal gave the appearance of relishing it? Or was it because they paid lip service to moral scruples by claiming that their urban area attacks were aimed at military objectives while Sir Arthur Harris frankly admitted that the cities themselves were the military objective?

The Secretary of State for Air, Sir Archibald Sinclair, once explained why he made a point of emphasizing in his public statements that the urban area attacks were aimed at military or industrial installations.

> Only in this way, he explained to Sir Charles Portal in October 1943, could he satisfy the enquiries of the Archbishop of Canterbury, the Moderator of the Church of Scotland and other significant religious leaders whose moral condemnation of the bombing offensive might, he observed, disturb the morale of Bomber Command crews. This latter consideration was, the Secretary of State thought, more important than another which Sir Arthur Harris had raised, namely, that *the Bomber Command crews might form the impression that they were being asked to perform deeds which the Air Ministry was ashamed to admit.***

Perhaps Sir Arthur Harris and his crews were right in thinking that they were asked to do what their superiors were ashamed to admit. After the war was won, Allied leaders may not have wished to be reminded that they had been forced to subordinate their moral scruples to the exigencies of a total war. Yet this is what Lord Trenchard had prophesied back in 1928, in the debate with which this narrative began:

> Whatever we may wish or hope, and whatever course of action we may decide, whatever be the views held as to the legality, or the humanity, or the military wisdom and expediency of such operations, there is not the slightest doubt that in the next war both sides will send their aircraft out without scruple to bomb those objectives which they consider the most suitable.

***Air Offensive*, Vol. 3, p. 284.

***Ibid.*, p. 116. Italics mine.

Part Two

REFLECTIONS

Introduction

In reviewing the events of World War II one is left with a sense of inevitability. The ultimate escalation to total war was not planned so much as it happened. It was the end result of actions that were taken in response to the pressure of events, often with little awareness of the possible consequences. Despite the great differences in their moral outlook and behavior standards, both sides contributed to the inexorable process of escalation, although from different motives.

To stress the inevitability of the outcome is not to suggest that the course of the war would have been the same regardless of who was at the helm. But it is important to understand that Churchill and Hitler, although they held unprecedented power in their respective countries, were also the victims, willing or unwilling, of pressures they could not resist and of events they could not control. Once the hounds of war were unleashed, the leaders were swept along at a pace or in a direction that was not always of their own choosing.

The story of escalation in World War II as pieced together in the foregoing narrative dealt with the circumstances in which the events occurred. It now remains to distill from the mass of evidence some of the underlying factors that could throw light on the phenomenon of escalation itself.

What was there in the nature of the war, in the characteristics of the nations involved, in the personalities of their leaders, or in the interactions among them to generate a process which, in retrospect, appears to have been inevitable? What were the pressures to which leaders succumbed, often against their better judgment? This will be the subject of the next two chapters.

But was the process of escalation inevitable because of factors uniquely characteristic of World War II, or are the underlying cuases likely to be operative in future wars as well? And if they are, could their effect be counteracted by new factors that have developed only in the nuclear age? The necessarily speculative task of inquiring into these questions will occupy the concluding chapter of this work.

10

The Asymmetrical Attitudes of the Two Sides

TO MOST PEOPLE in the West the term "escalation" connotes something both objectionable and frightening. It suggests an ever-mounting spiral of violence that may get out of control and end up in total war. It also implies a departure from civilized restraints and a resort to forms of warfare that are regarded inhumane. Escalation thus is condemned on grounds of humanity as well as of self-interest.

This was the way the British looked at escalation in World War II, although the term itself had not yet come into use.* But it had no such implications for the Nazis; the idea that restraint was desirable for its own sake, or that certain forms of warfare were inherently more objectionable than others, would have been regarded by them as a decadent notion. This basic difference in attitude between the two sides tends to be obscured by the apparent similarity of their actions after the war became total. But it played an important part in the developments that led up to it, and especially in British prewar planning.

Although the Nazis were not restrained by humanitarian scruples in their conduct of the war, there were occasions when military or political reasons made it expedient for them to practice restraint. During the Twilight War, for instance, it was to Hitler's interest not to provoke the Allies into a premature confrontation on the

*When speaking of what "the British" or "the Germans" thought or believed, I am merely using a shorthand phrase to indicate the prevailing, dominant, or operative opinion in those countries. This is not intended to minimize the diversity of opinion that existed in Britain on many of the issues discussed here. There was also, of course, disagreement within the German hierarchy, especially between the more conservative military professionals and the Nazi zealots. I have mentioned minority views only when they seemed to have a bearing on the analysis.

Western front until his own forces were ready for their big offensive. This served a political purpose as well, as his apparent restraint lent encouragement to those who believed in Hitler's professions of peaceful intent toward Britain and France, where the appeasement spirit was still rife.

Similarly, there were good practical reasons why the Germans waited a year before launching the all-out air assault that had been expected in Britain all along. The British attributed Hitler's restraint to his concern for public opinion in the United States and elsewhere. As we know, however, there were more compelling reasons why the assault was not undertaken earlier. One of them was that, until the Luftwaffe had acquired air bases along the occupied coast, it could not strike at Britain effectively.

In short, whenever the Germans exercised restraint, it was either because it served their interests or because they were compelled to; it was not because they saw virtue in moderation. Indeed, in their cult of violence on a heroic scale, it was lack of restraint that became a virtue.* All else being equal, the Nazis' instinctive preference was for using the maximum rather than the minimum of force. They were not content to defeat an opponent but, in Hitler's favorite phrase, wanted to "smash" him, or at least intimidate him through a display of German *Schrecklichkeit.*

The British were inclined in the opposite direction. Their innate sense of moderation and their moral scruples about certain forms of warfare impelled them toward restraint in the use of force. When they did raise the level of violence, they did so reluctantly and only in response to what they regarded as compelling necessity. The glorification of violence as an end in itself was alien and repugnant to them.

This difference in the attitudes of the two sides is often dismissed as irrelevant on the ground that it did not prevent the British from bombing civilians, and ultimately on a vaster scale than the Germans had done. Critics charge that the British were in favor of restraint only so long as it was to their advantage and that their profession of humanitarian concern was an example of typical Anglo-Saxon hypocrisy. For what happened to their moral scruples once they had acquired the means to perpetrate such horrors as the firestorms in Hamburg and Dresden?

It is certainly true that there were practical as well as humanitarian reasons why the British preferred restraint in the early part of the war. It is also true that, when the two were in conflict, expediency won out over moral scruples. But the scruples were nevertheless real, and strong enough to stymie Winston Churchill when he wanted revenge for the bombing of London. We saw, moreover, how long it took British leaders to make the mental transition to indiscriminate air warfare even after practical necessity had left them no other alternative. Whether these scruples would ever have been overridden if the British had not believed that they were fighting in

*I am indebted to my colleague Hans Speier for reminding me that this Nazi trait harks back to Hitler's favorite Nordic sagas with their glorification of the hero who goes berserk. See also Hans Speier, *Social Order and the Risks of War,* George W. Stewart, New York, 1952, pp. 118-121.

defense of Western civilization itself, as well as for their own survival, is a question that is, of course, impossible to answer.*

Though we do not know the extent to which their attitudes toward escalation influenced the decisions of the belligerents, we do know that whatever effect they had was exercised in opposite directions: as an inhibiting factor on the British side and as a spur to greater violence on the German side. The preference for restraint was at least one of the reasons why the British waited so long before adopting a deliberate policy of urban area attacks and why they clung so tenaciously to the fiction of precision bombing. Conversely, the Nazis' belief in the maximum use of force undoubtedly made the assault on London more attractive to Hitler and added to the zest with which Göring threw himself into that venture.

The role that these intangibles played in the war, however, was not confined to their direct influence upon decisions for or against escalation. They also affected the intelligence estimates on which these decisions were based, for each side, in assessing the opponent's intentions and actions, was inevitably influenced by its own attitude toward violence. But the common tendency to regard the enemy as a mirror image of oneself had more serious consequences for Britain than for Germany; a belligerent who imputes his own lack of scruples to the opponent is less likely to be caught out than one who relies on the hope that the enemy will share his preference for restraint. Moreover, even if the Nazis had recognized Britain's desire for more humane warfare, they presumably would not have felt compelled to reciprocate it and would not have allowed it to affect their own conduct of the war.

British misconceptions about the enemy did have a major impact on the course of events, for they provided the rationale for important decisions before and early in the war, when many British leaders clung to the hope that Germany, too, would wish to conduct the war in civilized fashion. It is, therefore, the British side with which we will be primarily concerned here in tracing the influence of characteristic national attitudes upon the assessment of the enemy's intentions and thus indirectly upon the conduct of the war.

The Effect on British Prewar Planning

At the time the British made their first serious plans and preparations to rearm against the Nazi menace, it was obvious that any war would be started by the other side. This meant that the enemy would have the initiative, and that the outcome might depend on how accurately the defender had anticipated the aggressor's moves. British planners, therefore, needed a realistic assessment of the enemy's intentions and preferred style of warfare; they had to know not only his capabilities but how he was likely to employ them.

Though the military planners were undoubtedly more skeptical of German intentions than their civilian superiors, the assumptions on which their planning was

*See above, pp. 42-43.

based reflected the vacillation of the Chamberlain Cabinet between the optimistic and pessimistic views of the impending war. Accordingly, the estimates of enemy intentions, and the plans based upon them, veered back and forth between the worst the British could conceive -- the knockout blow against their cities -- and the hope that Hitler's objectives would turn out to be limited and that he would show restraint in pursuing them. Both assumptions, though equally unrealistic, were based on the mirror image of the opponent, for both stemmed from Britain's own attitude toward warfare, one being merely the obverse of the other.

As we know, the pessimistic assumption -- that the war would begin with an all-out air assault against Britain -- was not supported by any evidence available to Britain at the time. Owing to the range and load limitations of German aircraft, which presumably were known to British Intelligence, the Luftwaffe was incapable of a massive, sustained assault on Britain until it acquired coastal bases in the Low Countries and France.* This meant that no such assault could be attempted until the Anglo-French armies had been defeated -- and to assume that this would happen was inconsistent with the prewar faith in the excellence of the French army and the impregnability of the Maginot Line. Even the most pessimistic British planners could not have envisaged that this splendid army could be routed so quickly.

Yet the idea of a knockout blow continued to dominate British planning in the face of all the arguments against it. One reason for this may have been the difficulty of obtaining reliable intelligence about the Luftwaffe, and the planners' tendency to mistrust the information that they did have. Conscious of their own weakness in the air, they were undoubtedly tempted to overrate the strength of the opponent. But there could have been another reason as well: that their assessment of the enemy's intentions was influenced by their own attitude toward warfare.

Strategic bombardment played a far more important role in British military thinking and doctrine than it did in German. Though senior officers of the older services discounted the claims of the strategic airpower advocates, their opposition did not arise primarily from doubts as to the military potential of this new weapon. In fact, most British leaders overrated its effectiveness. The reasons that they decided against the kind of air warfare advocated by Trenchard (except in retaliation for German bombing) were that they regarded Britain as more vulnerable to indiscriminate air attack than Germany and that their moral scruples inhibited them from making war on civilians.

What was more natural than to assume that an enemy who lacked such scruples would not hesitate to employ a form of warfare that most British leaders found repugnant? Here, after all, was what the British believed to be a potent weapon, whose use promised to give the enemy a formidable advantage, and one that the British themselves might have chosen if expediency and humanity had not argued against it.

*The range limitations of German fighters was to prove a serious handicap in the assault on Britain even after these bases had become available to the Luftwaffe.

Another consideration that may have contributed to the preoccupation with the knockout blow was that it represented the "worst case." Unrealistic though it was, most planners -- and not only in Britain -- would rather be charged with lack of realism, which is difficult to prove before the event, than with failure to have anticipated the worst. In this instance, they may have been influenced further by the nationwide fear of air attack, whose horrors were kept before the public through lurid press stories and the growing emphasis on air-raid precautions.

The alternative assumption -- that Hitler would refrain from initiating indiscriminate attacks on British cities -- might have been defended on the ground that the Luftwaffe lacked the capability to launch them from German bases. But this, of course, was not then recognized. Instead, the British believed, again under the influence of their own attitudes, that Hitler would be restrained from launching such an assault by a concern for world opinion. In view of the moral opprobrium attached to this form of warfare, they thought that, unless Britain provided Hitler with an excuse by initiating it, even the Nazis would be reluctant to resort to indiscriminate bombing and thereby incur the condemnation of the civilized world.

It will be recalled that in June 1938 Prime Minister Chamberlain had assured the House of Commons that in case of war Britain would bomb only strictly military objectives and would take scrupulous care not to inflict civilian casualties. One of the reasons for this policy was spelled out more clearly during the Munich crisis in September of that year, when Bomber Command was directed that in the event of war it was "to do nothing that might be construed as an attack on civilians *and so give the enemy an excuse to do likewise.*"*

There was, of course, nothing in Hitler's record, even as it was known before the war, to suggest that he would need an excuse for doing something he wished to do, or that he would hesitate to manufacture an excuse whenever he felt it expedient to have one. His long string of broken pledges provided ample evidence of his method. World opinion concerned him only when he was afraid that it might have practical consequences, such as to arouse his opponents to act against him before he was ready for them.

In retrospect, the notion of British leaders that they could induce restraint on Hitler's part by practicing it themselves seems almost preposterous. It was probably inspired by hope more than by conviction. Not surprisingly, considering Britain's military unpreparedness, her leaders alternated between hoping for the best and fearing the worst.

How strongly Britain's assessment of German intentions was influenced by her own attitudes is indicated by the fact that the planners' contradictory assumptions about the coming war both were rationalized in moral terms. Grossly simplified, the reasoning was that Hitler would wage indiscriminate air warfare because he lacked moral scruples; that he would not do so, unless the British gave him an excuse, because he would be deterred by his reluctance to incur the moral condemnation of mankind.

*See above, p. 19. Italics mine.

In the absence of a reliable and generally accepted estimate of the enemy threat, British planners did not know whether to prepare for a repetition of World War I, in which armies and navies would play their traditional roles, or for a new kind of war, characterized by the indiscriminate use of airpower on both sides.* Of the two eventualities, the latter clearly posed the greater danger to Britain. The Government could have prepared to meet this threat in one of two ways: by relying on defense, which meant building up Fighter Command; or by relying on deterrence, which meant improving Bomber Command's capability for retaliation. No explicit choice between these two strategies seems to have been made.

In one sense, of course, the peacetime desire for economy, and the lack of time in which to prepare, precluded a free choice. The procurement of an adequate bomber deterrent force would have been far more costly, and would have taken much longer, than an increase in fighter strength.** But, as the official History points out, "No doubt they [the British people] could have been induced to do much more if a clear call had come from the Government."*** If no such call was forthcoming, it was partly because "British policy meanwhile wavered between appeasement and panic preparations" and partly because the panic preparations themselves wavered between two conflicting images of the coming war.

In the circumstances, it is not surprising that this vacillation resulted in a typical compromise solution of building up both Fighter Command and Bomber Command but not doing enough for either to enable it to ward off the expected threat.**** As for Bomber Command, the numbers and kinds of bombers that would have been needed to deter a German assault on Britain probably could not have been made available in time in the best of cases, though it was fortunate that they were at least under development when war broke out. But lack of adequate aircraft was not Bomber Command's only handicap. What may have delayed its effective use even more was that its peacetime planning, crew training, and basic bombing philosophy were geared to a war fought in civilized fashion, in which bombers would be used only for precision daylight bombing of "strictly military objectives in the narrowest sense of the word."

The British were to pay for this erroneous image of the coming war in many ways. In the face of much evidence to the contrary, they clung to it partly because they

*The dilemma of British planners was by no means unique. The war plans made in peace-loving countries prior to the outbreak of conflict are seldom based on the "best" estimate of the enemy threat, as military folklore would have us believe. As a rule, they are a compromise between the desirable and what, in the complacent atmosphere of peacetime, is considered economically or politically feasible and palatable. The estimate of the enemy threat, itself rarely free from political bias, is used more often in justifying decisions reached on other grounds than in arriving at decisions.

**See the concise summary of "The Reconstruction of the Bombing Force, 1934-1939" in *Air Offensive,* Vol. 1, pp. 65-85.

****Ibid.*, p. 65.

****Though Fighter Command came off better in this compromise, it, too, would have lacked adequate strength if it had not been for the two months' respite after the fall of France, during which an all-out effort was made to push the output of fighter aircraft.

wished it to be true and partly because they allowed their own preconceptions and moral preferences to enter into their assessment of the enemy's intentions.

The Tit-for-Tat Notion

Another illustration of the asymmetry in the behavior standards of the two sides was the difference in their attitudes toward reprisals. Here, again, it was the British who were at a disadvantage in assuming that the enemy shared their concepts of proper retaliation. This could have been a disastrous mistake if the escalation of the war had not been preordained.

The British instinctively believed in the tit-for-tat principle of reprisals. The biblical concept of an eye for an eye, the notion that the punishment should match the offense, was deeply ingrained in them. The proper retaliation for the first bombing of London, therefore, was to attack the German capital, although the tactical problems involved made Berlin a most difficult and unprofitable target for Bomber Command. Even after it had become clear that the Germans were waging indiscriminate air warfare, Sir Charles Portal's proposal was to answer each Luftwaffe attack on a British city with a single attack on a German city. Churchill himself asked only for "the worst form of proportionate retaliation, i.e., *equal* retaliation." And when the Germans dropped parachute mines on London, which could not be aimed, he wanted Bomber Command to "drop a heavy parachute mine on German cities for everyone he drops on ours."

The tit-for-tat principle must have been strongly tied to a moral imperative, for the British applied it even when it was to their own disadvantage. The military effect of their reprisal raids on Berlin after the accidental bombing of London on August 24, 1940, for example, was bound to be negligible. The British may have hoped that the raids would have a psychological impact on the German people, but was this reason enough for them to invite an exchange of all-out blows in which they would be the heavy losers? They knew that from its newly-acquired bases across the Channel the Luftwaffe could do far more damage to London than they could possibly hope to inflict on Germany. Moreover, they had always leaned over backward to avoid giving the enemy an excuse for taking the gloves off. Yet they were providing one now, at great peril to themselves and with no hope of possible gain to justify the risk.

Having lived in daily expectation of the knockout blow, the British may have interpreted the accidental bombing of London as an indication that it had begun. If, then, Hitler already had decided to wage indiscriminate air warfare, their own reprisal raids would not have changed what he was going to do. But the first bombing of London was not followed up for two weeks, while the British continued their raids on Berlin.

Most likely, British leaders did not look on these retaliatory raids as giving the enemy an excuse for further reprisals. As they saw it, the Germans had started it by bombing London, and the British were merely evening the score. This should have ended the exchange at least for the time being. It should have -- if the Germans had been playing the game by British rules.

Obviously, they were not doing that. When he launched the all-out assault on London, Hitler used the British raids on Berlin to hang the reprisal label on an act that was bound to outrage world opinion. But, as we know, the Nazis always planned to proclaim terror attacks as reprisals. If no ready-made excuse had been available for the attack on London, Hitler would have manufactured one, as he had done on other occasions.*

The Nazis' concept of retaliation was that they were always the injured party, and that they alone were entitled to exact reprisals. When the opponent retaliated for an offense they had committed, it was treated not as a reprisal but as a fresh provocation to be punished severely. Hitler's vow to rub out British cities in punishment for their feeble retaliation raids on Berlin was not the only occasion when he demonstrated his own version of the tit-for-tat game.

At the time that Hitler launched his deliberate assault on London and other British cities, the British were unable to retaliate in kind. When they finally did, a year-and-a-half later, the Nazis behaved as if the British had initiated this form of warfare. The systematic destruction of London was conveniently forgotten. Sir Arthur Harris' attacks on the Hanseatic towns were treated as a new provocation, which had to be punished with the Baedeker raids on the English cathedral towns. If Hitler had had the capability, he might have turned Britain into the "place of ruin and sepulture" that some English writers had predicted. There was no "evening of scores" with Nazi Germany, as Hitler would always find grounds for further reprisals. When he was no longer able to exact them, it was equally characteristic that the German press began to protest loudly against Britain's inhumane methods of warfare. "The war has turned into something terrible which we did not expect. Is this, then, what total war is like?"**

Another peculiarity of the Nazis' code -- in sharp contrast to the British tit-for-tat -- was that what they chose to regard as an offense against them had to be repaid "a hundredfold." In the British retaliation raids on Berlin, fewer than a dozen people were killed, but the proper Nazi vengeance was to "rub out" British cities. The assassination of Gestapo chief Heydrich called for nothing less than the razing of the Czech town of Lidiče and the massacre of its inhabitants. Hundreds of innocent people in the subjugated countries had to pay with their lives for each offense against a single member of the German occupation forces.

The British idea of the tit-for-tat response to enemy provocation is shared in the United States, where it has been elevated into the strategy of "measured" or "controlled response." But many other nations, especially among potential enemies, lean toward the Nazi concept, in which reprisals are not equal or proportionate to

*See above, p. 79.

**From the Strassburg *Neueste Nachrichten* of April 15, 1943, cited in Spaight, p. 35. This was before the devastation of Hamburg in July 1943.

the offense but must exceed it many times over. The opponent is never entitled to retaliate; when he does, he becomes the aggressor and thus invites further reprisals.

Tit-for-tat is a dangerous policy to use against an opponent who plays the game by different rules, the more so if one mistakenly assumes that the enemy shares one's own rules of conduct. As it happened, the British tit-for-tat retaliation against Berlin had little bearing on the subsequent escalation of the war. A similar move in a future war, however, based on a comparable misconception of the enemy's standards of behavior, could have fateful consequences.

11

Pressures for Escalation

As MENTIONED at the outset,* the concept of a "controlled general war" rests on the tacit assumption that escalation to all-out war can be prevented if both sides wish to prevent it. This, in turn, implies that escalation results from deliberate policy decisions. But we have now seen that in World War II many other factors entered into it. War-generated pressures limited the leaders of both sides in their freedom of decision and effectively robbed them of control over events. In the crucial actions that led to the adoption of indiscriminate air warfare they sometimes became mere accessories after the fact. If they allowed the war to reach the level of violence that it did, it was not so much because they wanted it so as because circumstances, often of their own making, left them few choices.

One major source of the pressures for escalation was the belief of each side that its national survival was in jeopardy; the war was being fought for the highest stakes. But although this provided a compelling motive for pursuing victory at any cost, other, less obvious factors played an important and occasionally a decisive role in the escalation process by supplying additional motives, or removing inhibitions, or dictating the form that escalation was to take. On the British side, operational problems undoubtedly were the major reason for the drift into unrestricted area bombing. Erroneous assessments of the opponent's actions and intentions, the irrational element in decision-making, and purely circumstantial factors added their share.

This complicated interplay of motives and opportunities varied from case to case and permits few generalizations applicable to both sides. It will therefore be

*See above, pp. 1-5.

necessary to single out for separate discussion the key events in the escalation of the war, always remembering, however, that these events were merely steps in an almost continuous process, which might have been impossible to arrest once it had got under way.

The German Side

The great offensive in the West (May 10, 1940) was not the first major escalation of the war, since it had been preceded by the invasion of Scandinavia. But, though the latter should have been recognized as a forerunner of things to come, it could still be hopefully interpreted in Britain as merely another example of Hitler's strategy of piecemeal conquest. His violation of the neutrality of the Low Countries was a different matter, for this was read by the British as a sign that the gloves were off, and it therefore had a bearing on the subsequent escalation of the air war.

The reasons why Hitler decided to launch his ground offensive against the Allies may seem too obvious to need recapitulating. His far-reaching objectives called for elimination of the Anglo-French armies, and he was confident that his *Wehrmacht* could do the job. This would require a geographical escalation of the war and the violation of another solemn pledge to the neutrals, but, as Hitler himself said, who would care and what would it matter after he had won the war?*

The cynicism in this argument was typically Hitler's. But the belief that the latest step in the escalation would be the last, that it would bring victory and make further escalation unnecessary, was to be encountered repeatedly on both sides. A common illusion, it may play a role in future wars and deserves to be included among the important causes of escalation.

Hitler's motives for the offensive in the West may not have been as simple as they would appear. At the time he made this decision, after the Polish campaign in September 1939, he had every reason to believe that he could continue his strategy of piecemeal conquest with little danger of interference. The Allies' lack of offensive spirit and their inaction in the West must have convinced him that they would acquiesce in his conquest of Poland just as they had acquiesced in the fate of Austria and Czechoslovakia. By avoiding a head-on clash with the Allies, Hitler would have strengthened the appeasers in both England and France and might have reached an accommodation with them that would have permitted him to achieve the mastery of Europe without having to fight for it.

But it is also possible that he wanted to fight for it, just as he had wanted to fight in Poland. To inflict a spectacular defeat on the Allies would undoubtedly have given him an emotional satisfaction that a bloodless victory could not. Another explanation might be that Hitler lacked the patience for the bloodless course. He was a man in a hurry, who wanted to achieve his objectives for Germany while he was still alive to enjoy the triumph. Nor did he trust his compatriots to carry out his great design without himself at the helm.

*Jacobsen, *Fall Gelb,* p. 62.

We do not know if any of these were among his motives for the decision. We do know that the reasons he gave to his intimates* -- principally, that he wished to forestall an attack by the Allies -- were belied by his contempt for the decadent democracies and their lack of fighting spirit. If emotional pressures did contribute to his decision by reinforcing the political and military arguments for it, this would have been in keeping with Hitler's personality. It also would have fitted the pattern that characterized other instances of escalation in the war, on both sides.

* * *

Germany's next step toward escalation -- the air offensive against Britain *(Adlerangriff)* that began on August 13, 1940 -- was a good deal more significant from our standpoint. In itself, it was not a major escalation, except geographically. It did not introduce a new level of violence or alter the character of the war, for air attacks on military objectives, or to gain air superiority, had become accepted methods of modern warfare. It was an intensification more than an escalation of the war. By extending the combat zone to Britain proper, the Germans were undertaking what the British themselves considered a legitimate act of war, as it involved no violation of neutrality. It was significant, however, because in fact and in intent, at least as Göring saw it, the *Adlerangriff* was a prelude to the assault on London and therefore a link in the chain of escalation toward indiscriminate air warfare. Perhaps even more important, as we try to retrace that chain, are the reasons that prompted the Germans to take this step.

The ostensible objective was to defeat the RAF prior to launching SEA LION. But even if Hitler had believed that the Luftwaffe could accomplish what Göring had promised, this would not have been enough to enable him to go ahead with the invasion, unless Britain were to become so demoralized by the defeat of the RAF that she offered no real resistance with her remaining military forces. Hitler may have indulged in hopes that both would happen: that Göring would win air superiority, and that in the process Britain would be softened up to the point of surrender. But, at best, he cannot have had anything like the confidence in the successful outcome of this venture that he had had when he launched the great offensive in the West. There must have been additional and more compelling reasons for the air offensive against Britain.

For Hitler to seek a showdown with Britain at this stage of the war was to permit himself a diversion from his real war objectives, which lay in the East.** The risk of leaving an undefeated Britain in his rear while he was engaged in a Russian campaign could not have appeared very great to him. Britain's only means of striking directly at Germany was her feeble bomber force, whose raids had proved more of a nuisance than a threat. Even if the Russian campaign had to be postponed until 1941, there would not be time enough for Britain to develop an offensive capability that could seriously interfere with German operations against Russia.

*See above, pp. 33*ff.*

**Hillgruber, p. 167.

From a practical standpoint, it would have been to Germany's advantage to keep the war with Britain dormant until Russia had been got out of the way. Given his misconceptions about Britain, Hitler might have reasoned that a crusade against the common enemy, bolshevism, would appeal to the English ruling class and make its leaders more willing to come to terms with him. Yet he decided on the *Adlerangriff*, through which he foreclosed any hope of an amicable settlement.

This was a grave step for Hitler to take. He was aware that his objectives would be served better through a negotiated settlement with Britain than through military conquest. Even if he won, which was problematical, it was likely to be a Pyrrhic victory. He feared that its main beneficiary would not be Germany but Japan and the United States, who would fall heir to the remnants of the British empire which he himself coveted. The Führer also expected that, if faced with defeat, the British Government might move to Canada and continue the war from there with American help, so that Germany would still be involved in a war of indefinite duration.* For these and other reasons, Hitler was reluctant to seek a military showdown with Britain and would have preferred to terminate the conflict through negotiation.

It is possible that Hitler had abandoned hope that Britain would give up voluntarily even before he decided on the *Adlerangriff*. Given his personality and his capacity for self-delusion, however, it is unlikely that he would have abandoned something he desired until confronted with an accomplished fact. With the air attacks on Britain, he gave up any hopes he might still have entertained for an amicable settlement; he was burning his bridges behind him. The fact that an almost inevitable sequel of this decision was a more serious escalation might not have concerned him. But that its military outcome was dubious, that, even if successful, it would not promote Germany's best interests, that it was politically self-defeating, and that the entire campaign led away from Hitler's real war objectives -- these facts should have given the Führer pause. To undertake this venture when so much argued against it was, from almost every standpoint, an "irrational" decision. But, as we know, it was not the only time that irrational factors played a major role in the escalation of the war.

Among the contributing reasons that impelled Hitler to act as he did was again his impatience. Flushed with the success of his recent triumphs, he chafed at the prospect of remaining more or less inactive until his army was ready to tackle Russia almost a year later. The various alternatives with which he toyed at the time, such as ventures against Gibraltar, in North Africa, and in the Balkans, were not spectacular enough to satisfy his craving for new triumphs. Another emotional pressure on Hitler was his anger at Britain for having spurned his "peace offers" and thus forced him to take a course he disliked. That a nation he inwardly admired had rejected his suit must have added to his desire to punish her.

But the strongest pressure for *Adlerangriff* undoubtedly arose from his wish to escape from the SEA LION dilemma.** He needed a credible excuse that would

**Halder Diary*, July 13, 1940. See also Hillgruber, pp. 167-168.

**See above, p. 56.

allow him to postpone the decision on SEA LION, for which his commanders were pressing him, without confirming their suspicions that he had no intention of going through with the project or was at best lukewarm about it. So long as they could be kept in doubt as to his ultimate intentions, they would not dare to slacken in the preparations for invasion on which the Führer counted to bluff Britain into surrender. The battle for air superiority over Britain served the purpose admirably, for it made a postponement of the invasion decision logical. At the same time, it lent credibility to the invasion threat both in Britain and with Hitler's own military leaders. As noted elsewhere,* General Halder thought he detected a growing interest in SEA LION on Hitler's part, while the British were convinced that the air battle was the prelude to an imminent landing.

One German leader who was not taken in by this dual bluff was Göring. He was sure that there would be no invasion, with or without air superiority, since he counted on being able to bludgeon Britain into surrender through air attack alone. There is no evidence to show that Hitler shared Göring's thoughts or even that he knew them, but neither possibility should be excluded. If he was aware of them, this could have been an additional factor in the decision to launch the *Adlerangriff.* But, regardless of any hopes Hitler may have entertained as to the outcome of the air battle or its possible sequel, the mere fact that, for the moment at least, it got him out of the SEA LION dilemma would have been reason enough for him to approve it.

The invasion threat was an attempt at coercion that proved unsuccessful. But failure was not the only penalty, for coercion without the resolve to carry out the threat may boomerang. For Hitler, the need to maintain the deception had created a situation from which he could extricate himself only by reinforcing the threat and thus landing himself in an even worse situation. In short, the two escalations through which he sought to escape his dilemma resulted from circumstances which, though of his own creation, forced him into risky actions that were contrary to his interests and did nothing to further his real objectives.

* * *

The sequel to the *Adlerangriff* -- the assault on London -- was important not only because of the reasons why it was undertaken, but because it was the crucial step in the escalation of the war. With this act, the Nazis crossed the last firebreak at which the conflagration still might have been controlled. Henceforth, the only bounds on the level of violence were to be those set by technology and the skill of the belligerents.

The prospect of killing innocent civilians would not have given Hitler a moment's pause. What might have been expected to deter him, however, was that he was opening the door to indiscriminate air warfare by both sides. He was undoubtedly aware that an attempt to "rub out" London was the act best calculated to outrage the British people and stimulate a demand for revenge in kind. Perhaps he underrated the ability or willingness of the British to follow suit. More likely, he was under pressures that compelled him to take the risk.

*See above, p. 64.

We are familiar with the possible motives for the decision.* In the main, they conformed to the pattern exhibited in the previous instances of German escalation. But in the assault on London they were revealed in a clearer light and therefore provide a better insight into the various causes of escalation on the enemy side.

Once again, the belligerent's characteristic belief, or hope, that the currently contemplated act of escalation will be the last step needed to defeat the enemy was probably a factor in Hitler's decision. In the attack on London, however, such a hope was particularly self-deluding. We know that neither Hitler nor his Army and Navy commanders believed that a resolute enemy could be defeated by an attack on his capital unless he had already been brought to the verge of defeat by other means. Even if Hitler had credited the most optimistic reports of the damage done to Fighter Command, which is unlikely, Britain's actions and behavior during the weeks preceding the assault on London had shown that she was neither militarily nor psychologically anywhere near the verge of defeat. The hope that such an assault would knock Britain out of the war was too fragile to explain that step, just as the *Adlerangriff* could not be explained solely on this ground.

In contrast to the earlier escalation, however, the consequences for Germany in the event of failure were far more serious this time, and more easily foreseeable. Unlike the battle for air superiority, the assault on London would not be regarded by the British as a legitimate act of war and would spur them to attempt retaliation in kind. Their raids on Berlin were a token of things to come. Hitler must have known that in time, and with continued help from the United States, Britain would be able to repay him for what he was doing to London. Even if he shared the tendency of most government leaders to neglect the enemy's countermoves in their own planning, this tendency usually is an indication that the leaders are under pressure to make a certain move.

The pressure on Hitler in the late summer of 1940 did not stem from strategic considerations, since nothing had changed in the *military* situation to require a showdown with Britain at this point. Instead of attacking London, the Luftwaffe could have continued its battle with Fighter Command. Or, having already inflicted considerable damage, Hitler could have diverted his air and naval forces to a concentrated attack on Britain's maritime lifelines. From a military standpoint, it would have been perfectly safe for him, and more conducive to his war objectives, to let Britain wither on the vine while he went on with the piecemeal conquest of Europe and got ready for the showdown with the Soviet Union.

But the emotional pressures on Hitler were mounting. His rage against England was probably genuine, though not so much because of the raids on Berlin, which have been so often cited as the reason, as because the British had exposed him to ridicule. He must have longed to show them that they could not defy the master of Europe with impunity, much less heap scorn upon him, as Churchill was doing.

Miscalculations and wishful thinking undoubtedly played a part in Hitler's decision. A leader always has to guard against the danger of his subordinates' telling him

*See above, pp. 71*ff.*

what they think he would like to hear. Far from guarding against it, Hitler helped to create it by so intimidating his subordinates that they did not dare to give him unpalatable information. Göring's boasts of the Luftwaffe victory over Fighter Command and the reports of German agents in England and the United States about the war-weariness of the British people were what the Führer wanted to believe.

All these factors -- exaggerated hope of military success, impatience, a desire to punish Britain, miscalculations of her strength and determination -- undoubtedly entered into the complex motivation for the assault on London. But if there was any single factor that alone could have prompted Hitler to decide on this escalation, it could have been only the dilemma over SEA LION.

By the beginning of September, when he ordered the attack on London, the invasion bluff had got out of hand; he was no longer able to control the forces he had conjured up. In a few days he would have to cancel the project he had never intended to carry out. Yet he had built it up to a point where he could no longer abandon it without finding some compensatory act that would enable him to save face. The *Adlerangriff* had not got him out of his dilemma, for the British were still taunting him to go ahead with the invasion. The dramatic assault on London was his only hope of saving face, since it would divert attention from the invasion and serve as a substitute for it. With so much at stake for him, Hitler probably would have made the same decision even if he could have foreseen its consequences. To sacrifice a good portion of the Luftwaffe would not have appeared to him as too high a price to pay to escape personal humiliation. It would have been in keeping with his behavior toward the end, when he allowed Germany to go up in flames to provide a *Götterdämmerung* as a fitting finale for his regime.

We will never know, of course, what really went on in the Führer's mind when he decided on his two crucial escalations of the war. But if the reconstruction attempted here has any validity, it shows that escalation can happen without being really willed -- the result of circumstances that drive a leader to a course of action whose consequences he either does not foresee or disregards because of pressures arising from the war or inherent in his own personality.

This is not the way escalation is envisaged by those who are confident that leaders will be able to control the level of violence in future wars. But the lessons of World War II cannot be dismissed on the ground that Hitler's unique personality was responsible for the fact that these escalations happened and for the way they happened. It is possible that another leader might have written off SEA LION regardless of consequences, instead of allowing it to tempt him into fatal ventures. But it is not easy for any leader to retreat from an unsuccessful project in the middle of a war. The United States, too, has had great difficulty in finding an acceptable alternative to the bombing of North Vietnam.

The British Cross a Firebreak

Complex as Hitler's motives for escalation may have been, the pressures upon him were almost all in the same direction: toward increasing the level of violence.

The British leaders faced a more difficult problem, as they were torn between conflicting influences, for and against escalation.

Before the strains of war began to make themselves felt, the decision in favor of restraint was relatively easy to make; humanity as well as expediency argued convincingly for it.* It was only when Britain, under a tough leader, was confronted with the disaster in France that the pressures for escalation of the air war started to mount. The major issue then, and for some time to come, was not whether to use strategic airpower more aggressively, but how far to go and still make the escalation acceptable to the British Government.

In the prewar discussions of this problem, the Chiefs of Staff had identified four types of air action -- what might now be called an escalation ladder -- for possible use in a war with Germany. In a paper submitted to the Committee of Imperial Defence in July 1939, these actions, in ascending order of severity, were listed as (A) "not to initiate any offensive action in the air, except against warships at sea"; (B) "air action against purely 'military' objectives in the narrowest sense of the word" -- for example, against navy, air force and army units and their establishments; (C) to bomb objectives "as closely related as possible to purely military establishments [but which] will have a more important effect in reducing the enemy's capacity to carry on the war" (oil stocks and synthetic oil plants were cited as examples); and (D) "to 'take the gloves off' from the outset, and attack those objectives best calculated to reduce the enemy's war effort, irrespective of whether or not such action will cause heavy loss of life to enemy civilians."**

The crucial problem was, of course, posed by category "C", since it was in this kind of air action that civilians were likely to become the incidental victims of strategic bombing. The Chamberlain Government had seemingly resolved against such action when it insisted that civilians must be spared and that Britain must not be the first to take the gloves off. But it beclouded the issue when the Cabinet decided in the same breath that the strategic striking force would have to be used "in whatever way offered 'decisive' results" if Belgian neutrality were violated, or if France or Britain were faced with military action that threatened to be decisive.***

The first condition was met on May 10, 1940, with the German invasion of the Low Countries, and the second no more than two or three days later. Yet it was only after Rotterdam had been bombed that the new Churchill Government, on May 15, authorized air attacks on oil and communication targets in the Ruhr, the kind of air action contemplated under "C". This fact is significant, for it helps us to understand the British attitude toward escalation.

The violation of Belgian neutrality, the Luftwaffe's strafing of civilians on the roads of Flanders, and the German breakthrough at Sedan satisfied the formal conditions the Cabinet had stipulated as proof that Hitler had taken the gloves off. In

*See above, pp. 18*ff.* and 36*ff.*

***Grand Strategy,* Vol. 2, p. 56.

***See above, pp. 42-43.

the event, they proved insufficient. It took the bombing of Rotterdam before the Government decided on the escalation of the air war.

It was almost an article of faith in Britain that, when Hitler was ready to take the gloves off, he would go all out. And "going all out" meant the dreaded knockout blow against British cities. This was so much taken for granted that it would not have had to be stated explicitly. When the Cabinet mentioned the invasion of Belgium as a signal that the gloves were off, the implicit assumption may have been that it would be accompanied or immediately followed by the air assault on Britain. Once Hitler decided to abandon what the British mistakenly believed to be his policy of restraint, and once he was ready to defy world opinion by violating Belgian neutrality, they may have found it inconceivable that he would stop short of trying to knock out Britain herself.*

This interpretation is not as farfetched as it may seem, for a similar thought was voiced in a discussion between the Cabinet and the Chiefs of Staff a few days before the German offensive, which then seemed imminent:

> . . .the attitude of the Air Staff was not that it was desirable to open up the air war now but rather that, seeing that a German invasion of Holland -- the contingency then under consideration -- would be merely a preliminary to an air war against the United Kingdom, it was preferable to take the initiative at the moment most favourable to ourselves.**

British leaders must have been perplexed when the Low Countries were invaded and yet there was no sign that the expected air assault on Britain was about to be launched. Did this mean that the gloves were not really off, and that, in spite of having once again violated his solemn pledges, Hitler had decided to observe some civilized restraints after all? The British seem to have answered both questions in the affirmative, for they did not for their part step up the war until the bombing of Rotterdam, although they could have made out a legal case for escalation on the ground of previous German violations.***

It was more than an academic question for the British whether or not Hitler had taken the gloves off. Until they could be sure that he had, they lacked a moral justification for doing so themselves; furthermore, they would be inviting an aerial onslaught that they might otherwise hope to escape. Before they could bomb targets where civilians might be killed, they had to wait for Germany to initiate this form of warfare or show signs that she was about to do so; in the latter case the British would be merely "taking the initiative at the moment most favourable to ourselves."

*For the British attitudes on this subject, see Chapter 10.

***Grand Strategy*, Vol. 2, p. 171.

***As discussed in the narrative part of this study, the Anglo-French Declaration on bombing restrictions had been made contingent on its observance by the other side. Germany was held to have violated this undertaking during the Polish campaign, in Scandinavia, by her unrestricted submarine warfare against merchant shipping, and by the strafing of civilians in Belgium and France.

That moment seemed to have come when the Cabinet received apparently authentic reports that 30,000 civilians had been slaughtered in Rotterdam and that vast damage had been done to the city. Now there was no longer reason to doubt that Hitler had decided to throw all restraint to the winds, that the gloves were really off, and that the attack on the Dutch city was merely the forerunner of similar attacks on British cities. Considering the events of the preceding days, the tense atmosphere in London, the recent change in government, and British misconceptions about the enemy, it was an understandable mistake. The Cabinet's decision to "retaliate first," as it were, was undoubtedly helped along by the sense of moral outrage which the alleged Rotterdam massacre had aroused in Britain and elsewhere, making it easier for British leaders to square this decision with their conscience.

There were, of course, other reasons as well for this first British escalation of the war. Among them was the pressure on the Cabinet to do something that would have an immediate effect on the critical military situation in the battle of France. The strategic bombing of oil targets was going to be of little help, but this probably was not realized at the time, perhaps because the effectiveness of strategic airpower was still grossly overrated by its advocates and little understood by the layman. Even if it had been better understood, however, any action would have seemed better than none to a government that owed its existence to the sense of frustration created by the inaction of the Chamberlain regime. As Britain was faced with a military debacle in France, drastic measures were clearly indicated.

To the British, the initiation of the strategic air offensive may have seemed an enormous step to take. But by no stretch of the imagination could the attacks on the Ruhr targets be construed as a "decisive" use of Bomber Command. Only targets "as closely related as possible to purely military establishments" were to be hit. Although the British had every right to interpret the bombing of Rotterdam as the first act of indiscriminate air warfare, they themselves were not yet ready to take the fourth and final step on the escalation ladder.

One reason undoubtedly was that they wished to use Bomber Command against targets that were believed to have a bearing on the crucial battle of France; an attack on German cities would not have served that purpose. It is also possible that British leaders retained a hope, however small, that the bombing of Rotterdam might not, after all, mean the beginning of indiscriminate air warfare against Britain herself. But the strongest reason for their hesitation must have been that the British were not yet mentally ready to take the plunge into a form of warfare that was repugnant to them. Even after the Germans had removed any uncertainty with their brutal assault on London, the British did not make a clear-cut decision to follow suit but only inched into it over a period of months.

Considering the ineffectiveness of the first British bombing attacks on Germany, the importance of this escalation may seem to have been overstated here. Moreover, it appears to be belied by the fact that the man primarily responsible for the decision did not think it worth mentioning: In his chapter dealing with the eventful week of

May 10-16, 1940, Churchill makes no reference to the bombing of Rotterdam or to the initiation of the strategic air offensive against Germany.*

But it was not the immediate effect of the escalation that most concerns us here. More important is that, in deciding to go up the escalation ladder by bombing targets where civilians were likely to be killed, however unintentionally, the British made their first conscious departure from their traditional bombing policy. And by abandoning the strict definition of military objectives they unlocked a door that could be, and was, pushed open wider and wider, almost without volition on their part. In the current phrase, they crossed an important firebreak -- perhaps the last *identifiable* firebreak before unlimited escalation became inevitable. As we saw, the progression from targets "as closely related as possible to purely military establishments" to the deliberate attack on urban populations was so gradual that there was probably no logical point where it could have been halted.

If this escalation was as important in the light of its eventual consequences as has been argued here, it is significant that the decision to escalate was based on faulty intelligence and on an erroneous interpretation of that intelligence. As we now know, the reports of the Rotterdam "massacre" were wrong, both as to the event itself and with regard to its portent for the future. Decision-makers who must react to a fast-moving situation will often find it impossible to wait until the fog of war has lifted. They are apt to console themselves with the thought that the consequences of a decision are easier to control if one takes only a small step at a time. The British decision to bomb quasimilitary targets in the Ruhr may have appeared to the Cabinet as a small step, and was so regarded by Hitler, who dismissed the raids as pinpricks. But gradually, and perhaps inevitably, this first step led to the later steps, until Cologne was struck by a thousand bombers.

Escalation by Omission

In each of the German escalations -- the offensive in the West, the *Adlerangriff,* and the assault on London -- the change from one level of violence to another had been accomplished in a single step and as the result of a single decision. On the British side, this was true only of the first decision to initiate the strategic air offensive. The subsequent escalation of the bombing campaign was a gradual development that stretched over a period of almost two years. The transition from a policy of bombing only quasimilitary objectives to one of deliberate assault on urban populations was a continuous process, so that, in the absence of discrete steps, it is impossible to fix points in time when the changes from one level of violence to another occurred.

Another important difference between this and other escalations was that these changes crept in as solutions to operational problems rather than as the consequences

*Churchill, *Their Finest Hour,* Chap. 2. The omission, however, may have been deliberate, stemming from the distaste he later developed for this entire aspect of the war. (See above, pp. 132*ff.*)

of considered policy decisions. In fact, they occurred almost independently of the formal decision-making process. The Cabinet did give its official approval by incorporating the changes in new bombing directives, but these were generally issued after the fact and were little more than a ratification of practices already established. The Cabinet's operative decisions were made by omission rather than by commission; its formal decision did not precede the act but merely caught up with it.

Theoretically, British leaders could have halted the process of escalation by stopping the air offensive when it took a form that offended their moral scruples. But during the period of the transition to urban bombing, Britain was under the strongest political and military pressures to continue offensive action against Germany, even if the only weapon available for this purpose had to be used in a distasteful fashion.*

Though the process of escalation was continuous, it may be useful to identify certain milestones along the way. They do not represent points of decision, except in the sense mentioned above, but they are indicators that a significant change in the level of violence had occurred and had been sanctioned in a new bombing directive.

The first milestone was passed after the fall of France, when the narrow definition of targets "as closely related as possible to purely military establishments" was broadened to cover industrial objectives that were not so closely related. The directive of June 20, 1940, not only listed the usual oil and communication targets but also specified incendiary attacks on German forests -- a target whose relation to military establishments is not readily apparent.

Another milestone was the explicit recognition of the spill-over effect obtained from bombing industrial objectives that were situated in populated areas. Since this change occurred after the bombing of London, the British, understandably, were not greatly perturbed by the prospect of civilian casualties in Germany, so long as these were the "by-product" and not the "end-product" of strategic bombing. But the bonus effect that could be expected from the impact of such operations on German civilian morale was already valued sufficiently for the bombing directive of October 30, 1950 to single out industrial objectives in large towns, where the effect on the populace would be maximized.

Thereafter, it was inevitable that the by-product would soon be the end-product. This milestone was reached when the spill-over effect had become in fact, if not yet in name, the real objective of the bombing. Industrial objectives in cities continued to be listed as the nominal targets, but it was at least tacitly recognized that a mission had been successful if it accomplished widespread destruction in the cities themselves. If the industrial objectives were actually hit or destroyed in the conflagration, this was but a welcome bonus.

The last milestone was only an imperceptible distance away, but it must have been the hardest for the British to pass. They finally steeled themselves to it, in

*See above, pp. 88*ff.* and *passim.*

February 1942, when the Cabinet approved a change in the main aim of the bombing campaign. Henceforth, "the morale of the enemy civil population and in particular, of the industrial workers" was to be the primary object of the campaign. This was an admission that the cities themselves, and not the industrial objectives they contained, had become the real target and that the British would now engage in deliberate warfare against civilians.

Although the escalation continued thereafter, as the techniques of urban area bombing were perfected, it was an escalation in degree and not in kind. It did not introduce a new level of violence, for the ultimate had already been reached; it "merely" increased the measure of violence that could be accomplished at that level.

The circumstances that caused, or compelled, the British to take this path were discussed at length in Part One of this study. We recall Noble Frankland's conclusion:

> It therefore becomes clear that the decision to confine Bomber Command mainly to night action, which was taken in April 1940, resulted inevitably in a policy of attack upon whole German towns, the policy of area bombing. All the arguments based on strategic and economic reasons which have gone on since and, surprisingly, still go on, about the alternatives of this or that kind of attack are wholly groundless for operational reasons alone. The alternative to area bombing was either no strategic bombing or daylight bombing.*

Operational considerations indeed determined what form the strategic air offensive was to take. But that British leaders went ahead with the escalation despite their scruples against the form it was taking was due to a concatenation of factors with which we are already familiar.

The conviction that they were literally fighting for their lives, or at least for everything that made life worth living,** would have been motivation enough. But the British also knew that their survival and eventual victory depended on the continued support of Britain's friends, which could be ensured only so long as the nation's war effort demonstrated that hers was not a lost cause. The only instrument immediately available for offensive action against Germany was Bomber Command. For operational reasons, it would have to be used in an increasingly ruthless and escalatory fashion if the bombing offensive was to produce results that would convince the world of Britain's ability to stay the course and would also satisfy the domestic clamor for military successes. The exaggerated estimates of what could be achieved through attacks on German morale made this form of warfare all the more tempting.

*Frankland, p. 61.

**It is indicative of this mood that, at the time the invasion threat hung over England, Harold Nicholson procured suicide pills for himself and his wife in case the Nazis should succeed in conquering the island. (Harold Nicholson, *Memoirs,* Vol. 2, pp. 84 and 90.) The Gestapo plans for the occupation of England, captured after the war, show that British fears of the fate that was in store for them as a vassal of Nazi Germany were by no means exaggerated. (See Fleming, Chap. 18, and Wheatley, pp. 122-124.)

These incentives probably would have been powerful enough to force Britain into the course she took regardless of her feelings about indiscriminate air warfare. But these inhibitions had already been eroded. They had stemmed from considerations of expediency and humanity, and the former no longer applied, while the latter had lost their force.

Expediency had counseled restraint only so long as the British had to fear disproportionate retribution if they relaxed their own restrictions on strategic bombing. But with the assault on London they were already experiencing the worst of which the Luftwaffe was capable; their own actions could no longer affect the way the enemy fought the war.

Humanitarian considerations still played a role, for Britain's moral scruples were never completely stilled. But they were overridden by the passions of war. The Nazi atrocities in Europe and the destruction of London had stimulated a public demand for punishment of the offender that itself took on the tone of a moral crusade. The conviction that Britain was fighting in a righteous cause against an enemy of humanity made it easier to justify the use of previously unacceptable methods of warfare.

Perhaps the crucial factor in the British leaders' ability to overcome or ignore their moral scruples was that the escalation evolved in such a gradual manner as to require little affirmative action on their part. Once they had decided to abandon the narrow definition of military objectives -- a decision that did require affirmative action but was relatively easy because it was "such a small step" -- the last point where it was still possible to draw a sharp line had been passed. There was no identifiable firebreak between the third and fourth levels of air action, between bombing quasimilitary objectives and bombing any target that promised results, for in a population war there is hardly anything that could not be considered a quasimilitary objective in the broader sense of the word.

If there had been other firebreaks, an explicit policy decision would have been required before they could be crossed. In the absence of such decision points, the responsibility for selecting targets, and thereby changing the level of violence, fell to the operational commanders. This probably was not entirely unwelcome to the Government, for political leaders characteristically prefer to make unpalatable decisions by omission rather than commission, closing their eyes to what is going on until they are confronted with an accomplished fact, by which time it is too late to disavow the practice. We know that prior to the Cabinet debate of early 1942 many British leaders still deluded themselves that they were pursuing a policy of precision bombing and that the destruction of inhabited areas was accidental or a "by-product" of attacks on legitimate objectives.

This is not to say that British leaders would have decided against escalation if they had been confronted with that decision *before* the various milestones were passed. But when it came to a decision on urban bombing, their choice would have been only between further escalation and no strategic bombing at all, since the other alternative -- precision bombing -- was ruled out for operational reasons.

As we know, the possibility of stopping the strategic air offensive was considered in 1941, when Bomber Command's fortunes were at their lowest ebb. The reasons that made its cessation impractical then applied even more strongly in 1942, when the final escalation to urban area bombing received official sanction though it had already happened in fact. To abandon the bombing campaign in 1941, when it seemed a dismal and costly failure, would have been difficult enough. It would have been even more difficult in 1942, when success seemed to be just around the corner.*

In neither case could the British, about to be joined by the American bomber force, have seriously considered abandoning their huge investment in the bombing offensive as an alternative to further escalation. To do so would have been an admission of failure that the British could no more afford at this stage of the war than Hitler could have admitted a retreat from SEA LION.

* * *

If the strategic situation made it impossible for Britain to stop the escalation when she was suffering military reverses, why was there no de-escalation later on, when she had won the upper hand? Though British leaders had reconciled themselves to the policy of urban area attacks because there was no alternative, they had always hoped that it would be possible to return eventually to less objectionable methods of warfare. But that time never came. The destruction of German cities, by American as well as British forces, continued nearly to the end of the war, in spite of the increasing revulsion against it among the Allies. It went on even after both air forces had developed the capability for day and night precision attacks, for the lack of which the British had drifted into area bombing.

Inertia and the reluctance to give up a successful weapon may have been partly responsible. Another probable reason was that in the closing phase of the war the targets suitable for precision attack were few. Many had already been destroyed; others were hard to find and to hit, because Germany had dispersed her essential industries and put them underground.

But the strongest argument against de-escalation of the bombing offensive must have been that it might prolong the war. Though Germany was all but defeated, she was still holding on stubbornly, and every day that her resistance continued added to the toll of Allied casualties. Stopping the bombing would have meant freeing the tremendous manpower resources that were tied up in the air defense of Germany and thereby enabling her to hold out that much longer. No Allied leader could be expected to accept responsibility for incurring additional casualties so as to spare enemy lives.

Indeed, far from wishing to relax the military pressure on the enemy, the Allies wanted to increase it so as to break the war will of the German High Command and hasten the end of the war. Hence the idea of delivering a catastrophic blow against a single target, such as Berlin or Dresden. It was hoped that this would be the Allied *Todesstoss* that would finally induce the enemy to surrender. A more spectacular

*It will be recalled that the appointment of Air Marshal Harris as the Chief of Bomber Command and the availability of the new electronic aid GEE promised a more vigorous and more effective conduct of the bombing offensive.

version of the same idea was to be used in the war with Japan, when the atomic bombs were dropped.*

So far as World War II was concerned, there were compelling reasons why the process of escalation could not have been halted or reversed once it got under way, regardless of whether the *military* situation required its continuation. At the time the British started the process, they were probably not aware that they were crossing a crucial threshold and embarking on a course they would not be able to control. They thought that they were taking only a small step, which was true, and that they could stop at any point they chose, which turned out to be wrong.

The British decision to launch the strategic air offensive was made under hectic circumstances and at a time when the phenomenon of escalation was still little understood. We have a somewhat better understanding of it today, or at least of the fact that beyond a certain point escalation may be difficult or impossible to control. But will future leaders be able to tell where that threshold is and how close to it they can safely go? If the pressure to go beyond it is great, as it was in Britain, will they not be tempted to convince themselves that, though escalation may be difficult to control, it will not be impossible?

These questions go to the heart of the escalation problem. They will concern us now, as we turn from this examination of the past to speculations on the future.

*The major participants in the decision to drop the atomic bomb have themselves acknowledged that one of their main objectives was to avoid the casualties that would have been sustained in the planned invasion of the Japanese islands.

12

Speculations on the Future

Those who can not remember the past are condemned to repeat it.

George Santayana

Not all would agree with Santayana's statement. The uniqueness of history is often cited as a warning against drawing lessons from the past. Historical events, and the setting in which they occur, are indeed unique. But though the scene changes, the reaction of individuals and nations to given stimuli is apt to follow patterns that may remain unchanged for generations. Nobody can predict how future leaders *will* act under the pressures of war. History can help us, however, to identify what these pressures are likely to be and how leaders will be tempted to respond to them.

A more serious caveat against the misuse of history in our particular case is that the evidence is necessarily one-sided. It covers a single case in which escalation did occur. To avoid bias, one would like to have a case that illustrated the opposite: a population war between great powers in which the pressures for escalation were successfully resisted. If there had been such a war in recent history, it might have revealed factors making for restraint that did not emerge, or were obscured, in World War II.

The proponents of "controlled general war" believe that the fear of mutual annihilation will prove to be such a factor in any conflict between the major powers. They point to the restraining influence it has already exercised in various cold-war crises. They rightly assume that neither side will deliberately risk escalation so long as the strategic balance remains such as to convince both that the consequences might be fatal.

But all-out escalation could happen in other ways, as it did in World War II, through a sequence of small steps whose end result the leaders may be unable or unwilling to foresee. In the highly-charged atmosphere of a direct military confrontation between the major powers there will be pressures to raise the level of violence within safe limits. But what may seem to be a safe increment could turn out to be the beginning of uncontrolled escalation. The fear that this might happen will undoubtedly make both sides more cautious than in the past, but there is no guarantee that it will make them better able to recognize, and more willing to admit, that an action they are strongly tempted to take may not be safe.

Many U.S. planners assume that, if there is any danger that a "controlled general war" may get out of hand, it will be because of the enemy's actions. They regard American determination to keep the war controlled as a sufficient guarantee against risky actions on our part. This, however, can not be taken for granted. As we shall see, the pressures for escalation are likely to be stronger on our own side. Whether they would prove strong enough to drive future leaders across the threshold is not the question here; the question, itself highly speculative, is what may cause these pressures to build up in the course of a future war.

* * *

In World War II they arose from a combination of the practical problems, created by the political and military situation, with the intangible influences upon the leaders that governed their reaction to these problems and sometimes caused them to raise the level of violence even when this was against their own best interests. Both causes must be examined here, for they will be the major sources of potential escalation in a future war as well.

To begin with the political and military problems, it is, of course, impossible to predict the details of a hypothetical war between the United States and the Soviet Union. Certain basic features of the situation likely to prevail in such a war, however, are implicit in the concept of a "controlled general war" or follow from the assumptions that must be made for such a war to be credible.

In most scenarios, the war is assumed to take place in the NATO area. This is not the only locale where a direct military confrontation between the major powers could happen. But so long as both are anxious to avoid an overt clash, it can occur only in an area where their vital interests and commitments are such as to make it plausible for them to be drawn into conflict against their wishes. Europe is one of the few places where the stakes are sufficiently high for both sides to warrant a war on the scale implied by the definition of "controlled general war."

It is usually assumed that the war will have reached this stage inadvertently, as the result of a political crisis or a minor military incursion that has got out of hand. This seems more reasonable than to expect that the Soviets would deliberately engage in major aggression against the NATO area.* If they really intended the military conquest of all or part of free Europe -- hardly a realistic assumption in the foreseeable future -- they would proceed only if they felt reassured as to the likely

*Former U.S. Ambassador to NATO, Mr. Harlan Cleveland, put it as follows:

> Under present circumstances, the Soviet leaders' uncertainties about nucle?r escalation do persuade them that a large-scale attack on Western Europe is simply not in the cards. But they do have the capacity for limited operations – in Berlin or in the Eastern Mediterranean area, and to a growing extent at sea – and they have allies in Eastern Europe with forces that are strong enough for quick limited action. (continued on bottom of page 164)

American reaction. They might expect, for instance, that there would be no military response at all; they might think that because of domestic problems, or the state of the NATO alliance, or a critical situation in the Far East, the United States would no longer be able, or willing, to defend Europe. Or they might be led to believe that the only effective response the United States could make to an aggression in Europe would be to launch a massive thermonuclear attack on the Soviet Union, but that the strategic balance was such as to deter American leaders from such a course.

The assumption that a "controlled general war" could be triggered by a deliberate act of major aggression, therefore, would be tenable only in the unlikely event that the Soviets had grossly misjudged how the United States could or would respond to it. Not only that, but they would have to be willing to back their judgment at the risk of thermonuclear war. For they could never be sure that the strategic balance would indeed deter the United States from an all-out response, any more than they could rule out the possibility of local American intervention which, if it proved ineffective, might lead to further escalation.

This brings us back to the more logical assumption that the Soviets would not deliberately provoke a major confrontation with the United States in Europe and that the "controlled general war" would grow out of a minor crisis that got out of hand. If that were the case, it stands to reason that the original Soviet objectives in instigating the crisis, or in allowing themselves to be drawn into it, would have been limited, and that they would wish to limit their commitments and risks as well. In short, their political interests in such a situation would be served by restraint and not by escalation.

Nor are military reasons likely to require the Soviets to expand the conflict. If the war were fought on the periphery of Communist-controlled Europe, they would enjoy enough local superiority, at least initially, to achieve a limited objective. They would not need to raise the level of violence in order to get the better of their opponent. The burden of raising it so as to offset the enemy's military advantage would be on our side, as is so often the case for the defender.

Although the Soviets might have had limited objectives to start with, it is conceivable that, as the conflict turned into a "controlled general war," it would open up unexpected opportunities for more ambitious gains. The enemy's appetite could be whetted by the success of the initial aggression, or he might be tempted by his local military superiority to inflict a humiliating defeat on the United States. Such new objectives could provide the Soviet leaders with an incentive for escalation that they had previously lacked. In the circumstances assumed in the present scenario, however, any action by the Soviets that enlarges the area of conflict or raises the level of violence beyond that imposed by the United States would further increase the already high risk of all-out war. It is safe to assume that the Soviets would not

---

> It is a fair judgment, I think, that the NATO deterrent today is most dubious as a quick reaction to limited-crisis situations. Yet, as things stand, our political judgment would have to be that limited operations or blackmail situations are the most likely contingencies.

Harlan Cleveland, "The Nuclear War Game," *Interplay,* Vol. 1, No. 4, November 1967.

wish such a war to come about under conditions not of their own choosing or for reasons other than what they perceived as a threat to their existence.

In making such life-or-death decisions, the Soviet leaders would be governed by self-interest more than by the irrational factors that played such a role in Hitler's escalation of World War II. In any future war, the intangible influences upon Soviet leaders are likely to be on the side of caution and restraint, and against escalation and avoidable risks.

The Führer's personality was, and we hope will remain, unique among leaders of a major power. Stalin would have been too cautious to imperil his country and jeopardize his own rule merely to give vent to anger or to escape a personal embarrassment. And though he was equally devoid of moral scruples, the Russian dictator employed violence and cruelty as instruments of power but rarely for their own sake. The cultivation of the mystique of violence, divorced from the purpose it was to serve, was peculiar to Hitler's Germany. It was an atavism that a major power can no longer afford in the era of thermonuclear weapons.*

If it is unlikely that a Stalin would have acted in response to such emotional impulses as motivated Hitler's escalation in World War II, it is even less probable that a future Soviet leader would have the inclination or the freedom to act in this fashion. The trend toward collective leadership in Russia will make it more difficult for another individual to acquire the absolute power that Stalin possessed, and will also act as a check on impulsive actions by leaders like Khrushchev.

The irrational element in decision-making can never be ruled out altogether, regardless of the checks and balances imposed upon the leaders. But it is most apt to come to the fore when there are strong emotional or other pressures for a given course of action. Inasmuch as the political and military interests of the Soviet Union in a "controlled general war" will argue for restraint, pressures for escalation are likely to manifest themselves on the Soviet side only as the result of actions on our own part -- actions that deny the enemy a face-saving retreat or which he regards, rightly or wrongly, as a threat to his existence or as imperiling his control of the Communist bloc.

In the kind of war envisaged here, the United States, on the other hand, might be faced with military problems that could be solved only by raising the level of violence. Such escalation, in turn, could release counter-pressures, as the American actions might arouse the enemy's defensive instincts. This danger being the likeliest source of uncontrolled escalation in a future war, our next step will be to examine what might prompt such actions on the American side.

* * *

For the United States to act in a manner that could be construed by the Soviet Union as a direct threat to its vital interests would appear inconsistent with the basic concept of a war fought for limited objectives and at a carefully controlled

*It may be argued that Communist China, in her cultivation of the Mao mystique, is indulging in an atavism fully on a par with the Nazi aberrations. It remains to be seen whether it will be possible for her, in spite of this handicap, to acquire the technical and managerial skills needed by a major power.

level of violence. Yet this possibility cannot be excluded either as an unplanned or even as a planned course of action.

As for the latter, American leaders could deliberately decide on actions designed to show the enemy that the United States was more willing than he to risk further escalation. This might be intended as a coercive move that would capitalize on the enemy's residual fear of a thermonuclear holocaust and cause him to give up -- an exercise in "brinkmanship" of the kind discussed by various game theorists.* The enemy's nerves might be counted upon to prove weaker than ours, perhaps on the implicit assumption that, unlike ourselves, he would not be fighting in a righteous cause.

In defense of this extremely risky course of action, the proponents of "controlled general war" might argue that American escalation would be intended to show the Soviets that they were facing higher costs, and greater risks, than they had foreseen in starting the crisis. And since their original objectives had been limited, the prospect of having to fight for them at a much higher and more dangerous level of violence might coerce them into settling for a more modest gain or even into restoring the *status quo*. If they did not respond as expected to the American escalation, so the argument might continue, nothing much would have been risked, for the fear of mutual annihilation would keep the enemy from "overreacting" to the moves against him. Thus the war would still be "controlled," at the level of violence most advantageous to the United States. The underlying assumption, however, is that, while these various pressures were brought to bear upon the enemy, he would at no point be tempted by American actions to respond in a fashion that might start off a chain of uncontrolled escalation. It assumes that the Soviet leaders would not make what we would consider "irrational" decisions.

But the desire to engage in brinkmanship would not be the only reason for the United States to escalate the war in a manner that the Soviets might interpret as a threat to their existence. There may be no way to retrieve the local military situation except by increasing the level of violence. The hope of thereby achieving a coercive effect as well may simply provide an additional inducement.

Let us take a brief look at the political and military problems confronting the United States in the situation here envisaged. Under our assumptions, the original crisis had come about as the result of minor aggression by a member of the Soviet bloc. The Soviet Union would back its proxy, but with no intent of engaging in a direct military confrontation with the United States. In order to avoid this, the aggression therefore would probably be launched in an area, and in circumstances, in which the Soviets could reasonably expect to achieve their limited objective quickly, before the United States was able effectively to intervene. They would hope in this way to confront us with a *fait accompli,* to which we might reconcile ourselves in preference to trying to restore the *status quo.*

This would turn out to be a miscalculation, for, if the United States refrained from military intervention, the conflict would not become a "controlled general

*See Thomas C. Schelling, *Arms and Influence,* Yale University Press, New Haven, Conn., 1966, especially the chapters on "The Diplomacy of Violence" and "The Manipulation of Risk."

war." Nor is it unreasonable to assume that the Soviets would miscalculate in this case, as they have done on occasions in the past. They might feel safe in attacking an area in which no vital interests of the United States were at stake. This time, however, the international situation, or domestic pressures, or still other considerations, apart from the strategic importance of the area, might cause American leaders to decide that the enemy could not be allowed to get away with his aggression.*

Britain found herself in a similar situation after the fall of France, when external and internal pressures forced her to take offensive action against Germany before she had developed the proper capabilities for it. The operational problems she faced in employing the only suitable weapon she possessed prescribed the manner in which Bomber Command had to be used.

The United States, too, would encounter severe operational problems in a future attempt to fight a restrained war on the enemy's doorstep and still achieve its objective. We must assume, again to satisfy the conditions of a "controlled general war," that American intervention on the side of a threatened European ally had resulted in military actions against Soviet forces that were supporting a Communist proxy.** This could have come about, in spite of the Soviet desire to avoid such a clash, if the enemy had already committed himself too deeply to make a withdrawal politically feasible.

In a war fought on the periphery of the Soviet Union, however, and one in which Soviet forces were overtly engaged, the enemy could match or exceed any conventional forces or firepower the United States could bring to bear. He would have the additional advantage of being able to operate from more conveniently situated base areas and therefore with much shorter lines of communication.*** In these circumstances, the United States could hope to gain a military advantage only by raising the level of violence in ways that the Soviets, presumably because of their greater fear of all-out escalation, would be unwilling to match.

A logical first step in escalation, often threatened by official American spokesmen, would be to resort to nuclear weapons. In the beginning these would probably be used only against the enemy's armed forces or other "strictly military objectives" in the combat area. If this should prove ineffective in causing the Soviets to withdraw their support, other, more drastic steps could follow, for by then the United States would be so deeply committed that it might feel politically compelled to ensure the success of its intervention. What these other steps would be would depend on how one defined the upper limit of a "controlled general war." They could include nuclear attacks by strategic aircraft (because of the vulnerability or inadequacy of

*There is no implication here that this would be the outcome in real life and that it would not be equally credible for the United States to confine itself to diplomatic protests in the situation assumed here. But a scenario used for analytical purposes must devise a course of action that leads to the events to be studied, provided a credible justification for it can be found. The outcome of a hypothetical war is never a prediction, since it follows from the assumptions that are dictated by the research objective.

**See below, p. 168, footnote.

***The questionable reliability of allies, on both sides, may introduce additional complications, which, since they are obviously unpredictable, will be ignored here.

local bases) against military installations in the territory of Communist nations not initially involved in the conflict, but which the Soviets were using to support their forces. Even counterforce targets in Russia proper might be attacked with nuclear weapons. The strikes would be carried out, or ordered to be carried out, in a restrained fashion so as to minimize civilian casualties. Operational problems, however, could make this unexpectedly difficult to accomplish, as happened to the British in their strategic air offensive.

In American eyes, such actions would still be regarded as serving the limited objective of defeating the local aggression and restoring the *status quo.* The question is whether they would be so construed by the Soviet Union. Sometime during this process of escalation there would surely come a point when the Soviet leaders would have to decide that a drastic response was required and that two could play at this dangerous game.* American leaders could not be sure when this point would be reached; they would be tempted to set the enemy's threshold higher than it might turn out to be, in order to allow room for the additional escalation they might have to undertake to retrieve the military situation.

The reasoning behind the Soviet response would depend on the stage that the escalation had reached at the time they acted. Thus, the Soviet leaders might wish to withdraw on finding that the war had got out of hand, but would feel that, after having suffered punishing blows, a great power could not simply bow to American might without brandishing its own atomic power. Moreover, they might think that by giving the United States a dose of its own medicine they would get better terms at the conference table. Another possibility is that a geographical expansion of the war through American attacks against other Communist nations in Eastern Europe would cause Soviet leaders to fear for their control of the Communist bloc and for the stability of the regime in Russia itself. The most provocative escalation, and the one that would arouse their already highly defensive instincts more than any other act, undoubtedly would be an atomic strike against the territory of the Soviet Union.

Even then, however, it is unlikely that the Soviets would respond with an all-out thermonuclear attack on the United States unless American actions had convinced them, rightly or wrongly, that the final showdown was at hand and that their only choice was between being nibbled to death and striking the first blow. Their preferred response to the American escalation at any stage short of what they would interpret as a threat to their survival would probably be to retaliate in a fashion that would conjure up the spectre of Armageddon before the American people, causing them to prevail upon their leaders to conduct the war in a less risky fashion. The Soviet retaliation, whether tit-for-tat or an exercise in brinkmanship, would

*Again, this does not exclude the alternative outcome, which lies behind the concept of a "controlled general war," that the escalation would induce the Soviets to give up. But unless they make this decision as soon as the United States intervenes, and before their own forces are overtly engaged against American forces – a possibility which is credible but is ruled out by definition – they will find it politically very difficult to withdraw. By the time the escalation has set in, they will be deeply committed, perhaps too deeply for their regime to survive a humiliating retreat.

probably involve measures that the United States, in turn, would find unacceptable either because of the losses they inflicted on American forces or because they threatened vital American interests. In the sense that violence could reach a level that neither side desired, and higher than was anticipated in the plans for a "controlled general war," this could become a chain of uncontrolled escalation. At worst, American leaders could misread the enemy's retaliatory actions as a signal that all-out war was inevitable and that the United States had to strike before the other side did.

* * *

What has been said so far, far from being a prediction of what *would* happen in a "controlled general war," only dealt with one of the two sources of potential escalation: the political and military problems that such a war is likely to pose for the United States. Though these may prove to be the driving element, other pressures, both for and against escalation, will arise from the intangible influences upon American leaders, which we must now examine.

The experience of British leaders in World War II may help to throw light on this point. Some of the important intangibles that influenced their decisions will affect the reaction of American leaders as well, since they stemmed from national attitudes and behavior standards that are shared by both countries and are rooted in their common culture. The analogy cannot be carried too far, of course. But it is fair to assume that there are more similarities between British and American attitudes toward escalation than were found when comparing German and Soviet attitudes.

It will be recalled that the pressures for escalation did not arise on the British side during the early part of World War II, when both humanitarian and practical considerations had argued for restraint. It was only after the war had reached a critical stage for Britain that these two factors no longer reinforced each other but came to be at variance, and that humanitarian preferences began to give way to practical necessity.

In the kind of war assumed in our scenario, the critical stage will be reached when the Soviet Union and the United States are both directly involved, that is, when the conflict turns into a "controlled general war." Until then, the United States is likely to prefer restraint for the same reasons Britain did during the Twilight War.

The sense of moderation may not be as deeply rooted or as widely shared in America as it was in Britain, but there would be similar scruples against killing civilians or inflicting unnecessary hardship on innocent bystanders. This moral preference for civilized forms of warfare would be strengthened by sympathy for the common people of the small Communist nation involved, who would be thought to have been dragged into the war by a government they did not control and that was itself probably acting under Soviet pressure

Until Soviet forces became overtly involved, there would also be practical reasons for exercising restraint: The United States would try to forestall Russia's involvement by confining its own military action to the Communist proxy that presumably had initiated the aggression, and by limiting the scale of the conflict in other ways.

Such were the considerations that motivated American restraint in Korea and Vietnam. In the latter case, they did not prevent the gradual escalation of the bombing campaign against the North, but they must have been among the reasons why the President decided to stop short of attacks on populated areas. Aside from their provocative potential, such attacks would have been certain to cause a public outcry, in the United States and elsewhere, on humanitarian grounds. This prospect alone would have imposed restraint upon a leader who must be sensitive to public opinion.

The wars in Korea and Vietnam, however, were fought over issues which many people did not regard as vital to the United States or as involving a direct threat to their own security. A major war with the Soviet Union, although initially localized in Europe, would be a different matter. The American public would tend to see it as the long-feared showdown with our most dangerous and most implacable foe. This might cause the emotional climate to swing the other way, to where little heed would be given to humanitarian sentiments, as was the case when Britain found herself fighting for her survival against a ruthless enemy.

In a "controlled general war," American public opinion could become a major source of pressure for escalation. This is not to minimize the deep-seated fear of nuclear devastation which would undoubtedly cause a portion of the public to plead for restraint or even retreat.* But there would also be a popular clamor to bring the war to a decisive conclusion and thereby remove "forever" a long-standing threat to American security. We must assume that the more aggressive sentiment would prevail, for it is difficult to imagine that the United States could have engaged in a direct confrontation with the Soviet Union unless popular opinion had already been aroused to a high pitch and were backing a course of action that entailed great risk.

In a contingency such as the one here assumed, American leaders may inadvertently contribute to pressures that could compel them to go further than they consider it safe to go. Even if they themselves are not caught up in the emotional upsurge, they face the dilemma that usually confronts democracies as they try to pursue limited objectives in a major war. They need to arouse public opinion in order to assure themselves of the support needed for effective prosecution of the war or even for getting into it in the first place. In any war with the Soviet Union, they will probably try to do this by exploiting the latent anti-Communist feeling in the United States. Yet they cannot allow this feeling to turn into a crusading fervor, lest people demand a war to the finish in which the objective would be unconditional surrender or extermination of the enemy society.

Whether or not future leaders succeed in coping with this dilemma, their task is likely to be made more difficult by the enemy's own actions. World War II revealed the Soviet Union's capacity for inhumanity in warfare and its disdain for civilized conventions, and we have learned since, from our experience in Korea and Vietnam and our dealings with the Russians, what we may expect in fighting or in negotiating with a Communist enemy. If in a future conflict the Soviets follow previous patterns

*The role that this fear may play in a future war is discussed below, pp. 175*ff.*

of behavior and commit atrocities against prisoners or against dissidents in occupied countries, they will outrage the American public.

Although Soviet leaders presumably would not deliberately set out to provoke American hostility if they were interested in preventing escalation, they might not be aware of the likely effect of their actions upon American public opinion in an already highly charged situation. Also, they could easily underestimate the role that public opinion can play in a democracy by generating pressures that the leaders may find impossible to resist.

Popular sentiment in the United States in such an event will be torn between two conflicting emotions; a hatred of the enemy that will demand a vigorous prosecution of the war, and fear of nuclear devastation, which will argue for restraint or retreat. The passions so aroused will severely handicap those trying to conduct such a war with the steadfast prudence and calm deliberation needed to prevent it from getting out of control. Indeed, it may prove impossible to do so if the war comes to be widely regarded as a crusade against communism or as a "war to end wars" that must lead to a decisive victory.

* * *

Among other intangibles that would affect American decisions, both during the war itself and in the planning for it, is a common tendency to judge the enemy in terms of one's own rules of conduct and on the basis of certain misconceptions about him. We have noted how the British were misled by this tendency both in their preparations for the war and in their conduct of it. Ever since the Nazis' coming to power, in 1933, enough evidence had come out of Germany to show what their mentality was and to dispel the illusion that one could do business with Hitler. But it was not dispelled for many years, and even after the war was well along, most British leaders -- Churchill being a notable exception -- still failed to grasp the character of their opponent, which was utterly alien to theirs. They continued to impute to him their own standards of behavior, as, for instance, in such matters as reprisals.

Similar misjudgment of the Soviet Union, and of Communist modes of behavior in general, is widespread in the United States today. Though there is no lack of expertise on this subject here and in other Western countries, and in spite of the reams of paper devoted to studies of Soviet affairs, this knowledge is still confined to a relatively few specialists and does not seem to have penetrated the operative thinking of American leaders. It certainly has not dispelled the misconceptions about the Soviet Union that are encountered in official U.S. policy statements and in the behavior of American negotiators when they are dealing with their Communist adversaries.

Nor is it likely to do so. The tendency to view the enemy as a mirror image of oneself, to hope for reciprocal behavior on his part, to interpret his actions in terms of one's own motivations -- these are so deeply rooted in our habits of thought and behavior that they are not apt to be abandoned merely because the experts tell us that they do not conform to reality.

Our current planning for a "controlled general war," therefore, could well reflect the same lack of realism in assessing the enemy's intentions and style of warfare as beset British planners in their preparations for World War II. Without access to American plans it would be idle to speculate on whether or not this might be the case. If it were, however, it would result in our planning for the kind of war the United States was best equipped to fight, which might mean a higher level of violence than the enemy was willing to tolerate. The lack of an adequate capability for fighting at a lower level would itself add to the pressures for letting the war escalate to a level that is militarily better suited to our side.

Failure to understand the enemy's mentality would affect American decisions during a war as well. It might cause decision-makers to respond to what they considered provocative Soviet actions in the way the British reacted to the bombing of Rotterdam and the accidental attack on London. In any war, some events are bound to be wrongly reported or wrongly interpreted. If an immediate response is believed necessary, so that there is no time for verification of the facts or for a more sober reflection on their meaning, the enemy's intentions are likely to be interpreted on the basis of one's own preconceptions about his mentality.

In such a situation, American leaders would be tempted to follow their natural inclination to react to an assumed enemy provocation in a tit-for-tat fashion. (This tendency was demonstrated in Vietnam, when the United States crossed an important firebreak by bombing targets in North Vietnam in reprisal for the Tonkin Gulf incident and the enemy's attack on Pleiku.) The tacit assumption would be, as it was in Britain, that the enemy would play the tit-for-tat game by the same rules. In a war with the Soviet Union this might prove to be a fatal mistake. One would not expect future Soviet leaders to share Hitler's perverted notion that the national honor required a hundredfold revenge on the opponent. But Soviet actions in World War II and the behavior of other Communist nations in more recent conflicts show that the British notion of "equal and proportionate retaliation" is not a universal concept.

If the United States made a tit-for-tat response to a Soviet provocation, the enemy would not be constrained from retaliating by the thought that we had merely evened the score, though he might be restrained by self-interest. If he did decide on counterreprisals, such a violation of our notions of fair play could in turn stimulate pressure for further escalation on our part.

It is also possible for American leaders to interpret "fair play" in a self-serving manner by applying a dual standard of permissible conduct to the two sides. Confident that they were fighting in a righteous cause -- as in defending an innocent victim against aggression -- they might consider themselves entitled to raise the level of violence without granting the enemy the right to follow suit. If he did, his response could be regarded as a new provocation and thus could create pressures for further escalation.

For instance, the United States could find itself compelled by the military situation to use tactical nuclear weapons on Soviet forces in the combat area. If the enemy responded, say, with nuclear attacks on U.S. bases in Western Europe, or on the Sixth Fleet in the Mediterranean, this might be considered a challenge calling for American reprisals against Soviet bases in Eastern Europe or even in Russia.

We saw that in World War II the intangible influences were by no means all on the side of escalation. British leaders retained their deep-seated objections to indiscriminate air warfare even after the attack on London and when the practical reasons for restraint no longer applied. Probably, these objections would have given way to political and military necessity in any case. But what made it easier to overcome them was that the transition to urban area bombing occurred so gradually, and in such small increments, that the normal decision-making process was effectively circumvented.

In this last respect, American escalation in a "controlled general war" undoubtedly would be different. It would be tightly controlled, and each step would require an explicit decision from the top. A field commander would not be given the kind of latitude that Sir Arthur Harris enjoyed.

During the war in Vietnam, control from the top -- or overcontrol, as is often charged -- has extended to detailed operational decisions that formerly were left to subordinate echelons or to local commanders. This was the case in the Cuban missile crisis as well, as it probably will be in any future crisis or conflict in which delicate political-military issues are involved. No American President is likely to delegate responsibility for the conduct of a "controlled general war" in which a wrong move could have disastrous consequences. Civilian control at the highest level not only would be in line with the organizational trend in the U.S. Government toward more and more centralization of authority but would be regarded as a safeguard against unwanted escalation on the part of a hard-pressed military commander. But it is no guarantee that the level of violence will be kept within safe limits, for the civilian decision-makers may themselves be under pressure from various sources.

The likelihood of their yielding to such pressures would be greater if the escalation took place the way it did in Britain, in small increments spread over a lengthy period. That the progressive changes in British bombing policy occurred so gradually undoubtedly was a factor in gaining the Cabinet's assent after the event, and would have influenced British leaders even if their approval had been required before each change. While American leaders are not likely to let escalation in a future war be decided by default, they are no exception in preferring to make difficult decisions a step at a time and to keep each step as small as possible. This preference is reflected in the policy of graduated response and would be further reinforced by the fear of what the enemy might do if confronted with a sudden, sharp jump in the level of violence.

It is possible and even likely, however, that the pace of escalation in a "controlled general war" will be governed by the dynamics of the conflict, regardless of preferences. If U.S. forces were imperiled, or if the political situation demanded a more successful prosecution of the war, American leaders might find themselves under irresistible pressure to cross a firebreak by making an abrupt change in the character of the war. This could take the form of introducing nuclear weapons or of extending the combat area into the enemy's sanctuaries and perhaps even into the Russian homeland.

To cross such a clearly marked firebreak obviously would not be a small step. But American leaders might be tempted to persuade themselves that the step could be made to appear small if they inched across the threshold only a little way. They might plan, for instance, to confine themselves at first to small nuclear weapons, and to use them sparingly, as a warning to the enemy. Or, if they considered it necessary to attack targets in the territory of a Soviet proxy or in the Soviet Union itself, they might select "purely military objectives in the narrowest sense of the word."

This somewhat strained interpretation of the gradualism approach might or might not succeed in averting a drastic enemy reaction. If it did, it still might not achieve the hoped-for coercive effect and so would have to be supplemented by a militarily more effective use of force. In that case, the firebreak having been safely crossed, there would be a strong temptation to inch further along the same road and to make the military actions count instead of relying on their symbolic value. Once nuclear weapons had been introduced, for example, their numbers and size could gradually be increased, one small step at a time. Similarly, the definition of "military objectives," vague as it is, could be stretched to cover almost anything that appeared to be a lucrative target. However carefully American leaders tried at first to avoid targets where civilians might be killed, they could become less careful if they found this impossible or if they were frustrated by the Communist practice of placing antiaircraft sites and other key targets in or near population centers. If hard-pressed, they may even be tempted to minimize the importance of the firebreak itself by telling themselves that it is only a small step from, say, bombing a missile site in Eastern Europe to attacking one in the Soviet Union. But it may not seem a small step to the enemy.

The risk that a "controlled general war" may get out of hand is present not only when a clearly-marked firebreak has to be crossed. Indeed, this is the moment when decision-makers will be most alert to the possible enemy reaction. But once this hurdle is passed, they may be lulled into a false sense of security and resume the gradual escalation in the belief that they will be safe until they reach the next firebreak. Because each increment in the level of violence is considered separately, the leaders are likely to concern themselves only with the particular step they are about to take, rather than view it in light of the cumulative effect of changes that have already occurred. Yet we know that even a small increase in an already high level of violence may tip the balance and cause the enemy to react in a drastic manner.

American leaders cannot be sure at which point the enemy may decide that the process of escalation must be halted before it jeopardizes his survival or his vital interests. Their temptation will be to overestimate the enemy's tolerance so as to permit them to take the actions needed to get them out of a military predicament. They may therefore inadvertently inch their way beyond the danger point, whose location would be unpredictable and would not necessarily be marked by a well-advertised firebreak.

The principal danger posed by gradual escalation in a future war is not that it will allow the decision-making process to be circumvented, as was the case in World War II, but that it may exercise an insidious influence upon the decision-makers themselves. It could lead them to minimize the risk of escalation if the increments were small or appeared to be small, to ignore the cumulative effect and to drop their caution after a firebreak had been safely crossed.

In public discussions of a possible war with the Soviet Union it is normally assumed that only the enemy's actions could cause such a war to get out of hand; American resolve to keep it controlled is regarded as sufficient assurance against excessive escalation by our side. But this cannot be taken for granted. If American leaders are tempted by military necessity to take risky actions that the enemy could construe, rightly or wrongly, as a threat to his existence, they may persuade themselves that the risk is acceptable so long as the escalation is gradual and they are taking but a "small step." Common beliefs to the contrary notwithstanding, the risk of uncontrolled escalation therefore exists not so much because of the way the enemy is likely to conduct the war but because of the way we ourselves may be tempted, or compelled, to conduct it; it exists because our own actions may arouse the enemy's defensive instincts and set off a chain of events that cannot be arrested short of calamity. The appeal of the gradualist approach to escalation would be an important link in that chain.

* * *

On the American side, the pressures that have been examined so far would be predominantly on the side of escalation. This is especially true of the tangible pressures, those likely to arise from the practical problems posed by a "controlled general war" that has to be fought on the enemy's doorstep. We cannot be equally certain of the intangible influences upon American leaders, but the chances are that they will reinforce rather than counteract the other pressures.

Up to this point, it has been possible to draw on the experience of World War II, after allowing for the differences between that war and the conditions likely to prevail in any future conflict. One entirely new element in the situation, however, for which there is no precedent, is the role that the fear of nuclear annihilation will play in a war between the two major powers. This is the key factor on which the entire concept of a "controlled general war" rests, and on which the planners are counting to override all the pressures for escalation that may arise in such a war -- the factor that will make it both necessary and possible to conduct it in a restrained fashion. Regardless of the military and political mistakes that leaders may be tempted to make in the heat of conflict, it is argued, the instinct of self-preservation will save them from the fatal error of letting the war escalate into a thermonuclear holocaust.

This assumption, however fervently one may wish it to be valid, cannot be proved or disproved. But it is too important to this inquiry to be accepted without an attempt to examine what role this new factor is likely to play in a future war.

If the strategic balance between the United States and the Soviet Union actually is what we believe it to be, we are indeed faced with a novel situation. Both sides are credited with an assured second-strike capability sufficient to inflict mortal damage on the opponent almost instantaneously and regardless of what he may do. Both know that the other has this capability. Whoever started the exchange, therefore, would be committing suicide knowingly. Nations have committed suicide before,* but usually because they did not know or were not certain that this was the fate they were inviting.

The situation at the outbreak of World War II was different, for it was only the British who credited the opponent with the capability to inflict mortal damage upon the other side. But their expectations of what a German knockout blow could do to their cities were every bit as frightening as the current image of a thermonuclear attack, differing from it only in scale. We recall the lurid predictions in the popular press of devastated and burned-out cities, of millions of people killed or maimed by bombs and poison gas, of many more millions roaming the countryside in search of food, shelter, and medical care.** Even the more conservative government estimates of civilian casualties were so staggering that they had to be scaled down to make the planners' task less unmanageable. Unlike the known effects of nuclear weapons, the destructive possibilities attributed to the puny weapons of World War II were, of course, fantastically exaggerated, but, since they were the operative expectations, their impact was the same.

That the British nevertheless were not deterred from declaring war on Germany may have been because they were not certain that the worst would indeed happen. Hitler might yet choose to exercise restraint; his concern for world opinion might make him reluctant to take the gloves off by resorting to indiscriminate air warfare. This was a slender hope -- it was little more than wishful thinking -- but it was sufficient for the British to risk a course of action that they believed could result in the destruction of their homeland.

If the British precedent is any guide, American leaders, too, might bank on the hope that the worst could be avoided, and with sounder reasons. For so long as they refrained from provoking the enemy to an all-out response, they would not need to rely on his voluntary restraint, because they could expect him to be deterred from any other course by the certain prospect of devastating retaliation. Hence the fear of nuclear annihilation is unlikely to inhibit them in taking any actions they might consider appropriate in a "controlled general war." While they would be careful to stop short of what they considered the brink, the danger is that they might not know what the enemy regarded as the brink or how close to it they dared to go before he dropped his restraint regardless of consequences.

There is also the possibility that, if a future war lasts long enough, the fear of mutual annihilation will lose some of its sting. Again there may be a parallel with

*"In other words, a society does not ever die 'from natural causes,' but always dies from suicide or murder – and nearly always from the former. . . ." Arnold J. Toynbee, *A Study of History,* Abridgement of Vols. 1-6 by D. C. Sommervell, Oxford University Press, New York, 1947, Editor's Note, p. 273.

**See above, pp. 13-15.

World War II. During the eight months of the Twilight War, while the British waited for the knockout blow to fall, the event apparently lost its terrifying aspect. Perhaps the British had lived with it so long that familiarity had blurred its vivid colors. Or the air actions that took place during the Twilight War were too ineffective to keep alive the exaggerated image of what air power could accomplish. Whatever the reason, the fear of the knockout blow must have become less compelling or the British would not have initiated strategic bombing. They had good reasons for doing so, and they also believed that the blow would fall on Britain no matter what they did. But they would have been unlikely to risk precipitating it if they had still been sure that it would mean the total devastation they had envisaged prior to the war.

It is not impossible that events in a future war similarly could make the danger of mutual extinction seem increasingly remote and thereby counteract its deterrent effect. If nuclear weapons at first were used only sparingly and with the "surgical precision" military men are fond of promising, the spectre of a holocaust that is associated with their use may be gradually dissipated. The very fact that an important firebreak had been safely crossed without the war's getting out of control might convince an American leader that he could safely "take as much or as little of the war as he will."*

The fear of mutual annihilation is certain to deter both sides from a deliberate decision to initiate a massive thermonuclear exchange. But this presupposes that such a decision would involve an abrupt change from some permissible level of violence. And this may not be the case if the pressures upon American leaders tempt them to inch up gradually to the forbidden threshold, trusting that they will be safe so long as they do not cross it. The fear of mutual annihilation would deter them from crossing the threshold, but it might not deter them quite so effectively from getting closer to it than the enemy considered compatible with his security. The deterrent must not be regarded as permitting the leaders on either side to "take as much or as little of the war" as they will.

* * *

If these speculations into the future have any validity, they show that it will not be easy to keep a "controlled general war" from getting out of hand.

Political considerations will demand successful prosecution of the war. But the military situation, and the operational problems it is likely to pose, will make this difficult or impossible without our raising the level of violence, and continuing to raise it as the opponent becomes more deeply involved. The difficulty would be aggravated if misconceptions about the enemy had resulted in America's planning for the wrong kind of war or taking wartime actions on the basis of unrealistic estimates of the opponent's likely reaction. The gradualness of the escalation process might create a false sense of security, which would be heightened if American leaders came to feel that the identifiable firebreaks were the only danger points, and that

*A phrase used by Francis Bacon, in his essay *Of the True Greatness of Kingdoms and Estates,* to describe the benefits of having command of the sea.

once a firebreak had been crossed it would be safe to carry the escalation up to the next firebreak.

Against these factors making for escalation there would be such countervailing influences as the moral preference for restraint, close control from the top over wartime decisions, and the fear of nuclear annihilation. These influences, however, are always strongest prior to the outbreak of a war. Humanitarian feelings tend to melt away in the heat of battle or in the passions aroused by the enemy's inhumanity. Tight central control over the decision-making process has its disadvantages, for domestic pressures are felt most keenly at the top and there is temptation to indulge in false optimism when faced with unpalatable decisions. Finally, even the fear of mutual extinction could lose some of its restraining effect if this dreaded possibility came to be discounted, or if the leaders believed, or deceived themselves into believing, that the escalation could be halted at any point they chose.

It would be a rash man indeed who would attempt to predict the weight of these opposing influences in a future war. One can hope that the forces for restraint will prove sufficient to prevent a deliberate decision to initiate an all-out war. But that is not the main danger. The question is whether they will prove sufficient to prevent the process of escalation from being carried beyond the danger point, where an irreversible chain reaction may set in.

The answer does not lie solely in the interplay of forces over which men have little or no control. It will depend on whether the decision-makers of the future understand the process of escalation well enough to avoid the mistakes into which they may be tempted by the unfamiliar problems of a "controlled general war." If they are willing to learn from the past, they will find that these problems are not without precedent.

Appendix A

A NOTE ON GERMAN EXPLANATIONS FOR THE ASSAULT ON LONDON

The long list of fairy tales, distortions, and calumnies that are passed down to us as historical facts* is in process of being swelled by a new addition: the explanations "Made in Germany" of why London was bombed. There is not much time left to set the record straight. As this note will show, there are already signs that gullible historians and revisionists in other countries are swallowing the excuses put out by German apologists during and after the war.

Distortions of historical events are easier to perpetrate where there is a dearth of factual evidence that discourages objective historians from investigating them. This may be why the best accounts of German actions in the summer of 1940 -- those of Ansel, Telford Taylor, and Wheatley -- concentrate their attention on SEA LION, for which there is an abundance of documentary material, but not on the decision to attack London, which can only be reconstructed from circumstantial evidence. All three authors provide invaluable insights into the background for the decision from which I have benefited greatly in my own account, but, unfortunately, they touch on the decision itself only as it bears on their main interest. Taylor, who devotes only a single paragraph to the reasons for the assault,** was led to remark:

> For the Germans the Battle [of Britain] is no such source of pride, and their works on the subject are generally superficial, or too narrow and personal. It is more than a little ironic that Sea Lion, which was never attempted, has been comprehensively examined in excellent works in both languages, while the

*For an enjoyable case study, see Josephine Tey, *The Daughter of Time,* The Macmillan Co., New York, 1952, in which a Scotland Yard detective applies his talents to an investigation of the calumnies spread about Richard III.

**Telford Taylor, p. 158.

> decisive and dramatic Battle of Britain still lacks a comprehensive account focused on those who initiated it.*

Telford Taylor's assessment of the German sources, which I share, fails to mention their obvious bias. Their reticence on matters connected with the assault on London is indeed remarkable. Field Marshal Kesselring, who, as the commander of *Luftflotte* 2, was one of the principal actors in these events, devotes less than 10 out of 469 pages in his Memoirs to the bombing of London, and most of what he has to say is devoted to operational problems and the inadequacy of the Luftwaffe for the task assigned to it. The 700-page "History of the Second World War" by General von Tippelskirch passes over the subject in one-half page. The OKW diarist Helmuth Greiner dismisses it with a few sentences. Karl Klee, the author of a 20-page chapter on "The Battle of Britain," manages to dispose of the assault on London in a single page.

This reticence regarding an event that had such far-reaching consequences for the course of the war is not the only manifestation of bias. I mentioned elsewhere** that, with a single exception, none of the German sources available to me makes any reference to the accidental bombing of London on August 24 -- an omission that cannot be ascribed to an oversight when the writer is an otherwise meticulous scholar. That less scholarly authors showed their bias in a more direct fashion, by either repeating the Goebbels propaganda about the assault on London or inventing their own excuses for it, is therefore not surprising.

The reasons most frequently given by German authors to justify the assault on London can be compressed into three principal arguments: that it was "a reprisal for the British raids on Berlin"; that it was "not a terror attack but was aimed at economic and industrial objectives"; and that it was meant "to flush out the remaining British fighters."

The Assault was a Reprisal for the British Raids on Berlin

Hillgruber is the only German author I have read who does not resort to this explanation. The others mention it at least as a subsidiary and sometimes as the only reason. But the assault can be described as a reprisal only if one forgets about the accidental Luftwaffe attack on London which preceded the Berlin raids and clearly inspired them. The alternative premise -- that only Nazis were entitled to exact reprisals and that other countries had no right to retaliate -- may have reflected Hitler's own belief but does not require comment here.

In my own reconstruction of the decision to attack London I mentioned that Hitler's desire for revenge against Britain, due probably more to her obstructing him than to the raids on Berlin, may well have been a factor in the timing of his decision. As Telford Taylor puts it,

**Ibid.*, pp. 79-82.

**See above, p. 65.

> It is true that the RAF's Berlin raids provoked Hitler into lifting the ban on London as a target, and but for them the concentration on London might have been delayed; but reprisal was only one of several motives.*

But, as we also know, attacks on British cities had been considered by the Nazis ever since the fall of France and had been vetoed by Hitler only because he wanted to reserve them for the *Todesstoss,* for which he judged the time was not yet ripe. If there had been no other reasons for launching the attack when he did, Hitler probably would have ordered it in any case as soon as he thought that Britain was ready for the *coup de grace.* His attitude on this subject is well illustrated by a phrase used in the OKW Directive of September 14, 1940: "Terror attacks against purely residential areas should be reserved as the ultimate means of pressure and therefore should not yet be applied."**

A far-fetched variant of the reprisal argument is presented by an American author, who goes the German writers one better by blaming Churchill himself for the assault on London:

> In fact, Churchill's decision to bomb Berlin almost certainly was a conscious effort to bait Hitler into an immediate shifting of the Luftwaffe attack on to London, away from the RAF Fighter Command bases which were beginning to collapse under the strain.***

The sole evidence on which Quester bases his certainty is the fact that Churchill has described the relief he felt when Göring stopped the attacks on Fighter Command and bombed London instead. To assume that because Churchill welcomed the German action he must also have engineered it is quite a feat of logical legerdemain. And if Churchill had been the kind of man willing to sacrifice the civilian population of London, Quester's theory does not explain how he got the other members of the War Cabinet to go along with him.

There are other reasons, however, for dismissing this unsupported tale. The relief that Churchill expressed after the Luftwaffe switched to London was inspired by the serious condition in which Fighter Command found itself on September 7 as the result of two weeks of systematic attacks. But the decision to bomb Berlin, supposedly to "bait" Hitler into ordering the switch, was made on August 25, when Fighter Command was still in good shape and before there was any conceivable need for such desperate measures. The new phase of the *Adlerangriff,* when the Luftwaffe began to concentrate on Fighter Command ground installations, had only started the previous day. On that first day, August 24, one of the less vital fighter bases -- Manston -- was put out of action and two of the more important stations -- Hornchurch and North Weald -- were damaged, but not critically. Twenty-two

*Telford Taylor, p. 158

**In *Dokumente,* p. 407.

***George H. Quester, *Deterrence Before Hiroshima,* John Wiley & Sons, Inc., New York, 1966, p. 117.

British fighters were lost, against 38 German aircraft.* This was the picture that Churchill had on August 25; it certainly did not add up to the conclusion that the fighter bases were "beginning to collapse under the strain."

Moreover, the British had no reason to expect that the strain would continue after that first day. They did not know that Göring had decided to change his tactics. The August 24 attack might have been simply another part of the planless bombing that the Luftwaffe had conducted since August 13 against a variety of targets. Also, London itself had already been bombed the night of August 24. So far as the British knew, that bombing was intentional and would be repeated -- another reason why there was no need to "bait" the Nazis into doing something they were already doing.

Quester's version of the reprisal explanation would not deserve mention here, except to show the lengths to which some revisionist authors in the West have gone to absolve the Nazis of guilt for the assault.

The assault on London was not a terror attack; it was aimed at economic and industrial objectives

We have seen how long the British clung to the fiction that their strategic air attacks, however indiscriminate, were aimed at industrial or military objectives and that the damage to the cities was incidental. And even after the leaders recognized the fiction for what it was, it was retained for public relations purposes. The urban area attacks by the U.S. Air Force were justified on similar grounds. It was natural that the Germans should resort to the same subterfuge.

We therefore need not take too seriously Field Marshal Kesselring's claim that the assault on London was undertaken with the objective of waging economic warfare *(Wirtschaftskrieg)*** and that, "although in isolated cases the Commander-in-Chief of the Luftwaffe [Göring] did order pure terror attacks in reprisal, these orders were modified by the Luftflotten [meaning Kesselring himself] which selected militarily important targets."*** Nevertheless, it is a fact that Hitler did indeed order Göring to attack industrial and economic targets in London and to concentrate on the docks and port facilities. There are also indications that at first the Luftwaffe crews tried to comply with the order, at least in daylight attacks. To judge by the results, they must have given up trying when they found that it was impossible to identify specific targets in a city overhung with smoke from previous fires. British bomber crews learned the same lesson when they attempted to attack industrial targets through the smoke-laden atmosphere of the Ruhr before they had the H2S radar navigation and bombing system.

That the Luftwaffe itself did not take Hitler's orders any more seriously than Göring intended that it should is indicated by its official log, which reported on

*Collier, *The Battle of Britain,* p. 104.
**Kesselring, p. 100.
****Ibid.*, p. 107.

September 8, 1940, that 21 planes "carried out an attack in excellent visibility with great success. . . .Center of effort on Kensington, Buckingham Palace and Westham . . . .In the west part of the city 15 to 20 fires. . . ."* Military objectives, indeed! Nor did Göring hesitate to acknowledge proudly in his broadcast that London was in flames and that he had struck "right into the enemy's heart." The photographs in the British and American press bore him out.

Yet in spite of all this evidence Hitler continued to believe, or affected to believe, that his original order to attack only industrial and economic objectives was being carried out. General Halder reports an exchange that took place between Hitler and General Jeschonnek, the Chief of Staff of the Luftwaffe, at the Führer Conference on September 14, after London had been subject to day and night bombardment for a whole week:

> *Jeschonnek:* The material successes surpass our expectations. But so far no mass panic because residential areas have not been attacked and destroyed. Wants free hand in attack on residential areas.
>
> *Führer:* Yes, but attacks on strategic targets are always the most important because they destroy values that can not be replaced. So long as there are strategic targets left they must be attacked. Railroad stations, targets in the suburbs, water and gas works. Attacks aimed at mass panic must be left to the last (possibility of retaliation against German cities). The terrible threat of bombing the population itself must be left to the last.**

In view of what the Luftwaffe already had done to London, this exchange has an air of complete unreality. Jeschonnek certainly knew that one of his assigned target areas included residential districts and that most of the time the crews were hitting "secondary targets," which meant that they dropped their bombs anywhere over the city. And Hitler undoubtedly had seen pictures of the burning city and was aware that Buckingham Palace itself had been hit on September 11. Can he really have thought that the British would not retaliate against German cities for the devastation already wrought in London, and would do so only if he ordered "attacks aimed at mass panic"? Did he really believe that the Luftwaffe was only bombing strategic targets, as he had ordered?

In view of Hitler's ability to deceive himself, this last possibility cannot be excluded. The deception would have been the easier for him to maintain as he was ignorant of aerial warfare and apparently little interested in it.

> Hitler himself made no effort to understand the Battle, much less (saving the semipolitical question of bombing London) to guide its course. Göring, vain as a peacock, would hardly have enjoyed the Führer's direct involvement in Luftwaffe planning, and in any event Hitler seemed totally uninterested, and even antipathetic toward the German flyers. Ruminating on the matter at

*Ansel, p. 250.

***Halder Diary*, September 14, 1940.

> Nuremberg, Göring opined that Hitler's lack of comprehension of aerial warfare stemmed from his inability "to think in the third dimension."*

The likeliest explanation is that Hitler did not really care what Göring was doing to London so long as it met three requirements: The British had to continue to believe that the invasion was coming off (which is probably why he emphasized the attack on docks and port facilities); they had to suffer a punishment severe enough to reinforce the pressure on them to give up, and spectacular enough to attract world attention; and some ultimate degree of horror had to be held in reserve to be meted out when Hitler judged the time ripe for the *Todesstoss*.

To Göring, however, the assault he was delivering against London already *was* the *Todesstoss*, and he threw everything he could into it, convinced that it would force Britain to give up. Thus the only real difference between him and Hitler was that the Führer believed the Luftwaffe was holding back some last degree of violence, whereas it was already doing all that was in its power to destroy the city.

The assault on London was not economic warfare, or an aerial blockade, aimed at strangling Britain's supply system. It was a terror attack in intent as well as execution.

London was attacked in order to flush out the remaining British fighters

When Göring met with his two principal *Luftflotten* commanders at The Hague on September 3, 1940, to plan the assault on London, there apparently was sharp disagreement between Field Marshals Sperrle and Kesselring. The former thought Fighter Command still had a thousand fighters left and therefore wanted to continue the attack on airfields; Kesselring, however, probably eager to back up his chief's claim that air superiority had already been won, insisted that "the English have next to nothing left."

> Göring capped the argument by declaring that so far Fighter Command had saved itself from destruction only by withdrawing to airfields beyond the range of the Luftwaffe's single-engined fighters. Daylight attacks on London, he insisted, would compel the R.A.F. to throw in "its last reserves of Spitfires and Hurricanes."**

Göring's thesis that the assault on London would finish the battle for air superiority seems to have been widely echoed in the Luftwaffe as a rationale for that assault.*** It has found its way into most of the German literature on the subject.

*Telford Taylor, p. 185.

**Chester Wilmot, *The Struggle for Europe*. Harper & Brothers, New York, 1952, p. 49. This account is evidently based on Sperrle's verbal report, since no written record of the conference exists.

***See, for example, Galland, p. 41.

If the following remarks by the English military historian Captain Cyril Falls are any indication, it may even become enshrined in history as *the* reason that London was bombed:

> Among the points made by Dr. Klee on this extraordinary and unique battle, one is well known to students but may be worth repeating for a wider public: that the aim of the Luftwaffe was to wear out the British fighters before committing its own bombers and that it finally found this impossible without attacking London, which was of such importance from many points of view that the British War Cabinet had to take the risk of fighters being worn down in its defence.*

This explanation may be "well known to students," as Cyril Falls asserts, but it should not be accepted by a wider public, for it is wrong. That the personnel of the Luftwaffe believed it was probably an honest mistake on their part. Unlike their Commander-in-Chief, the German pilots -- men like Adolf Galland -- knew that they were far from having won air superiority. They also knew that the British avoided combat with the German fighters whenever possible and tried to concentrate on the Luftwaffe bombers. They may have reasoned that, if their bombers attacked a target that the British had to defend at all costs, such as London, the British fighters would be forced to accept battle and thus would gradually be whittled down.

Their reasoning was wrong, but combat flyers are not expected to be intelligence experts as well. What they did not know, and what Göring should have known, was that the Fighter Command ground installations were the most important targets for Air Marshal Dowding to defend and that, whenever large Luftwaffe formations were headed for essential sector stations, he sent up all the fighters, even from adjoining parts of England, that the threatened sector could handle.** In other words, the targets that Göring was forsaking on September 7, 1940, in order to attack London were the real Achilles heel of Britain's defense; they were precisely the targets that would flush out all available British fighters if the size of the attacking force warranted it.

Some German accounts give the impression that the Luftwaffe, believing it had already won local air superiority over southern England, wished to attack London in order to win superiority over that area as well. But that was what it had been trying to do between August 24 and September 6, when it attacked the airfields and sector stations in the immediate vicinity of London which served not only for the defense

*From Cyril Fall's Introduction to *Decisive Battles of World War II: The German View*, H. A. Jacobsen and J. Rohwer (eds.), G. P. Putnam's Sons, New York, 1965, p. 8. The quoted remarks refer to the chapter by Karl Klee, "The Battle of Britain," pp. 73-94.

**Nor could he [Dowding], without sacrificing the advantages of the control system, use entire squadrons from quiet sectors to increase Park's strength beyond the number of squadrons his sectors could handle – and that number was likely to grow smaller rather than larger as more and more stations were bombed and perhaps forced to rely on standby operations rooms." Collier, *The Battle of Britain*, p. 115. It will be recalled that Air Vice-Marshal Park commanded No. 11 Group, which defended all of Southeast England and included the sectors surrounding London.

of that city but would also have been essential in case of invasion. By attacking London itself, the Luftwaffe was not enlarging the area of combat; it was merely changing targets within the same area, served by the same sector stations and by the same fighter squadrons.

There are so many contradictions in the German explanations of why London was bombed that one would suspect them on that ground alone, even if they did not fall of their own weight. Karl Klee, for instance, himself a Luftwaffe officer who served during the war, asserts on one page: "There was only one target which would quite certainly force Fighter Command to send all it had into the air in its defence, and that was London." But he admits on another page: "It did not take the Luftwaffe long to realize what these [radar] stations meant, but it did not attack them vigorously enough, and its attacks were sporadic and unsystematic."*

Nor could the Luftwaffe High Command have been entirely unaware that the British would be forced to defend their sector stations in the London area. On August 7, 1940, the Luftwaffe liaison officer at OKW reported on the plans for the *Adlerangriff*: "The attacks were to be directed at the vicinity of London, without touching London itself, *in order to force the enemy to put up strong fighter formations.*"**

That the attack on London served a purpose other than the winning of air superiority is also implied in a report by Kesselring's Chief of Staff, Lieutenant General Wilhelm Speidel, that was published in the *OKW Diary* of September 23. Speidel summarized the air war to date as having consisted of three phases: the first, the battle against the British fighters; the second, the assault on London; then:

> This development [the unexpected strength of British defenses] led a few days ago to the need to renew the battle against the enemy fighters. Now, in the third stage of the air war, strong bomber formations and strong fighter formations are employed simultaneously, although the bombers are mainly used at night.***

Some honest but misguided Luftwaffe pilots may have believed the rationale given for the assault on London, but they must have known that it could be applied only to the daylight attacks. If the purpose really was to force the British day fighters into battle, why was London bombed at night, when it was defended only by antiaircraft artillery and a few improvised night fighters? The night attacks started on the first night of the assault and were kept up for almost two months, whereas the daylight attacks were essentially discontinued after a week.

There is no need, however, for additional arguments. We know what Göring really hoped to accomplish with the assault on London, whatever rationale for it he may have invented afterwards. And as for Hitler, it strains the imagination to believe that purely tactical reasons would have prompted him to make a decision that had

*Karl Klee, *The Battle of Britain*, pp. 87 and 92.

***OKW Diary*, August 7, 1940, in *Dokumente*, p. 26. Italics mine.

***Wheatley, App. D.

such enormous political implications. He may have believed Göring's contention that it was essential to finish off the British fighters, but he would not have considered that a sufficient reason for playing his trump card against Britain.

Appendix B

SELECTIVE CHRONOLOGY

1939	
23 August	German-Soviet pact
25 August	Anglo-Polish alliance
1 September	World War II starts with German invasion of Poland
1 September	President Roosevelt issues appeal to refrain from bombing civilians or unfortified cities
17 September	Soviet Union invades Poland
18 September	Polish government flees to Rumania, as isolated pockets of resistance hold out in Warsaw and elsewhere
27 September	Fall of Warsaw after bombing by Luftwaffe
27 September	Hitler orders plans for offensive in the West
6 October	Hitler makes "peace offer" to France and England
30 November	Soviet Union invades Finland
December	Hitler authorizes planning for occupation of Norway
1940	
12 January	British Cabinet abandons plans for stopping Swedish ore traffic with Germany
1 March	Hitler issues directive for occupation of Norway and Denmark to precede offensive in the West
12 March	Russo-Finnish war ends
9 April	Germany invades Norway and Denmark
14 April	Allied landings in Norway

1940 (continued)

10 May	German invasion of Low Countries and France ends the Twilight War
10 May	Chamberlain government resigns; Churchill becomes Prime Minister
14 May	Rotterdam bombed by Luftwaffe
15 May	British start strategic air offensive against German mainland with attack on oil and railway targets in the Ruhr area
26 May	Evacuation from Dunkirk begins
11 June	Italy declares war
16 June	Pétain government asks for armistice
20 June	Admiral Raeder discusses with Hitler plans for invasion of Britain
3 July	British put French fleet out of action at Mers-el-Kebir
16 July	Hitler issues vague directive to prepare for SEA LION
19 July	Hitler makes "last appeal" for peace
1 August	Hitler's directive for intensified air and naval action against Britain
13 August	*Adlertag* - Battle of Britain begins
24 August	First bombing of London, probably accidental
24 August	Luftwaffe begins to concentrate attacks on Fighter Command ground facilities
25 August	RAF launches first retaliatory raid on Berlin
30 August	Hitler postpones decision on SEA LION
30 August	Hitler authorizes all-out air assault on London
7 September	The London Blitz begins with day and night attacks
15 September	Climax of Battle of Britain - thereafter only night attacks continue
17 September	SEA LION postponed but effectively canceled
19 September	Churchill vainly seeks tit-for-tat retaliation against Germany
12 October	SEA LION formally cancelled for 1940
30 October	New Bomber Command directive leans toward urban area attacks
14 November	Heavy Luftwaffe attack on Coventry
16 November	RAF forms first photoreconnaissance unit to evaluate results of "precision" bombing

1941

9 March	Bomber Command diverted to Battle of Atlantic
6 April	Germany invades Yugoslavia and Greece
22 June	Germany invades Soviet Union
9 July	New Bomber Command directive selects civilian morale and inland transportation as primary objectives

1941 (continued)

18 August	The "Butt Report" confirms growing doubts of effectiveness of British bombing
13 November	Bomber Command ordered to conserve force until following spring
7 December	Pearl Harbor - United States and Japan enter the war

1942

14 February	New Bomber Command directive singles out civilian morale as "main aim" of bombing campaign
March-April	Bomber Command under Air Marshal Harris makes successful incendiary attacks on Hanseatic cities
30 March	Lord Cherwell recommends heavy build-up of Bomber Command
30 May	Air Marshal Harris launches "Thousand Bomber" raid on Cologne
17 August	U.S. strategic bombers fly first daylight mission from British bases

1943

January	Casablanca Conference decides on combined Anglo-American air offensive against Germany

Appendix C

SOURCES*

Ansel, Walter, *Hitler Confronts England,* Duke University Press, Durham, N.C., 1960.

Boyle, Andrew, *Trenchard,* W. W. Norton & Co. Inc., New York, 1962.

Butler, J. R. M., *Grand Strategy,* Vol. 2, *September 1939 - June 1941,* in *History of the Second World War,* United Kingdom Military Series, Her Majesty's Stationery Office, London, 1957.

Churchill, Winston S., *The Second World War,* 6 vols., Houghton Mifflin Company, Boston, Mass., 1948-1954.

Collier, Basil, *The Defence of the United Kingdom,* in *History of the Second World War,* United Kingdom Military Series, Her Majesty's Stationery Office, London, 1957.

Collier, Basil, *The Battle of Britain,* The Macmillan Company, New York, 1962.

Craven, Wesley F., and James L. Cate (eds.), *The Army Air Forces in World War II,* Vols. 1-3, The University of Chicago Press, Chicago, Ill., 1948-51.

*This selective listing includes only the major sources for this study, omitting, among others, some of the references cited in the text that bear on a single incident or a minor point. Nor have I attempted to identify the many familiar war books, diplomatic histories, and memoirs of participants which have been part of my general reading over the years but were not consciously consulted in the preparation of this work.

The sources listed vary greatly in their reliability and importance, as will be apparent from my discussion of German authors in Appendix A. The frequency with which they are used in the text, however, should guide the reader to those I consider the most reliable.

This note on sources would not be complete without acknowledgment of my indebtedness to the authors of the *British History of the Strategic Air Offensive Against Germany,* whose scholarly work was the single indispensable source for this study.

Fleming, Peter, *Operation Sea Lion,* Simon and Schuster, New York, 1957.

Frankland, Noble, *The Bombing Offensive Against Germany: Outlines and Perspectives,* Faber and Faber, London, 1965.

Greiner, Helmuth, *Die Oberste Wehrmachtführung, 1939-1943* (The Supreme Command of the Wehrmacht), Limes Verlag, Wiesbaden, Germany, 1951.

Halder, Generaloberst Franz, *Kriegstagebuch* (War Diary), 2 vols., ed. Hans-Adolf Jacobsen, W. Kohlhammer Verlag, Stuttgart, Germany.

Hillgruber, Andreas, *Hitlers Strategie: Politik und Kriegführung 1940-1941* (Hitler's Strategy: Politics and the Conduct of the War, 1940-1941), Bernard & Graefe Verlag für Wehrwesen, Frankfurt, Germany, 1965.

Hinsley, F. H., *Hitler's Strategy,* Cambridge University Press, Cambridge, England, 1951.

Harris, Sir Arthur, *Bomber Offensive,* Collins, London, 1947.

Jacobsen, Hans-Adolf, *Fall Gelb: Der Kampf um den deutschen Operationsplan zur Westoffensive 1940* (CASE YELLOW: The Conflict over the German Operations Plan for the Western Offensive, 1940), Franz Steiner Verlag, Wiesbaden, Germany, 1957.

Kesselring, Generalfeldmarschall Albert, *Soldat bis zum letzten Tag* (Soldier to the Last Day), Athenaüm Verlag, Bonn, Germany, 1953.

Klee, Karl, *Das Unternehmen "Seelöwe"* (Operation "Sea Lion"), Musterschmidt Verlag, Göttingen, Germany, 1958.

Klee, Karl (ed.), *Dokumente zum Unternehmen "Seelöwe"* (Documents on Operation "Sea Lion"), Musterschmidt Verlag, Göttingen, Germany, 1959. A useful selection of official German documents pertaining to Operation SEA LION, this includes OKW directives, situation reports and entries from the OKW, Army, and Navy diaries. Published as a companion volume to Karl Klee's historical narrative of Operation SEA LION (see above).

Klee, Karl, "The Battle of Britain," in H. A. Jacobsen and J. Rohwer (eds.), *Decisive Battles of World War II: The German View,* G. P. Putnam's Sons, New York, 1965.

Lee, Asher, *The German Air Force,* Harper & Brothers, New York, 1946.

von Manstein, Generalfeldmarschall Erich, *Verlorene Siege* (Lost Victories), Athenaüm Verlag, Bonn, Germany, 1955.

de Mendelssohn, Peter, *Design for Aggression,* Harper & Brothers, New York, 1946.

Spaight, J. M., *Air Power and War Rights,* 3d ed., Longmans, Green and Co., London, 1947.

Taylor, Telford, *The Breaking Wave: The Second World War in the Summer of 1940,* Simon and Schuster, New York, 1967.

Titmuss, Richard M., *Problems of Social Policy,* in *History of the Second World War,* United Kingdom Civil Series, His Majesty's Stationery Office, London, 1950.

Webster, Sir Charles, and Noble Frankland, *The Strategic Air Offensive against Germany, 1939-1945,* Vols. 1-4, in *History of the Second World War,* United Kingdom Military Series, Her Majesty's Stationery Office, London, 1961.

Wheatley, Ronald, *Operation Sea Lion,* Clarendon Press, Oxford, 1958.

Wheeler-Bennett, John W., *The Nemesis of Power: The German Army in Politics 1918-1945,* Macmillan & Co. Ltd., London, 1953.

Index